AIR FLORIDA #90 CRASHES INTO DC'S ↓ POTOMAC • ADOBE FOUNDED • MARCH 10TH: ALL 8 PLANETS ALIGN ON SAME SIDE OF SUN CREATING JUPITER EFFECT • MARCH 26TH GROUND-BREAKING CEREMONY FOR VIETNAM VETERANS MEMORIAL IN DC • CHARIOTS OF FIRE WINS BEST PICTURE AND BEST ORIGINAL SCORE AT 54TH ACADEMY AWARDS • ISRAEL COMPLETES WITHDRAWAL FROM THE SINAI PENINSULA • THE FALKLANDS WAR STARTS, GOES ON AND ON • KGB HEAD YURI ANDROPOV BECOMES SECRETARIAT OF THE COMMUNIST PARTY OF THE SOVIET UNION • ISRAEL INVADES LEBANON • NUCLEAR DISARMAMENT RALLY TAKES PLACE AT CATHEDRAL OF ST. JOHN THE DIVINE, NYC • US VOTE FOR EQUAL RIGHTS AMENDMENT FALLS SHORT • JULY 6: LONGEST LUNAR ECLIPSE OF THE 20TH CENTURY • PROVISIONAL IRA DETONATES BOMBS IN LONDON, KILLING 8 SOLDIERS, WOUNDING 47 • MEXICO TRIGGERS DEBT CRISIS THAT SPREADS TO LATIN AMERICA • FIRST CD'S PRODUCED IN GERMANY • FIRST INTERNATIONAL DAY OF PEACE PROCLAIMED BY UN • NFL PLAYERS ASSOCIATION STRIKES FOR 57 DAYS • TYLENOL LACED WITH CYANIDE KILLS 7 IN CHICAGO • EPCOT OPENS • POLAND BANS SOLIDARITY • HOMOSEXUALITY DECRIMINALIZED IN NORTHERN IRELAND FOR THOSE 18+ • VIETNAM VETERANS MEMORIAL DEDICATED IN WASHINGTON DC [NOT OFTEN A FRONT-PAGE STORY. BREZHNEV'S DEATH AND YURI ANDROPOV'S REPLACEMENT SEEMED MORE NEWSWORTHY.] • LECH WALESA RELEASED AFTER 11 MONTHS OF INTERNMENT • 88 COUNTRIES MEET IN GENEVA ON FREE TRADE • MICHAEL JACKSON RELEASES THRILLER • BARNEY CLARK RECEIVES FIRST PERMANENT ARTIFICIAL HEART • DIOXIN IN TIMES BEACH, MO CONTAINS 300 TIMES SAFE LEVEL, EPA RECOMMENDS EVACUATION • FIRST EXECUTION BY LETHAL INJECTION IN U.S. • M7 EARTHQUAKE HITS NO. YEMEN KILLING 2,800 • TIME'S MAN OF THE YEAR IS THE COMPUTER • GALLUP POLL: 51% OF AMERICANS DO NOT ACCEPT HOMOSEXUALITY AS NORMAL •

3003 Days of
Mike & Me
/ And the Wars Between Us

11/13/1982 ~ 2/4/1991

Martha Voutas Donegan

WITH LETTERS
By
Michael E. Creamer
FORMER AIRBORNE RANGER COMBAT MEDIC

For Dennis who has given me the time to write.
I have been richly blessed by you.

For information about this title or to order other books
and/or electronic media, contact:
Martha Voutas Donegan
1495 Books, LLC

Printed in the United States of America

ISBN: 979-8-9875936-0-8

Cover Art: Mike Creamer

Editor; Marcia Rockwood

Interior Design: Van-garde Imagery, Inc.

Contents

Soldier Boy

Soldier boy.
Boy soldier.
Shaped so, by a uniform.

Till war came.
Then war left.
And left you there alone.

Proud in life.
Proud of death.
Lingering glacier, inching.

Telling truths.
Truth be told.
Impossible to tell You

know now why I hid from you.
No words to tell.
Soldier boy.

＊　＊　＊

PART I

CHAPTER 1

"Hello, Mrs. Creamer?

This is Martha, um, I mean Muffy Voutas. Is Michael home?"

Oh, man! It struck me, just six words into the damn phone call, that I probably wasn't prepared to invite him to visit me. (I inhaled deeply.) I'd already regressed to that stupid nickname I went by in high school. Clearly, I didn't know this guy. I must be crazy. Since graduating fourteen years ago, I had seen Michael once—last Saturday in DC. Today was Tuesday. I guess it was only realistic that I went by a different name now, not Muffy. Between us, Mike and Me, we had countless other differences it would probably take one lifetime to reveal. First and foremost, he had gone to Vietnam, and I had gone to New York City.

Dot Creamer cut in, sweetly. "Oh yes, Muffy, I know you. I came to see you in *Wildcat*." (A musical Michael and I performed in together my junior, his sophomore year.) I heard her unabashed enthusiasm; was it for *Wildcat* or what she said next?

"Michael told me he met you at the Vietnam Veterans Memorial dedication in Wash-ing-ton." She said Washington like Jaqueline Kennedy said Washington—as if it were hyphenated. "Let me get him for you."

Quickly, I thought of how to do it. Then, for about the rest of the time it took for Michael to get to the phone, I planned my exit strategy. I could just touch base, ask him how the bus ride back was. Finally, I grew ecstatic waiting to hear his voice again. Michael Creamer fascinated me; here, at last, was a Vietnam combat veteran *I could talk to.* One

1

who would tell me things I didn't know about the War. More than that, I felt bonded to Michael by what had happened during our extraordinary reconnection just three days ago. He picked up the phone.

"'Lo," he said, "this is Mike," sounding as though I woke him.

"Hi," I said, "it's Muffy Voutas." I stuck with the nickname.

"Hi," he said with more energy, "hold on a sec." I'm sure he had to get his cigarettes because I heard the Zippo and his inhale into the next, "Hello. Hey, how are you doing?" (Exhale.)

"I'm excellent." I replied.

"You got to the rehearsal dinner on time?" he asked.

Oh, I thought. He remembered. "Yes. Yes, just. And the wedding was nice on Sunday, but I drank too much," I said. "How about you? Found the bus back to Marlboro, huh?"

"Yeah, a much better trip back. Thought a lot about our meeting up," Mike said.

Hmmm. Music to my ears, "Me too."

Mike continued, "Slept finally too; I'm afraid you met a sleep-deprived version of myself."

"I was pretty tired too," I said. "It was remarkable to have met up like that."

Mike said, "Papers say there were 150,000 people at the dedication."

"I'm telling everybody how awesome it was that we found each other." I blurted out, "But you know, it's like they don't get it. Like, it was an amazing day. So strange, I felt compelled to be there; all day long. Like I had this absolute sense of peace and place and," I paused long enough between the "likes" for him to jump in...

"I really am grateful you went down to support us Vietnam veterans. It made all the difference. I told Pete and Vinnie you'd come from New York City. They send their regards. Don't know if I told you, but they're the ones who put me on the bus to DC. They were flabbergasted that we met by chance. You know crazy Vinnie; he went ape-shit!" he added, "It was great." Michael was laughing. Wonderful.

* * *

Peter and Vinnie were old friends of ours. Vinnie and Mike joined Youth Theatre Workshop in their freshman year when I was a sophomore. Peter was already a member when I joined my freshman year. I always liked Peter; we dissected a cat together in Advanced Biology. He was funny and older by a few years; dark and nicely odd-looking. Boys were hard to come by in YTW; most started as crew members. (Vinnie boasted that he liked girls in leotards; he switched to cast member to peek at girls' crotches as they warmed up.) For years, I dreamt of becoming an actress, of going "Legit" in NYC and hitting the boards. I danced and sang reasonably well, but I *really* could act! YTW became an incubator for kids in Marlboro with talent and feelings. I also tried out for cheer team at the end of my freshman year, having deduced that cheerleaders got their pictures in the *Marlboro Enterprise* at a higher rate than any other girls. I was driven for fame.

"That line at the refreshment stand was unbelievable," I said to Michael.

"To think I almost didn't get there. After the parade, I was talking to a woman from Pepperell who recognized my patch. Her husband was killed in action in '67. I've been trying to connect with someone who might have served with him," Michael said. "I'm in the process of writing her back." He added, "I wrote you a letter this morning. Was going to call you and get your address."

"You did? Thank you. I love letters," I said, thrilled that Michael was writing already. And me nervous that he didn't want to hear from me again. I gave him my address.

The day before DC, wreath-laying in Marlboro. From left, Bob Killerby, Terry Adams, Mike Creamer, and Richard Temple

"I do too," Mike said, "letters were my lifeline when I was in Africa."

He'd mentioned Africa in DC, he seemed eager to talk of it. And I wanted to hear about Mike's time in Africa, but not now. My ears were on Vietnam, and the excitement I felt since last Saturday's hook-up; I jumped right into the invite.

"Listen, do you have plans for Thanksgiving? I was hoping maybe you'd come to visit me in New York City if you didn't. You could take Amtrak. I used to take Amtrak when I first moved to New York;

enjoyed the time to myself. Ate my tuna fish sandwich and beer. And oh, they serve beer." I didn't hear him answering me, so I went on. "I'm cooking Thanksgiving dinner with my neighbors; I think you'd like them, Diane and Gregg." Michael's hesitation was apparent; I decided to give him a chance to think it over, not push too hard, leave the door open enough and still have a way to say no. "Hey, think it over, maybe call me when you decide. Gotta run right now."

Nothing like jumping in with both feet. Airborne! That's what Mike would say, right?

CHAPTER 2

Mike the Day Before The Wall

Mike Creamer was up early that Friday, pulled on his jeans, his jump boots, climbed into his BDU jacket, threw five packs of Camel filters, and an extra Zippo lighter into a small rucksack he'd packed the night before. He glanced at his Rolex to see what time he needed to arrive for the wreath-laying, then peered down the hallway of his mother's house and exited the front door, setting off towards Marlboro's downtown.

Mike had not slept at all; the thought of having something to do, a purpose to perform, was refreshing. Mike had a brilliant mind, but he was bored to death. He'd spent so many days alone in the last six months; it sucked not working when all his friends had jobs. Daily, Mike would hump a half-mile to buy beer, up a brutal little hill on Glen Street, then back down, nurse the beer till it was gone, and crash. Ten and a half years out of Vietnam, his hips hurt like hell; he said they never were good after jumping out of choppers, "My medic's bag was heavy on top of a rucksack and my gun." He tried to explain it away. Often, he wanted to escape the bedroom he'd retreated to after dropping out of nursing school, with its paper-thin walls and the constant drone of his mother's whispered rosaries. He knew the rosaries were for him; Mike thought she was wasting her time. Some nights when he couldn't take it any longer, Mike slipped out to the backyard, climbed into an old government-issue bag, and stared, sorting constellations.

"I hate being home," he said, as he hit the hill and started up it.

Mike usually loved the outdoors and the crispness of autumn, the smell of his first cigarette of the day mingling with the outside air. He loathed the smoke-filled cell of his room. Man, he hated his mom's little voice. "Are you going to Washington?" She had asked. Every inquiry was so saccharine, so holier-than-thou, it eroded Mike's sense of human understanding.

His friends called him on it, "Mike, that's your mother you're talking about; have some human understanding."

Mike would answer, "I had human understanding; she used her's up."

And Nell. Nell was such an angry baby—and Richard, his brother, too. The lot of them walked on f'n eggshells. How do you walk on eggshells all your life? Or maybe it was him. Perhaps it was **his** problem, and walking around f'n Claymores finally got to him. Mike drew in hard, almost audibly on his cigarette. He wished the comment he'd made last night about their dad hadn't set Nell off on her pissy, cry-baby tangent. Gawd, it was more like a diatribe she'd learned by rote. Like his mother's f'n "Sorrowful Mysteries." What a stinkin' life; couldn't she just get over it?

"Yeah?" Mike had said, "our father left. What about it?"

"You want to blame it on Mom all the time," Nell answered.

"Yeah. Well, I would have left here too," Mike fought back.

"Well maybe you should leave," Nell said, emphatically. Each. Word. Separated. And slammed the door to her bedroom.

Mike had been thinking about suicide for a long time. "I've found my own little place in the woods," he prodded his friends. The ultimate discourtesy of suicide speaking. Mike had written to his fellow ex-pat and sometime girlfriend Maryanne, in Swaziland, that he was planning to kill himself. Right after this trip to DC, "It's the last thing I'll do." Once up and over the hill, on flatter terrain, Mike's hips didn't hurt as much; he broke into a stride.

✳ ✳ ✳

It was the worst Pete and Vinnie had seen Mike. He would talk louder and more often about doing himself in. They knew that this time Mike was not joking. All three were veterans: Pete, Airforce; Vinnie, Marines; Mike, Army. Only Mike had seen face-to-face combat; Vinnie remained stateside, and Pete, good at linguistics, sat in remote eavesdropping enclaves, his choice over a dishonorable discharge for getting high and getting caught. Pete's dad was a turret gunner in WWII.

That morning, Mike had been asked to lay the wreath on Marlboro's Vietnam War Memorial, honoring the seven men the city had lost. Bivouacked at his mom's, he memorized the details of their deaths. It made them more human: Richie Demers, a Marine, killed in '66; Mike Minehan, high school hockey star, a Marine, '67; Jimmy McDonough with the 82nd Airborne, lasted twenty-seven days in '68, the same year as 1st Lieutenant Kappy Kales. Marine Rifleman Bill Leonard survived forty days in '70 (three and a half months before Mike got over there). Mike never knew the odd men out: E5 Michael Neil Faherty, 22, died of Malaria in '68, and an old-timer, George Hanlon, who at 37, was killed in a non-hostile car crash in '67. Minehan, McDonough, Kappy Kales, and Leonard **together** survived 337 days in Vietnam, 28 days shy of the mandatory 365 for a single member of the regular services (58 days if you were a Marine).

"Shit, the average age when they died was 20 years old," Mike had computed, "I was already home at 20." Mike was mindful of the day he'd join them.

✳ ✳ ✳

Immediately after the wreath-laying—which wasn't such a big deal after all, because Mike didn't do it alone as he had thought. Three other vets shared the honor ("At least they were combat vets," Mike said afterward, showing some respect). "Who cares who lays a wreath anyway?" Mike said to himself.

Then Pete and Vinnie put Mike on the bus to DC, stocked with free food and beer, for the vets' trip down to the Vietnam Veterans Memorial dedication. Best hope Mike had was that he would hook up with The Herd, his Airborne unit, the guys of the 173rd he had served with in Nam. It was November 12, 1982.

Then Mike would come home and be done with it all. The whole shitshow. Least of all, he wouldn't have to deal with "the world" or interview for one more stinkin' job; Mike thought while settling into the seat.

The summer before, in 1981, hunger-striking members of the VVAW (Vietnam Veterans Against the War) on the west coast brought attention to hard realities Mike faced. The story was reported in one of the magazines Mike collected—*Time* dated July 13, 1981—its cover story "Viet Nam Vets: Fighting for Their Rights." It awoke a broader consciousness towards veterans who had been struggling since their return.

CHAPTER 3

I Had to Get to The Wall

Along with running a graphic design business, I had been writing a book, or trying to. It was about Vietnam and the damage it did to our generation, the deep cuts it left in our lives. I had a good premise: Vietnam affected all men and women of our generation. We were all shaped by that War. We all enlisted, just kind of served with different units—some fought the war, some fought Vietnam. But we were all changed by it.

I had about seven interviews done with men, all of whom hated or avoided their military experience. My theory was that every man and woman born within certain years had been subtly and blatantly affected by choices over Vietnam. It was interesting interviewing the men, but I needed to put in more effort, find guys who counter-weighed their opinions. I was very busy; it was my fifth year of business. MVP had doubled its earnings each year. I'd just moved both my apartment and the studio. Our clients were mostly fashion designers, very finicky. Still, we were growing.

When the TV coverage at Washington's National Cathedral started to air, in the days preceding the Veterans Memorial dedication— "The Wall"— I raced home from my studio after work to watch the vigil. It was mesmerizing, beckoning to me: The one-by-one calling out, the reading of each name of a service member who'd died, followed by a muffled hammer-strike on an enormous bell. It was scheduled to go on non-stop for five days and nights, leading up to the dedication, pausing only to change readers, or bell-strikers, to honor the 57,939 we lost.

Hearing all those names, watching the family readers, the sound of the bell, I felt summoned to get to DC, whatever it took—I didn't know how I would get there, the flights were all booked. *I listened to my heart compelling me to go and not to end up wishing I had been there.*

In watching that meditation of many lives lost, I figured out a few crucial aspects of my life:

1. That Manhattan's men weren't my men; my men never made it to Manhattan.

2. That Vietnam was a working-class war fought by working-class boys like those from my working-class town.

3. That **my men** got caught up in the draft and came out damaged or married or both.

4. That that war severely changed a lot of people.

I had to go. But I wasn't sure how to get there.

And then like manna from heaven, He gave me Nancy and her Audi wagon.

CHAPTER 4

Mike

It had been nearly ten years since Mike Creamer's discharge from the Army after Vietnam. He'd held down tough jobs: His two tours of Vietnam set him up for the three years he spent as a medic in Zaire. He worked miles from civilization, an ex-pat on a powerline crew, able to purchase a Fiat Spitfire and ship it home tax-free. Mike relished the bravado that surrounded him. That's when he bought his Rolex; he showed it around when he came home to recover from malaria, along with his elephant tusks (legal then, if amoral) and his zebra rug.

Then, after serving as the safety engineer on the Cambridge/Somerville subway project, somebody talked Mike into enrolling in nursing school at the hospital associated with the project. They were thrilled to have him. He was making straight A's; the doctors sought him out to assist in the OR. But by the second semester, when Emergency Room duty brought on flashbacks, Mike made the mistake of sharing a few stories about Vietnam with his fellow students. That triggered their stupid-ass "Baby Killer" talk, and Mike went ballistic. He'd worked hard to fit in. He didn't have the patience to teach idiots that **he** fought to keep Communism at bay, keep the world free. Just because someone fought in Vietnam didn't make them an f'n Baby Killer. People were so quick to label every vet as *crazed* as if the whole lot had gone bad over there. That crap pushed him farther to the outside; Mike was always ornery, now he was rip-shit ornery. He just shut up. Stewing.

On top of everything, Mike had to get a job. It was Ronald Reagan's first year as president, and unbeknownst to Mike and the many veterans who voted him in, Reagan secretly mandated the cutting of Veteran's Administration funding.[1] The president of the United States considered Vietnam vets crybabies.

Mike found a job as an EMT on a street ambulance outside of Boston. It was the wrong move. He was an outstanding EMT; people praised him, and Mike loved praise. But with praise came nights he barely managed; nights with gunshot wounds and the inevitable guts dredging up memories, dragging Mike all over the f'ing Nam again. Night terrors that had never fully subsided after deploying to Nam and the B Med MASH Unit now haunted him nonstop. Mike would jerk awake, soaked in sweat. He didn't want to sleep; he read his textbooks way in advance of assignments. Then read them again. He grew further and further away from his classmates. But none of that mattered. Nothing did. Mike couldn't function; he didn't eat, just smoked cigarettes and drank beer. Big Mike of the Jungle saw no alternative but to quit school and retreat home to *Mumbleboro*, as he called it, to Marlboro, to his mom's.

That's when Dot Creamer's novenas started.

"Gawd," Mike said, "too little too late." Mike didn't have much fight left.

Usually when Mike had an audience and a few beers in him, he would reel off the statistics from *Time:* the post-Vietnam death rate was twice as frequent in the six years between 1973 and 1979 as during the war: 57,000 vets dead from suicide or "death under mysterious circumstances,[2] " including single-car accidents (like the one Mike walked away from unscathed, that put his pretty little Spitfire in the junkyard),

---

1   Nicosia, Gerald, Home to War, A History of the Vietnam Veterans' Movement (New York: Crown Publishers, 2001) p,107.
2   Nicosia, p. 426.

and the increased oddball cancer cases. Vets had an unemployment rate two times the national average. One out of four vets earned less than $7,000 a year, which probably contributed to a divorce rate two times the national average. Add to that, one-third of the adult male prison population were Vietnam veterans. An estimated half-million vets manifested "a severe inability to assimilate back into American Society.[3] "

"Aw shit," Mike thought, "I don't need any more reasons to hang around."

The fact that Mike couldn't sleep much now, or fit in well with even his non-combat buddies—Pete and Vinnie—wasn't outside the norm: statistically, he fit right in. Mike's take on life did not fit with the people around him; it was set like concrete in his mind, and he'd lugged it onto the DC bus with him. Now he folded his arms across his chest, closed his eyes, and allowed the bus to rock him into a fitful sleep, his first in days.

---

3   "Delayed Stress" is the common name for Post-traumatic Stress Disorder (PTSD): a delayed and often chronic reaction experienced by normal people exposed to abnormally intense amounts of stress, such as encountered in war zones, natural disasters and other catastrophic situations. A delayed stress reaction may surface after many years. Source: Brochure, "Vet Center, Serving the Needs of Vietnam Era Veterans. Hartford, Connecticut. no date.

CHAPTER 5

Nancy, a Friend with a Car

Nancy was a bit of an anomaly-friend. Eventually, she would come to work for me, but at that time, she worked for fashion designer Perry Ellis, my client of four years. A single mom, divorced from her Marine husband, whose thirteen-month tour in Vietnam she had endured; Nancy knew what it was like to have a husband at war. I didn't. Now, she was dating another Marine, Jim, who had opted to drive to the dedication with his buddies. Nancy knew I wanted to go to DC badly; she did too and offered a ride.

Of course, my staff knew about my Vietnam project and the events in DC from my rantings all week. Now they could relax, "I am going to DC to find the men of my generation. My men!" I cried out as the elevator closed behind me.

Leaving the island of Manhattan via any of the bridges or tunnels on a Friday when you think you've escaped early is a joke. You never can leave the city early, especially on a holiday weekend, and this was Veteran's Day; we had Monday off. Nancy and I were heading south for the Holland Tunnel; we got thick into traffic while still in New York. But it was okay to be with Nancy and catch up on the news at Perry Ellis. I had designed his brand the first year (1978) I set up my graphic design shop. Since then, I had become a kind of a designer's designer. Perry's Spring 1983[1] runway show, just weeks before, had been a huge

---

1   NYC fashion shows were always a half-year ahead.

success; he paired absurdly unsellable, flaring farthingale skirts with the music from the soundtrack of *Chariots of Fire.*

The traffic never let up on the New Jersey Turnpike as the day squeezed itself out on the horizon. The spaces between cars grew less and less until it diminished to stop-and-go, halfway down the Pike. Conversation faded between Nancy and me. The rain, forecast for all night, reflected brake lights in puddles on the roadway. The closer we got to DC, the more rain fell, as if Mother Earth was crying out her full measure of sorrow in anticipation of the Vietnam service for so many men and the women who'd died in our generation. It was an exhausting drive, made more so since I wasn't behind the wheel and wanted to be.

After paying the toll at the end of the New Jersey Turnpike, Nancy and I stopped to use the restroom in the I-95 service area in Delaware. We witnessed a strange phenomenon. It should have been evident in the jammed parking lot, but once inside, Nancy and I doubled-over, laughing at the non-existent line for the women's room, while the men's room line snaked back to the entrance and down the outside stairs. Men. My men. All our age too. I was ecstatic!

As Nancy and I pulled back onto the highway, we understood that the cars packing the road were filled with vets. It was so congested, and traffic moved slowly enough for us to see the men's faces. All of us were headed for DC, and nobody seemed upset with the traffic; in fact, everyone looked elated. "Look," Nancy said, nodding to a Jeep on our right. The five vets crammed inside raised their beer cans in a toast, and we toasted back with our to-go cups. When the traffic got too snarled, Nancy knew an alternate route to Virginia, where we headed off to her mom's, to spend the night.

CHAPTER 6

DC and Mike

For Mike, the trip to DC was uneventful. There were no other paratroopers on the bus, just "legs," guys who didn't jump. They were parading vets in parade uniforms with garrison caps that folded flat between parades, caps embroidered with VFW and Marlborough, the long, puffed-up spelling, and post numbers, and "Korea" or whatever. Mike stayed to himself in his camouflage BDU jacket with its embroidered CREAMER and CMB, his Combat Medic's Badge, blue jeans, and the black beret with its red-rimmed Ranger tab raked over his right eyebrow. When he lifted that eyebrow, it snuck underneath the cap in an almost cartoon-like way, though there was nothing funny about it. That usually meant Mike was sizing you up. It was a sneer of sorts without a move of his mouth or sleekly slim nose. It put people off, which is exactly what Mike meant for it to do.

A hell of a lot of change had gone down between Mike's getting out of high school in 1969, going to war, working in Africa, the tunnel projects in California, and Boston, nursing school in 1981. That dozen or more years of change made for sharp divisions in folks. Hawk, Doves, Gays, Straights, Right, Left. Frankly, Mike didn't want to speak to anyone about change, politics, or anything remotely involving. Mike wanted no debates. Not on some legs' bus, especially given the deep pounding in his heart for what lay ahead.

As Mike fell in and out of sleep, he heard the men on the bus going on about the Memorial, "How could anyone dredge such a trench;

it's like a mass grave. You think that survivors could find comfort in that?" Someone said.

"Well, it's not for them; it's for the dead," said another.

"Really? You think it don't matter to the survivors? Well it does."

"That just makes for more of the same old, same old we got in the first place."

"What do you mean? Still get. We got a wall."

"Survivors want peace, closure…"

"Stop already with the surviving. Get on with the living."

Mike had read all about the monument and its 19-year-old designer from Yale, Maya Lin. He'd clipped the reviews out of *The Boston Globe* and the *Worcester Telegram & Gazette*, whose opinions were split down the middle. Just like the country for the past sixteen years. Vietnam sure screwed up America, Mike thought to himself.

"This Memorial is more like a bunch of black headstones strung together," came one from the skinny guy in the back of the bus.

Mike thought, however majestic or "designed" it was, it wasn't going to be the thing he'd hang around for, God knows.

Mike felt no compunction about spending any time arguing with the plebeians from Marlboro. There was too much death in his head for Mike to make room for anything else, just the dead men he'd come to honor and the dead man he longed to be. His eyes were locked in a deadness, a stare that let no one in for fear they might die from it, and it left Mike trapped on the other side of that stare, waiting his time out. All Mike wanted was to see the memorial, pay his respects, maybe catch a few beers, go home, and finish what he'd put off too long.

Eight hours later, stepping off the bus, the sun was low in the sky, and the wind had picked up. Mike barely heard the details of the return to Marlboro, where to meet up, or where to assemble for the state-by-state parade on Saturday before the dedication at 2 o'clock. "Remember we'll be marching with Massachusetts, between Maryland and Michigan…"

"Too little, too late," Mike said under his breath. "After a decade of fighting a friggin' conflict in Vietnam—a conflict, Gawd, they didn't even have the balls to call it a war—just shitloads of soldiers, pulled out one-by-one after their 365 days, and shipped home to what? Nobody gives a flying fuck what we were fighting for, forget about survivors. We were barely welcomed home," Mike said to himself. "I wasn't, that's for damn sure." There were no parades; this one tomorrow would be the first.

Mike hoisted his small pack over his back and headed off to see The Wall; see what he'd helped pay for. Back when word came out that Jan C. Scruggs had brainstormed the Vietnam Veterans Memorial and was raising funds (VVMF) to honor the men lost in Vietnam, Mike donated, especially when he heard there'd be no government funding for it. Mike liked the Vietnam Veterans of America's (the VVA's) motto: *Never Again Will One Generation of Veterans Abandon Another.* It always made Mike tear up.)

In his first months over there in B Med, the Herd's MASH Unit where Mike started his Vietnam tour, he'd signed off on many of the wounded on their way to The Wall. Or home. Hopefully, a few had beaten his triage call and made it safely home. Fucking triage: How do you decide who would live or die?

Mike walked towards the National Mall; the rain that had followed him down all day wouldn't let up. It had rendered the sloping hill facing the Memorial into a quagmire—like the monsoon season in Nam—the grounds crew had cordoned off the fragile sod with plastic tape. It was impossible for Mike to get into the crag of the Memorial—the part Maya Lin called her "park within a park"—and pay his respects. It wouldn't have taken him long. He'd already studied the configuration and how the names laid out in chronological order of death. The beginning of the war, 1959 starting from the tallest right middle panel, then onto the panels to the right of it, all the way east to the shortest panel; then the names crossed over to the shortest panel on the west, continuing with names, ending in the middle. The end of the war, 1975, meeting up with its start, 1959. Mike just had to find 1970, which started on line 113 of panel 15W.

One of the articles he'd clipped from the papers commented on how asinine the layout was, preferring an alphabetical or state-listing. But to the Nam vets, it was okay: it was about **their** time there, they could find **their** guys all together—made sense—if anything about their time over there could.

Mike gave his head a shake. Maybe it was a mistake to have come; such a cold black aftermath stood in the mist before him. The Wall was massive; it had to be to hold all those 57,939 names.[1]

Cordoned off and kept for Saturday, November 13—the day when busloads of veterans and families would appear—the Memorial formed a formidable black bird-in-flight, a sliver, carved into the soon-to-be-hallowed ground between the Lincoln and Washington Memorials. Thus far, only the press and officials had been allowed to walk the Vietnam Memorial's sloping pathways. Those who had, reported of emotions rising up as they descended and saw themselves superimposed with the soldiers' names reflecting in the polished rock. Maya Lin was pretty genius; she wasn't designing a mere memorial. She was creating the reimagining of a soul-sick generation. Stone that polished to a mirror-like quality was chosen just for that reason.

---

1   Maya Lin's original design of the Vietnam Veterans Memorial contained 57,939 names, the dedication day total. Her design, laid out chronologically, included "negative space" enough to allow the etching of additional names to compensate for recovered MIAs, veterans who later died of their wounds, and errors. At the time of this writing, there are 58,271 names. Source: thewall-usa.com

There was hardly a guy who'd served in Nam who didn't need some answer to be found here, and women too—not just nurses who'd served or died there—but women who'd grown to love, or used to love, or remembered a Love, dead or alive, who'd flown too close to the fire, and who came home all done in. Maybe did themselves in. They came seeking answers to their nightmares, or those of their husband's or lover's or child's.

Without access, Mike started to wander away up Constitution Avenue, then he stopped, stood there in the rain, thinking about what it meant to go home. As Mike slowly began to walk again, a short, balding vet with a "Herd" patch—a white wing emblazoned on a blue shield with a red sword slashing across it—ran up to him.

"Hey, Doc," the eagle-eyed paratrooper had spotted, not just Mike's Herd patch, but Mike's CMB. "When you over there?"

"February of '70 till they disbanded," Mike answered. He liked being called 'Doc,' he put out his hand, "Mike Creamer, N/75th Rangers with the 503."

"Frank Baker," he said, offering a cigarette to the younger man. "Came in with them from Okinawa with the 503rd; made the jump in '67.[2]" There they were, the two Rangers: The Alpha and the Omega of the infamous 173rd Airborne Brigade, a cadre so feared and revered in Vietnam, the enemy called them The Herd, thought they must be animals. Michael smiled, cocking his head at the implication of such a chance hook-up. Baker too, a smart guy, not so unlike Mike Creamer, had figured the same for himself. Smiling, he asked, "What are you doing out here in the rain, Creamer?"

Mike laughed aloud, "I just got off a legs' bus down from central

---

2   Operation Junction City was the only official jump of the Vietnam War. Robert J. Martin, ed., "Operation Junction City," History of 'The Herd' (Paducah, KY: Turner Publishing Co, 1993) p. 18-19.

Mass." He went on, "Thought I could see the memorial tonight, before the crowds. Not good with crowds."

"No, me neither." Baker added, "The Sigholtz Chapter has a suite at the Sheraton tonight. Open bar."

"Chapter?" Mike asked. "I didn't know there were Herd chapters."

"Oh yeah. Much better than the VFW." Frank grimaced wryly. "Made our own group. Where you been Creamer, under a rock or something? Come on; check it out."

"Excellent," Mike smiled, the first of many smiles that night, and one more heartfelt than he'd felt all year. It lifted him and his spirits to the proud height of a paratrooper.

"We can walk there," Baker said, starting off, grasping the foundling by the shoulder and drawing him in. "Good to find you, Creamer. Good to find you."

"Same, same," Mike said.

Baker led Mike away from the muddy crevice and into the smoky Sheraton DC, that hosted the Sky Soldiers of the 173rd hospitality suite: non-stop free beer, camos, (of course), bush hats, black berets, red berets, unit colors, no bullshit, paratroopers with unabashed tear-strewn faces, welcome embraces—long and lusty. The *ad hoc* ballroom décor alone had Mike in tears; Scotch-taped to flocked wallpaper were maps, company rosters, campaign streamers of battles won, and home-sweet-home. Swept back and into a proud culture where he could, at last, breathe deeply, Mike let go of the incomprehensible tension that had, for the better part of a year, nearly consumed him, almost eradicated his quick wit, whatever remained of his love of life and a driving wanderlust that had plunked him fatefully close to paths of glory and finally led him here. This was home. Mike's hometown friends' hopes and his mother's prayers aligned, suspending him in a nexus of new life. Mike had rejoined The Herd; he was the elite LRRP[3] Ranger Medic, a survivor of two Vietnam tours, who had come back stateside through the spitting and name-calling on another dark night in San Francisco ten and a half years ago. This was different; this was the homecoming he never got, this was changing everything. Here he didn't have to explain. Mike was in the arms of his Sky Soldier named Frank Baker. They laughed and cried into Saturday morning, telling their stories, meeting his men, slugging back beers, taking long drags of cigarette after cigarette. When Mike took a moment to lift his head and peruse the room, he saw dozens of others, just like him, crying into their beers, in the arms of their angels.

---

3   LRRP (pronounced lurp) stands for Long Range Reconnaissance Patrol, a covert operations unit comprised of Rangers in Vietnam. LRRPs scouted secretly behind enemy lines.

CHAPTER 7

A Glorious Day

The next morning, Nancy and I were clueless, not knowing the schedule of events for that day, or where we were going to park, or how we would find The Wall once we got to DC. We knew there was a parade, but military parades had become oddities in New York City. Only a thin stream of people would line parade routes, interspersed with obvious gaps. We didn't know this would be so different a parade. Besides, we needed to leave immediately after the dedication, so this was the time we planned to visit. I sat with Nancy and her mom, eating breakfast, trying to be patient, but nervous we'd miss the dedication ceremony. Nancy knew the way into the capitol, so happily, I drove, and she navigated.

Miraculously, as we crossed Constitution Avenue, a parking space opened before me (it was like the Red Sea parting). We didn't know it at the time, but this was **the** closest parking space to the Vietnam Veterans Memorial. I felt washed with, well, call it wonder, my first sense of being where I was meant to be, maybe ever. It was the start of a Glorious Day.

Neither Nancy nor I could see The Wall; it was cut below the rise across Constitution Avenue. Suddenly there was a flood of men, and assorted family units huddled around an entrance to the National Mall. It took a few minutes to realize that we were at the terminus of the veterans' homecoming parade, the event leading up to the dedication. Men marched towards their memorial and were finishing where we stood on Constitution Ave., amid a contingent from, wow— "Those guys are from Marlboro, my hometown." I called out to Nancy. Right. I felt it again, "God must have put me here."

The Marlboro men, many neat in their dress uniforms and suits, weren't my expectation of Vietnam warriors. Still, I ran up to one folding a VFW banner and said, "Hi, I'm from Marlboro too." I was ready to explain, "I moved to NYC and then…" He could have cared less. In retrospect, those Marlboro men were merely a celestial compass point, folding their flags, that I'd just tripped over. Now I had Marlboro on my radar.

Nancy pulled me further into the mall just as it started to spit rain; The Wall was at best, forty yards from where we parked. We could see the area filling fast. Massachusetts was not even mid-way of states about to flow onto the memorial grounds. They were mostly men, though some had marched in family units, dressed in partial or complete uniform, engaged in mini-reunions, back clapping, bear-hugging men welcoming each other home. Many wore camouflage outfits and raggedy fatigues. Some wore suits. Nancy and I looked longingly across to the memorial's ramp, closed until after the dedication.

Respectfully we nudged around people up to a precipice, away from the walkway now swarming with parade participants. From there, we could see the complete Memorial. It was stunning; its polished black granite winked at us when the sun peeped out behind sometimes sobbing clouds. We wandered to seek different perspectives, and from every angle, we felt overcome by separate sagas happening all around us. Here was a story, and there was a story. Someone handed us little pins in plastic bags: MARCHING ALONG and TOGETHER AGAIN nicely laid out, stacked over and under the colors of the Vietnam Service Ribbon.

I spotted Jane Alexander, my favorite actress and soon to be president of the NEA (National Endowment for the Arts), standing off to the left in the Lincoln Memorial's direction. But the vets were the stars that day, and we, the humbled audience, whispered to one another to maintain reverence.

Catching snippets of a story of loss, or hearing as guys from the same unit hooked up—it was impossible not to eavesdrop given the situation—I started to shiver. The rain and the obvious pain of the men alternated a current of emotion around us. It put a layer between me and the rest who'd come because of some attachment—I knew almost no one who'd served. I'd gone to DC hoping to find Vietnam vets to talk to; now there was no chance in hell that I could casually approach one, interrupt something far more important. I would have to settle for on-looker. Inside, I was saddened by this realization; I wanted badly to connect. Nancy and I drifted into speechlessness, words trapped with no way to respond, our throats sore from what we were witnessing. All around, the aftermath of Vietnam was playing out live. Parents of lost boys appeared with pictures pinned to their chests, hoping to attract anyone who might have known their sons. Firefight combatants were coming together on this muddy knoll; there a survivor and maybe a widow, here a husband and a wife or a dad and a daughter holding onto one another, explanations impossible— or perhaps a start. From the beginning, it was hard to swallow; I looked at Nancy, whose eyes were filled and reddened with tears. What did she feel/remember/know that I didn't?

Between electrified pops and crackles blaring on the loudspeakers—perhaps impaired by so much rain—the *Chariots of Fire* soundtrack began its haunting strains. I looked at Nancy; her mouth was open! The overture moved me at Perry's fashion show last week, now it took my breath away, whatever breath I had left since losing most of mine on a legless man in a wheelchair who when I went to shake his hand, there was a stump instead. I needed a drink. And maybe some napkins. The Kleenex I'd brought were already soaked wads in my jacket pocket. I could only swipe at the stuff that ran continuously out of my nostrils with my cold, reddened fingers. I didn't need to worry about anyone approaching me; at that moment, I was far from attractive.

I said to Nancy, "We still have time. I can barely swallow; let's find something to drink."

"I'm with you."

We walked up the paved path, atop which, a beer company was pouring out free drinks from a keg at the top of the knoll. We thought it best to pass. The beer was not meant for us. Besides, we needed to use the women's room.

In motion now, even to find the refreshment stand, seemed to give us cause. We were not just gaping oglers. As we maneuvered around vet vignettes, the Lincoln Memorial was to our right. We laughed aloud, again that the men's room line was way back to the roadway and the women's room had stroll-in status.

"You know," Nancy said, "we will **never** in our lives see this oddity a third time; I'm sure of it." We went to pee. That accomplished, we approached the refreshment stands, where we found another set of lines, each longer than the next.

"You pick the line," Nancy said, and I wished she hadn't.

Already my day was as near to perfect as I could have wanted: I'd been moved to tears, I had laughed, (we'd found a parking space). It was a Glorious Day, and I knew it then, and that's how I'd recall it. But by the looks of it, it would take a good twenty, twenty-five minutes to order. Still, it wasn't a day to worry about stupid things like lines not moving, or anything else, though our line moved slower than the rest. Patience, I said to myself. Be content to take it all in: This was **their** big Homecoming.

A photo of Michael, whom I had buried in the sand on a Youth Theatre Workshop outing, with me snuggled up to his "bulky" frame... Summer of 1967.

CHAPTER 8

Mike and Me

In the next line over, I spotted a guy who stretched his skinny arm in the air to check the time on his Rolex. What? Double-take. A Rolex? I flashed back to a Thug boyfriend of mine, who had tried to kick in my apartment door after I'd split with him. He had huffed and puffed about me buying him a Rolex—Ha, like I had $2,500 extra to buy a Rolex! What's all the rage about a Rolex, anyway? I peered to see who it was, making sure it wasn't that creep.

The culprit was a thin, blondish man in a black beret and a camouflage jacket—lots of pockets and flaps—with blue jeans tucked into black lace-up boots. *Polished*, black lace-up boots. He turned to stuff his hands back into his pockets, and as he did, I caught the ID, embroidered in black, on a green band above his chest pocket: CREAMER. Odd name. Rolex, huh? I had no way of knowing that a Rolex was the *de facto*, must-have timepiece for soldiers of fortune. If you worked in the jungle, you needed a Rolex so it wouldn't rot off your wrist; then too, you could use it to pay your ransom out. These men bought Rolexes whenever they achieved the pay grade to afford them. To the Thug back in New York City, it was merely a status symbol.

I looked back; Mr. Creamer wasn't making eye contact with anyone. His glassy Steve McQueen eyes were focused on something way in the distance. It's what was known by combat vets as "the thousand-meter stare, with which a man learns to look beyond an endless field of hurt.[1]" I didn't know that at the time; just wondered what his stare was all about.

Wait, Creamer? I knew a Creamer once upon... "I think I know that man," I whispered to Nancy, breaking from the silence we'd kept what with our throats so dry. "I think."

"From where?" Nancy asked.

I didn't know. Boston Conservatory? Massachusetts College of Art? Someone I worked with in summer stock? Maybe theatre...but...

"He's hard to place," I said. Then I recognized something about him. Yes! That was it; he was that kid from Marlboro who'd gone off and...someone told me he had become-—I gushed, excitedly— a hero. Those were her words, but my remembrance of him: skinny, short, in a football town where skinny and short don't cut it... We'd both acted in Youth Theatre, years before. When I played Ursula, sophomore year in *Bye Bye Birdie*, our director, Judy, made him hide in the prop railway handcar I pumped across the stage—my ballast to keep from tipping over. Ha! Yes, wait, she told me he'd enlisted to go to Vietnam and **saved** a bunch of guys. Wow, him. Michael Creamer.

Remembering, I didn't even let Nancy in on it. I bounded out of the slowest line in the world that had perfectly positioned me, side by side, with this "hero" from my hometown I hadn't seen in—gosh, I couldn't think of how many years. "Are you Michael Creamer?"—I pronounced it as I would the thing alongside a teapot, not knowing yet that the Army had toughened him and his name into CRAMER. "Creamers don't become Rangers," he would tell me afterward, "Cramers do."

But now he said nothing.

"From Marlboro, Massachusetts?" I stammered.

"Yeah." There was a long delay between that and the accusatory, "Why?"

Shrinking back a bit, I said, "I'm Martha," no reaction, "Muffy

---

1   Nicosia, p,107.

Voutas." Still, he showed no sign of recognizing, but I was intent on getting through to him "from Marlboro." I, too, had changed my name from one he might recall to the more dignified name I hated as a child, that had always come out of Massachusetts mouths as Maaaatha.

* * *

From the moment of reconnect, the reality of how much we'd both changed was apparent. Our single binding factor was a hometown he planned to return to kill himself (of which I knew nothing, at that moment). It was a town that had I stayed, I, too, might have had to kill myself. His was a serious consideration, mine a nonsensical thought because it was never my intention to stay in Marlboro in the first place. Yet here we were, together, in parallel hot dog lines on the National Mall.

Recognizing the Marlboro link, Michael's far-away gaze altered for a moment, first deciphering the consequence of talking to anyone from Marlboro, then transforming into a closed-mouth smirk/smile I'd later know meant, "Okay." I introduced Nancy, who had held our place in the slowest line in the world. As those in front of us slipped away, our two lines advanced to the counter in a dead heat, and there wasn't much else we could say. We had to order. Mike asked, "Can I buy you two beers?"

Laughing, Nancy replied, "We should buy *you* one," and we walked away with two beers, a Coke, and two hot dogs.

"Not drinking?" I asked him.

"Whoa no! I did my share last night," he said.

"Two hot dogs?" I always order too much. Had a bite of one and trashed it; the second I stashed in my jacket pocket. Couldn't eat, too nervous, excited. A safe combat vet to talk to!

"Why are you here?" Mike asked. "Did you serve in Vietnam? Do you live in DC?"

"To honor the vets," Nancy said.

"We live in New York City. We work together." I said, "I was, I don't know, compelled to be here. I don't know why, well, no, I know why, but...." I was losing myself. Michael had a certain intensity. Now everything coming out of my mouth took on new importance. "I just wanted to welcome you veterans back in a way that didn't happen back then."

"Hell, no!" Mike blurted out. It was good to see his emotions, hear him laugh. "You have to forgive me, see, I just marched with my unit, the 173rd Airborne, we double-timed in front of the viewing stand, and..."

"I saw the guys from Marlboro when I came in." I said.

"I didn't march with those pencil-pushers. I marched with the 173rd Airborne." Mike was ecstatic and alive; his broad beaming smile stayed pasted on his face. "We did the Airborne Shuffle for old Westy. General Westmoreland got up and whooped!"

"You're out of breath," I said.

"Shit, it's way more than breath. It's a long story."

"Oh, good," I said. "It's just why I came."

We were almost back to where the dedication was about to begin, to where Nancy and I stood earlier. *Chariots of Fire* wound to the *denouement*, the part in the story when things become clear. The passion of the music was perfect; its airy trills tinkled down from above, its bass notes underscored Mike's new-found pride. The hot dog grew cold in my olive-colored leather jacket, but I was on fire. It was so worth coming. I was going to find out about Vietnam. (And this man!) Atop the Memorial, speakers were getting set, and we three stood waiting, making small talk. Then Nancy turned ecstatically, "There's Jim, I'll see you later!" Angels working yet and still. Glorious.

Now Mike and I were alone. "When did you graduate?" I asked, trying to seize on moments my memory robbed me of, praying he wouldn't walk away.

"The year after you, 1969. I early upped. Did two tours with the 173rd." Mike was beaming when he spoke of his unit, but he spoke in such staccato terms, each time waiting for my reaction. It was awkward. I didn't know what his words meant exactly: upped, The Herd, pencil-pushers. We were both nervous. I was caught between not wanting him to know why I'd come—I was writing a book that, so far, had told us that serving in Vietnam was on the losing side, while I delighted at meeting someone I knew from whom I might hear the flip side. I hadn't seriously comprehended the reality of both sides. Michael might put it together that I was meaningless, which is to say I didn't serve. Now, with Michael and Marlboro—honesty would reveal that I just wanted out. Back then, I gave no thought to Vietnam except that it robbed me of my first love, David. Vietnam taught women to take care of themselves; I ran to college. I ran to New York. And over the past nine years, I had almost given up looking for someone to love.

"Should I be impressed?" I finally asked, not trying to be facetious, "Because I..." He looked silently back. "I went to art school." Get it all out. Quickly. It was all I could say short of saying I was a hippie and marched in protests and chanted, "Bring the boys home. Now." But that was enough; he got the message.

"Oh," Mike said, tilting his head like Steve McQueen. Then he smiled, "Well, you're here, aren't you? More than I can say for a lot of people."

"I donated to build The Wall," I said, then ventured, "I've been trying to write about how Vietnam changed us, and well..." I wasn't sure how to talk to a combat vet; anything I said would show how little I knew. "I've only really talked to one combat vet. A door-gunner. He was *really* intense. Kinda scary."

"A door-gunner?" Mike laughed. "He would be scary." Mike raised one eyebrow and looked at me. "You know what door-gunners do? Don't you?"

I nodded. "In fact, once I knew what a door-gunner did, I became very unsure as to..." I stumbled, "...like, what I'd say to a veteran like that." Mike just stood there, checking me out, "I hope you aren't a door-gunner. Are you? I mean, were you?"

Mike laughed, "They wanted me to train as a helicopter pilot, but the school was going to take too long. I wouldn't have gotten over there. I couldn't miss the war," Mike was McQueen again, staring far and away, and I loved Steve McQueen. I day-dreamt I'd marry Steve McQueen.

Miss the war? Everyone I'd interviewed thus far had tried with all their lives to miss the war.

"I chose to be a medic instead." Mike pointed to the CMB pinned to his jacket, "This is my Combat Medic's Badge," he said. "They needed medics; walking targets over there." Mike rocked gleefully on his heels, grinning. "Pretty much guaranteed I'd get to Nam."

"Mmm," I didn't know anyone like him. Since landing in New York City back in 1973, and working in the fashion world almost exclusively, my jungle was Manhattan. I barely left it even for the outer boroughs. (The outer migration was years away.)

"I marched with my unit today for the first time." Mike said, "It was great."

I didn't exactly know what that meant either. Didn't understand the implication of not marching with one's unit, or why? or what might have caused it. Maybe the pins they handed out after the parade were...? Right, Marching Along Together Again. I reached into my pocket and offered Mike one.

"Oh, I picked up a few myself," he said, showing me. "But thank you."

The stuff I didn't know about Vietnam was about to expand exponentially. I was so excited; my heart raced. Yes, I was going to learn about what it was like coming home from War. But my heartbeat had quickened for reasons beyond my writing project.

Mike paused again, then, "Thank you for coming all the way to DC."

"You came a lot further than I did," I said, not acknowledging the compliment.

Then realized it. Realized him. "You're welcome," I said.

CHAPTER 9

Michael is Coming

"Hello," I answered the phone next to my bed.

"Hello, Muffy?" It was Mike. Oh God, it was Michael. I sat up. Would he come?

"Oh, hi, Michael." I was overly eager, "You know I was thinking about what we'd do if you came. We can go to the Macy's Thanksgiving Day Parade; I live close by, we can walk over, see the big balloons," I said.

"Well…" Michael said. It sounded like a no. I gritted my teeth.

"The parade doesn't matter," I said, cutting in. "I mean if you want to come down."

"Yeah, I want to come down. Just had to check on the specifics of how I'd get to the train," Michael said. "Sorry, it took some calls, but yeah, it will be nice to talk."

"Right. (Yay, yay, yay) It will be," I said.

"And you can tell me about *Mademoiselle*, and *Vogue*, and the magazine world," he said.

"Okay," I said. "Great, a meeting of the minds. I'm looking forward to it."

And that was that.

Are You Mr. Goodbar?

✴   ✴   ✴

Back in the 70s, I was a war protester. I wanted the war to end. I wanted our pass/fail college scoring to disappear because if all it was doing was keeping kids in school and out of the draft, it confused me. I wanted to know my marks; I was competitive. I watched as protesters projected onto the soldiers their hatred for the war. I tried not to. If others knew the damage they were doing to the vets, they might have stopped. Maybe they didn't care. I did, and I stopped protesting. You could see that same hatred on TV news stories and motion pictures. It was rampant. Society didn't trust vets trained to kill, guys who could "lose it" in a second. People called them "crazed Vietnam vets" and "ticking time-bombs."

Thinking more, I grew nervous about whom I had invited into my life. *Rambo*? That weird Richard Gere/Vietnam vet in *Looking for Mr. Goodbar*? Wasn't the shooter at the top of the tower at the University of Texas a vet?

After my staff had gone for the day, as I sat assessing Martha Voutas Productions' (MVP) state of finances, I called my sister Dottie and told her I'd invited Michael. Dottie lived nearby in New Jersey; her husband Bernie was our accountant. Dot and I were close like girlfriends.

"Well, you did theatre with him, right? He was that little guy, played Oliver?" She was living at home at the time of *Oliver*, dating Bernie, who was in the Army. He'd been stationed in California, escorting caskets of KIA (killed in action) home. Dottie knew Michael.

And I knew Michael; I remembered him in YTW. I found a photograph of us taken at the beach party we held every summer with YTW. I'd buried him and carved an enlarged, hulky body of sand around his skinny little one. Then I, in my two-piece, hand-made bathing suit, nuzzled down in the crook of his flexed arm, and someone took the shot. I remember building his body; it was the thing a flirtatious girl who wanted to be a Broadway star would do, but I didn't remember the action of lying there with him.

My concerns dissipated when I remembered Michael in DC. And the most memorable occurrence of that day...

✶ ✶ ✶

With Nancy still off with her Jim, Michael and I stood together listening to the final cut of *Chariots of Fire*, when a man, a veteran, approached us.

"There you are," he said to Mike, clutching his arms and grasping him. "I've been looking all over for you." The vet embraced Mike in such a way that spoke of a deep love between them. Without Mike, I was only a bystander; I felt I needed to turn my head from the intimacy coming from between them, not to intrude.

After what felt a long while—vets seemed slow to respond—fighting back his emotions, the vet managed to voice, "I was looking all over. I'd know you anywhere. You saved my life."

Mike smiled. The two of them clasped each other's forearms, looking into each other's eyes now. "Well, I worked on a lot of guys over there," Mike said in a humility I didn't recognize.

I said to myself, "Thank you, God, for showing this to me," and barely moved.

"LZ English, November 1970?" He paused; Mike shook his head in agreement. "We were in the Suoi Ca Valley."

"*Beaucoup* shit went down there," Mike said, now picking up his tempo. "Thanksgiving?"

"Five days. *Beaucoup* shit," he nodded. "When did you get back?" the stranger asked.

"When they disbanded over there, March of '71," Mike said. "And you?"

"Shrapnel opened me up; I lost part of my intestines. I thought I was going to die," the vet said, "and," he labored still to get his words out, "*you saved me.*"

Mike held the vet's sobbing being with one hand (his whole body shook), and with the other, he rubbed his back. It was a gesture to mask his own pain, it seemed.

The man braved, "You worked on me until they could get a chopper in."

"I...," Mike started then stopped. The vet gave him time now to process what he was going to say, "I was a medic. Out there, it was either save a life or shoot like shit to hold onto yours. I'm sorry," Mike said, his bravado releasing painful memories, "I don't remember you."

It didn't matter, "I do. I'd know your face anywhere."

"Yeah?" Mike made light of the intensity, removed his Ranger beret, and rubbed his thinning blonde hair. "I had more of this then." I liked him more without the beret; he had a handsome smile. The tough guy we'd met at the concession had nearly disappeared.

"You saved my life, Brother. You and The Herd." They embraced even harder and longer than before.

Michael was crying now. We all were. "Yeah," Mike said, "they kind of saved my life too, last night at the Sheraton. And today, doing the Airborne Shuffle in front of Westmoreland's viewing stand!"

"Sorry, I missed both those things. Barely got in for the Dedication." The two hugged again, and over Mike's shoulder, the vet spotted me. "This your wife?"

"No," Michael said, then without pausing, "she's my friend."

I was taken aback, that in the last half-hour, Michael unhesitatingly called me—the hippie art student and war protester—his friend. I liked that. I liked that a lot. I hoped to be.

The vet turned to include me in their closeness, opening the circle of the two of them, inviting me in. "Hi." He shook my hand and held it still. "Do you know who you're with?"

"Yes." I smiled, cheeks quivering, about to tell him of our meeting. Then, "No. Not really..."

He cut in, looking at Michael, "This man is the closest thing to God I know."

(God again. So that's why You gave me that parking space.)

The three of us embraced, each one crying over the shoulder of the other while *Chariots of Fire* swelled to its final crescendo. The sound of the flyby filled the void, as the Navy's Blue Angels filled the sky overhead. Three heads looked upward.

"Look, lost man formation," I said.

"*Missing* Man Formation," the two vets said in unison.

The emcee came to the microphone to start the dedication—the invocation, the presentation of arms, a posting of each of the fifty states' flags, "Star-Spangled Banner," the speakers, "America The Beautiful." Then the echoing "Taps," which brought us again to tears. I don't remember how the vet vanished, or if Mike got his number. He had come to find Mike, to share his testimony of Michael's heroism for my sake, no doubt, but also for Mike, who seemed to grow from that reminder. Mike *saved* people.

Nancy came back, and I explained to Mike that I had to leave for NYC. I was to serve as maid of honor at a friend's wedding, and the rehearsal dinner was to be that night at 7:00. We had just enough time to get me there. I hugged Michael, and he hugged me back with one of those vet-clutching embraces I'd witnessed all day and I was part of now. It was a sweet embrace.

"I'd love to talk more," I said. "Next time I get to Marlboro, I'll call." Mike looked back with only a half-smile. Still, it was a smile, as measured as I cared to measure. He hugged Nancy, thanked us again for coming. I knew clearly that I didn't want to leave.

Neither Nancy nor I got to see the names on the monument; it was far too crowded. I had gone to DC, remembering only one name on The Wall from Marlboro: Richie Demers. Richie fought with his brother in the playground of my K-12 elementary school. Bloody nose violent, those Demers brothers, you could barely tell them apart. Richie would have to wait; the lines were too long. Long lines—the credo of the day.

My resume photo for acting taken by Bruce Plotkin, a few years before I met Mike Creamer

I like to say that God gave me a clarity that day, the clarity of being exactly where He wanted me to be, of seeing with eyes all around me, and sensing His presence in every step. My takeaway of November 13, 1982—Day 1, of 3003 we'd have together—is when we discover something inside that speaks to us and we take action (as in getting to DC), the possibilities are endless. Call it fate if you will, but I think God guides us. For me, meeting Mike was like that.

Inviting Mike, the closest thing to God, into my home? No problem.

Then Mike's first letter came. I ripped it open.

11/19/1982

Hello Muffy,

Still can't get over meeting you in DC! I'm <u>very</u> much looking forward to seeing you next week! We certainly have a lot to talk about, and Thanksgiving will be a special time. Hope you have a slide projector—I rummaged through closets and came up with close to 100 Ektachromes of the Rangers, which is about the extent of my Nam photo library.

Thank you again for making that long trip to be with us on our special day. You'll never know how much it was appreciated! So, take care, 'till we meet again next week!

—Mike C.

CHAPTER 10

Me

I guess Vietnam had been in my blood for years. My brother Stephen enlisted in the Air Force to avoid going to combat. He left before my senior year in HS (1968). Back then, everyone had someone who was dealing with the Nam. It wasn't always obvious, since "dealing" sometimes involved personal choices, private issues men didn't want exposed. (Faking health reports, escaping to Canada.)

In my senior year of college, I had written about the Kent State shootings back in May of 1970, when the Ohio National Guard killed four students during a Vietnam war protest. The Guardsmen opened fire on the crowd; they were supposed to be carrying blanks. Kent State shut down my freshman year at Massachusetts College of Art and hundreds of other colleges and universities across the country. That's how widespread the anti-war movement was.

In my piece, I wrote about how Kent State enlisted all of us students hanging out on the edge to join in war protests: "They are killing students. It's a state college, just like us!" The aftermath helped turn the tide on Vietnam. I wrote that the student strike socked me with a nearly debilitating confusion. There was side-taking. I drove out to see my mentor, a Mass Art grad, when the school struck. I had forgotten her husband was a National Guardsman.

"They should have shot them all," the Guardsman bellowed.

"How could you let them close your school?" she said. "You make them open your school. *You* paid tuition." I was crushed. There would be no more late night Black Russians shared listening to Rod McKuen. No more discussions of *The Fountainhead* or *The Prophet*. Kent State ended that.

Writing about the widespread anger and how it affected me throughout my college experience won me a *Mademoiselle* Guest Editorship in 1973, which took me to New York City for a month, including a trip to Paris. *Mlle* lateralled me to *Vogue*, a magazine owned by the same publisher, where I began my design career.

At *Vogue*, I read all the manuscripts under consideration for publication. I lined up front and back-of-the book illustrators and photographers in case we needed them. My Marlboro, Mass schooling barely prepared me: Travel, Cooking, Beauty, Health, Exercise. Though I did little actual design work, it was mind-expanding. I studied Monday nights with the Graphic Design Guru of all time, Milton Glaser, who on week two, unpinned my assignment from the wall, raising it up, and asked, "Who did these (there were two)? Come up here and explain it, please."

My embellished Xerox copies, self-portraits of both sides of my brain were mounted in 3-D foamcore frames. I had inserted magnets to repel if the two faces met, and to snap together when placed opposite. I explained, "We have these two sides of our brain, but in life, we're oblivious to them. We don't look at ourselves knowingly."

Milton held them, playing with the magnetic properties. Then he held them up, "See this, class; this is the kind of work I expect out of each of you, every week."

✳ ✳ ✳

One day in 1975, our production manager at *Vogue,* my friend, Gerry Slater, a WWII vet, ran into the office, "Come look, they're evacuating Saigon, throwing helicopters off ships. You must see this." Someone had wheeled a TV out into the hallway near the Beauty Department. We watched in awe—the Art Department, the writers, the Beauty

Editors, the Managing Editor—our whole corner of *Vogue*, caught up in the chaos. That was the end of Vietnam, a war that had run its course throughout my lifetime—from twelve until I was twenty-five.

I moved into a sweet fifth-floor walk-up on West 89th Street in the last block before Riverside Drive. I left *Vogue* at the end of the year; I'd saved enough from freelance illustration for *Mlle* to last a year. I went back nights to acting at Herbert Berghdorf Studios with a great teacher, Carol Rosenfeld. I didn't have a lot of extra time, but it was my time. That was a valuable commodity, and I treasured it immensely.

I knew very little about Vietnam until I found a paperback: *Chance and Circumstance/The Draft, the War and the Vietnam Generation.*[1] Its cover photo was of dog tags, a peace symbol, and dice sitting atop a US Army fatigue jacket. *Chance and Circumstance* was a compilation of data researched by President Gerald Ford's Clemency Board to determine the fate of the 209,500[2] accused draft avoiders—deserters and others—those whose lives were still in limbo. It was published in 1978, three years after the war ended, the same year Martha Voutas Graphic Design (before a name change) started up.

In *Chance and Circumstance*, I found oceans of data and just dove in. I learned about 365 days—the length of a tour of duty for a soldier sent to Vietnam. The book became my bible, a thesaurus for learning the language—arriving in-country alone, every "Newbie," was the "F'n New Guy," or, situations like how a "Cherry" would need to win the trust of the men he was going to be fighting beside. Would he freeze? Was he reliable? Could he maintain silence or would he cry? I learned about how experienced soldiers were reluctant to embrace any FNG—another way of putting it—who seemed to lack the skills to survive. Frightening. I marked up my book with notes in the margins. One note: "365 days of dread."

---

1   Baskir, Lawrence M., and William A. Strauss. Chance and Circumstance the Draft, the War, and the Vietnam Generation. (New York: Vintage Books, 1978). My primary source of statistical data that first inspired me when I picked it up in 1978.
2   Baskir et al., p. 4, chart 1.

* * *

I decided to start interviewing men—finding out what Vietnam meant to them. When I asked Richard, my college roommate's new husband from California, about the draft, he replied, "I don't remember," he paused, "but I remember something on television..." Then he recalled. His hands flew to his face in an Edvard Munch-like scream, "I never wanted to have anything to do with *that* war," Richard said, angry, tearing up. He fumbled on details, but I knew what he meant. The image had seared my memory too: A captured Asian man dressed in black, hands tied behind his back, and a soldier with a gun to his head. The captive shakes visibly, "No, no," then is shot in the side of the head. The second-of-impact photo was violent. It received coverage everywhere.[3] There was a video as well; I was frightened to have viewed it once, but it played repeatedly on TV. It would push America a digit further against the war.

Most striking of my interviews was with Allyn, who told his tale from Detroit, where as a senior in HS he got a girl pregnant. He married her, but knew he was gay, and the marriage was eventually annulled. That's when the draft notice came, and Allyn traveled to his physical on a bus with others from his high school. They were told to strip down to undershorts, and each was given a manila folder with a sheet for health issues to be checked. The men paraded single-file around a gym going from one health inspection to another. Finally, they were offered an option to go to a section of the gym to discuss psychological issues.

As he sat waiting in the folding chair and moved closer and closer to the doctors, Allyn eyed the three men in white coats, sizing up which one was likely to give him what he hoped for: Understanding Compassion. When he was next in line for the meanest-looking of the three, Allyn excused himself and went to the men's room. Returning,

---

3   Photo by AP's Eddie Adams shot in 1968 during the Tet Offensive; Adams won the Pulitzer Prize and the front page of *The New York Times*.

he found he was next for the compassionate one. Allyn discussed with him what had happened, why he couldn't serve. After some discussion, the doctor asked for Allyn's folder and stamped across it on both sides, in 3" red letters: HOMOSEXUAL. Allyn, finished with the physical went to get dressed. Angry, he hurried to leave, coming to a turn-style, and a military guard who said, "Go in and have lunch."

Allyn stood by the cafeteria door and said, "No, I don't want lunch."

The guard said, "You have to have lunch."

"I want to wait on the bus," Allyn said.

"Well you're not allowed," the guard said.

Allyn flashed the homosexual folder in the guard's face proclaiming, "I don't *have* to do anything." And left for the bus.

A young superintendent, now in an upscale Connecticut school district, said he never intended to teach but told me he received a draft exemption for working in a low-income, inner-city school. He had married to stay out of the war, though he knew he was gay. "I ruined my wife's life," he said, crying. Each of the men I interviewed cried.

These were moral issues that I wanted to pursue; it was essential to complete more interviews, but that summer—1982— I moved to a new apartment and found a new design studio for myself. I went to Paris and researched products for Trimfit, the legwear licensee for Perry Ellis—as Perry grew and flourished, so did we. We became an official advertising agency, and were headed to gross one million dollars by year-end. We had a staff of five. MVP paid their living. I had responsibilities.

There was in that time, the din of the Equal Rights Amendment.[4] Proponents were drumming up votes for the ERA; the vote was in June. I had an opinion on the Gender Gap, and maybe I should have gotten involved. It seemed so elementary; to me, the gender gap was blatantly apparent. In my generation, boys turned eighteen; they got draft notices. Girls turned eighteen; they didn't. With the draft hanging over their heads, American boys had to start deciding at sixteen and seventeen, which way to turn. Maybe they enlisted in the non-combat service arms or evaded the war by going to Canada or Sweden. My generation had a very early wakeup call. They called us the Vietnam Generation.

In *Chance and Circumstance,* I read that one in every four men admitted he avoided the draft by hurrying into marriage, having unwanted children. (I found those facts played out in my own family's circumstances, or friends' divorces. I was not anxious to get married early on.) At a very young age, a boy dealt with lifelong choices. It affected us women too. When my high school sweetheart left for the Navy during my senior year, I was hurt and angry that he hadn't said good-bye; I felt oddly betrayed, and knew, without coaching, that I had better take care of myself.

A month before meeting Mike, a girlfriend from home said, "Muff, get over Vietnam; it's a done deal. Stop living in the past." But the stories from men I had already interviewed were far from a done deal, and except for the door-gunner, they hadn't even *gone* to war. And what about the data in *Chance and Circumstance?* Or Jan Scruggs who'd raised the $17 million to build our tribute to the dead, then built it in less than nine months?

No, Vietnam was not a done deal.

---

4   The ERA would fail to get its 38 states in a vote in June 1982.

CHAPTER 11

Landing Zone

Mike debated seriously about calling me back and reneging on coming to New York. He hadn't fully recovered from his last trip to New York City in early 1981, when he was flown in as the honored guest of Morrison-Knudson (M-K), his former employer on the powerline project in Africa. A few months prior, machete-wielding Angolan rebels attacked the M-K compound near Kinshasa, Zaire, the former Belgian Congo, killing anyone in their path, particularly foreigners. Mike and another Nam vet stepped in to rescue the team, first evacuating workers' wives and children on some small aircraft. Abandoning everything, they led the men on foot through dense jungle. Hotly pursued, the two vets blew up bridges behind them before they could cut a safe landing zone (LZ). Then they called in the coordinates for air rescue. This was precisely why M-K hired Vietnam vets as medics—not just for their tropical medicine experience, but to counterweigh the hazards of working in what was called a "third world" country.

To reward the heros, Morrison-Knudsen flew them to New York City to celebrate with a three-day, all-expense-paid trip, culminating in a company banquet. On January 30th, Michael checked into the posh Waldorf Astoria, the same day 21 of the 52 hostages from the Iranian Hostage Crisis, recently released as Ronald Reagan became president, checked into the *same hotel*. The two celebrations were way too con-current for Michael; his whole celebration "shit the bed." The hostages were honored with a ticker-tape parade through Lower Manhattan that was, "More festive than anything since WWII.[1]"

From my office on 23rd Street, I heard the motorcade sirens. I hopped on the subway, and down on Broadway, I snapped a roll of slide film I had in my camera; I wanted to know what this patriotism stuff was all about. I did not know that Michael Creamer was in Manhattan. I knew nothing of his journey at the time. And I was only just getting into Vietnam.

Vietnam vets raged, "Where the hell is my parade?"

For Mike, it was very immediate: Caught smack dab in the middle of New York with the hostages was humiliating, intimidating, and infuriating. The Iran Hostage parade torpedoed his pride; Michael's celebratory feast grew meaningless. He cut his visit short by a day and flew back into Boston. If Mike never saw New York City again, it wouldn't have bothered him.

Until now, *now* there was Me, this woman he'd met in DC, who wanted to talk about Vietnam. The trip to DC had halted his suicide; maybe this was alluring enough to break the hex Mike had put on NYC. Or the thought of maybe having a little sexual activity was more than Mike Creamer could resist. His letter sounded excited.

Michael copied a few of his humorous two and three-page, single-spaced diatribes from Zaire and enclosed them with his second letter to me.

> Ron— *(to whom Mike wrote)*
> 2 Oct 75: Start a campaign for me—I want every woman you know (sexy ones anyway) to send me a little lock of their hair. That's what's incredibly hard to take here—no variety. ...After two joints, a Simba (beer) and a glass of Cognac, I'm feeling okay; 'cept I lust mightily for your

---

1   Nicosia, pp. 395-6.

sister, Carolyn. Ah, to feel those arms, those lush lips again!

PHOTO RON BUCCINO

Michael at Cape Cod National Seashore, Marconi Beach, Wellfleet, summer of 1973.

And

<u>10 November 76:</u> Been busy here—my partner in Kolwezi was on a month's leave, and things were hopping. I've been helping with fieldwork and statistics along with the WHO[2] and CDC in conjunction with African Hemorrhagic fever here[3]: I worked with the WHO to fight what is believed to be the last reported

2   WHO—World Health Organization, CDC—Center for Disease Control
3   The Hemorrhagic fever Mike was working on would later be known as Ebola, which had its start in Zaire.

new case of smallpox in the world! Right here in Kolwezi. Jesus, I know now why it used to strike terror in the past—this guy was covered with quarter-sized vesicles, he was comatose, and his face and genitals looked like they had been napalmed. We had a whole string of traumatic accidents: broken legs, internal injuries, eye injuries and the like; a big run on medical emergencies (appendicitis, abnormal pregnancies, crisis stage septicemia, you name it), and overall, I saw a record 3,241 patients from 26 Sept. to 25 Oct. Busted my ass, but I found a few moments for swimming, smoking, screwing, and Simba-chugging. I don't want to hear you bitching about 60-hour weeks! Mine run 80-85 hours on average, counting time spent on night and Sunday calls. —Mike

Boy, that Mike could write.

CHAPTER 12

Right Now

Michael's letters impressed me. While I was pretty much over the anxiety of bringing a crazed vet into my life, my neighbor, Diane, came up with a scheme that if Michael were truly crazed, I could develop some rare kidney attack or whatever it took.

"He was a medic in Vietnam, remember?" I argued.

"Gregg could come out with his rifle—make Michael leave us alone?" Diane said.

"Yeah, that's good, Diane," Gregg said, "let's bring out the guns. Do you forget I keep ours hidden because of NY state gun laws? You want me to spend a year in prison?"

I could only laugh. By then, Michael and I had had several telephone conversations and letters that allayed my fears. The four of us were to celebrate Thanksgiving in my apartment; I was responsible for the turkey and dressings, Diane, the vegetables, and dessert.

Diane was a beauty from Ohio; she designed retail spaces for Bloomingdale's. Every morning she left looking gorgeous, all made up. I, on the other hand, rarely wore makeup and looked like I'd rolled out of bed, which, as often as possible, I had. Gregg was a graphic designer who dressed as smashingly as Diane. They were a stunning pair—a virtual Barbie and Ken. I smoked an occasional joint with him and drank white wine over Scrabble with her. Diane and I, total Scrabble *aficionados*, would join two boards together using color copies, and we'd triple the triple-point blocks. We also played thematic Scrabble, whereby words within a predetermined theme—say architecture—would warrant 50 points. I couldn't want for better neighbors. They were as competitive as I was.

My remaining anxiety focused on how to get a 20-pound turkey, wine bottles, a case of beer, and all the rest from individual stores on Third Avenue to my apartment between Park Avenue South and Broadway. Due to commitments, Diane and Gregg couldn't help, so I called Mike.

"Michael? It's Martha. Muffy. How are you?"

"Oh, okay. I guess." I just woke him again. Didn't I?

"I was wondering," I said, "I know I said you should come down on Wednesday."

"Yep, the 24th," he said.

"Listen, I was beginning to stress about it," I said.

"It's okay. I don't have to come." So quick to judge themselves, those crazy Vietnam vets. Mike showed early signs that he didn't trust romance, or himself in a romance, but I failed to recognize them.

"No, I *want* you to come. That's not it," I explained. "I'm sorry. See, I don't know how I can get the turkey from the store to my house. I mean and all the stuff."

"Yeah, like stuff-ing?" Michael said. Ah, wry humor; this could be good.

"Yeah, funny." I still had mine. "All the stuffing and ingredients for *hors d'oeuvres* and drinks, and I was hoping that you might come down a day earlier, and you could help me with that." I didn't let him answer. "Here I am, assuming you're free."

"Nothing else planned," he said after a pregnant pause, "I can come on the 23rd."

✳ ✳ ✳

Great, then we can shop after you get here. I gave my staff Wednesday and Friday off, so I won't be so stressed." I *was* stressing. "When you get to Penn Station, give me a ring. My studio's not far. The station's on 33rd, and I'm on 28th. Right down Broadway. Except don't look for Broadway. Aim for Seventh Avenue then head east to Broadway. But how will you know where east..." I was a lunatic.

"It's okay. I can find it," Mike said, "I've been trained in the jungle."

"Oh. Right," I exhaled; he was making another joke. Oh, good! "Or I can pick you up if you want?"

"No need," he said.

"And don't worry, I have a separate bed—well, it's a futon, al-most—in the living room, and you can sleep there. I promise not to attack you," I said.

"Curses," Mike said, half under his breath. Only half.

"I've been insane, telling everyone about the 173rd and meeting you and... Ah.... Gregg and Diane are looking forward. They're both designers, and she's a great cook too."

"You're a great cook, then?"

"I'm a good cook; I can say that. I cooked when my mother went to college. I perfected my skills as forced labor," I bragged.

Mike asked me for the address of the studio and said, "What else?"

"Nothing, really. I appreciate it." I added, "Thanks."

"For coming down early?" he asked.

"No, for being so easy to get along with. Thank you."

Truth be told, I hadn't found men so easy to deal with. I was all of 32, and things weren't exactly falling into place. Before going down to DC, I had kept a year-long celibacy, one self-instilled after tangling with a boyfriend of less than a year, with whom I was "engaged." It was the Thug from earlier, but my celibacy's real cause was him beating me up. Celibacy was a hot topic trending on the news.

It's a dreadful thing getting beat up. Low class. Demoralizing.

Embarrassing. Frightening. The rush of anxiety as you realize your eyeglasses are flying from your face, the look of terror, and a fist at arm's length coming at you with full force. It was in our apartment on West 14th, in a building big enough for some anonymity. Crazed vets didn't have to be vets; they could be vet's sons. The Thug was the son of a violent man (his mother told me), who had survived the Battle of the Bulge in WWII. He came home from war unhinged. He was dead now; I never met him. PTSD hadn't been coined to the vernacular yet. Still, the father had PTSD, and the son, like many offspring of servicemen and women surviving horrible scenarios, who inherit the parent's disease. The fears of the fathers chiseled into the next generation.

After the celibate year, I didn't date for romance; I didn't even touch myself for sexual pleasure. I met Michael a month later. After it was up. Before the Thug, I'd describe myself as desperate, lonely. I found poems I wrote about that time.

Somewhat Drunk in a Cab Going Uptown

I pass thru this city
In pulsating rhythm
Left hand out front—
My right hand behind me
Moving thru space in
A current of motion
Like blinking my eyes
And the pupils stand clear.

I am made for the city
My pulse and my rhythm
On again, off again
Trying with all me
But the motion at times

Leaves me lost and unwilling
And I down a few wines and
I leave myself still.

While the mind keeps on moving
In force-beats that drive me
And the clogging is deadened
It opens my mind.
I am off on a trip
That the dullness affords me,
I'm facile and moving
The city surrounds me.

I'm moving and striving
And nothing around me
Can block out my tempo
It's so much behind me.
My rhythm, my tempo
The dullness affords me
And I write poems in taxis,
Leave Midtown behind me
And climb to a place where
My tempo surrounds me
Behind me, around me
I'm forced to ignore
That I live alone.

So, the *getting along* part I'd thanked Michael for? It was bigger than I was willing to admit. I, too, had inherited my demeanor; my father was a yeller. My mother once told me she'd love me a lot more if I didn't have my father's temper. That hurt, and it made me angry. So, yeah, it was at least fifty percent me. At 32, out of college for ten years, maybe I had grown tough being alone. I owned a business alone; my word was final. See, it wasn't just the vets who were changed; maybe I was too. And my poetry reflected a solitude and sense of need that were inextricably linked. This poem is another one I wrote before meeting Michael in DC.

Red Ink Poem #1
From Martha's Lovelorn Series 1973-1982

I cup you into my hands
In dreams—and lift you up and away.
I hold you dear in palms so strong
That all those years
I've dreamt I'd use them—
To cup you into my arms
In dreams—when arms fall short
Of holding, dear. I hold you dear,
I cup you close,
In arms so strong and long
As years I spent—looking down
At fingers flushed with flowing stuff
That throbbed inside
When I was cold.
So many days spent cold and dreaming.
Cold and dreaming days
Fidgeting fingers
And time away—dreaming then
Of cupping someone in my arms,
Who'd cup me back with
So-strong arms
And he delighting all the while,
That I'd grown strong enough
To cup him into my arms anew
To rock his fears away.

CHAPTER 13

NY 1

Michael arrived at my design studio, MVP, on the Tuesday before Thanksgiving dressed in faded dungarees and a worn plaid flannel shirt. He carried a full Army rucksack on his back, one not in keeping with the trendy knapsacks that adorned New York City backs in the '80s. Instantly judging, I wondered if he and I would hit it off, then I caught myself! "Come on, Martha," I said silently. "Get to know this man. Once upon a time in YTW, you two were friends. This is 'your generation' that you went looking for in DC. *Remember?*"

I introduced Michael to my staff; it was late in the afternoon. They were readying to go home for the long holiday. I was surprised that Michael spoke with them of design and designers in the fashion world. He was smart; he wasn't just trying to impress me. I wondered if Michael, humped over from that olive-drab Quasimodo bag, had caught my slight shiver when he came through the elevator door? In that fleeting moment, we were still Marlboro's senior class vice-president, and the underclassman, Youth Theatre Workshop's leading lady, and the *second* male lead. I was not seeker-woman welcoming the hero-come-home. Damn. If I were to grow into the woman as I truly saw myself and find my soul-mate, I needed first to find my soul.

"Your backpack looks heavy; do you want to catch a cab home?" I asked.

"Heck no. This is my ruck," Michael said like it was a favored appendage, a remnant of war. "It's just bulky from everything I brought to show you. Say, if we're going to view my slides here, I can leave them. They'll be safe, right?"

"Yes, sure. They'll be safe here."

Michael opened the sack and removed ten or twelve yellow boxes of photographic slides, quite a lot. Then we closed the office, everyone else was gone, and we walked home—down Broadway, past the Flat Iron Building, and left, on till morning.

I lived on the second floor, in a one-bedroom apartment, the former front drawing-room (replete with French doors that opened in) of a newly refurbished brownstone in the up-and-coming Flatiron District. I had rented it after the Thug incident, though I thought I couldn't afford it. It was a place that made me feel important; I needed it for self-esteem. Its high ceilings and dental crown moldings spoke grandeur more than any place I'd lived before. I hired a designer friend to install track lighting with dimmers. Didn't have a bed frame, but that lighting was essential.

Past the bedroom on the right, the dining and living areas flowed into each other with a kitchenette and bathroom in the building's windowless middle. I used a futon-like thing sitting on the wood floor as a couch. Two giant India-appliqued pillows leaned against the wall, and there was an excellent pine table and four dining chairs bought from the new Conran's. I owned not-bad stereo equipment (my first major purchase from freelancing into the night when I worked for *Vogue*), bookshelves, a wicker tri-fold screen for privacy, and a small Sony Trinitron TV on a rolling cart.

Michael and I each popped a beer, sat down, and began to get to know one another again.

"Do you see any of the gang from YTW?" I asked.

"Peter and Vinnie, I told you, but I haven't seen them much once I moved home," he started to explain. "I was going to nursing school in Boston, but don't get me started on that. Not yet." He changed the subject, "You seem to be doing well."

"I am. Not sure it's exactly what I want to be doing. I mean…" I was heading off on a tangent about wishing I was writing more, and I wasn't ready to go there. And just as he had stopped, I stopped—both of us afraid of leading with less than our strong suits, hoping to keep the getting-to-know-you ball in the air.

Besides myopic poetry and Communication Plans for would-be clients, any of my recent writing had been of non-vet interviews. All of whom were vehemently opposed to the war. In the little we'd shared in DC, I knew that Michael was proud of his service, and I wanted to understand where *he* was coming from. He would be the ballast for non-vets, and I needed Michael not to take offense with my findings to date. He needed to be the combat veteran he was and share his War with me, the one I didn't know that *I hadn't* come home from. Yet.

"How'd you end up in fashion?" Michael asked. "You mentioned winning that competition. As a writer?"

"Yes, *Mademoiselle* magazine's Guest Editorship.[1]"

"What did you write about?" he asked.

"The first part was humorous. *Mlle* suggested topics; one was 'Write a handbook for your college.' I wrote how transferring from one college to another was like transplanting a seedling. It began, 'I am the daughter of a demi-farmer.' I illustrated it too."

"You know," Michael said, "I worked for your father in the greenhouse."

"I didn't know that."

"Yeah, I dated your sister Jeanie," he said.

"When?" I asked, surprised. "Well, it must have been when I was away at the Conservatory."

---

1   *Mademoiselle's* Guest Editorship: A national competition for college students that ended in 1975 before *Mademoiselle* ceased publication. Open to men in 1972. In 1973 we numbered fourteen, with two men.

Mike nodded.

"You worked in his greenhouses?" I asked.

"And I helped clean out his bedroom. He gave me a bunch of old magazines," Mike said.

"Oh, not those *True Man* magazines." I coughed, a bit embarrassed. Mike nodded, fiendishly, "Those."

"Aw, no. Women tied up with leaches on their breasts," I winced.

"And *Argosy*. Good stuff," he joked. Or I hoped that was joking. I had read too much of those magazines as a youth, pornographic content, filled with aggressive, destructive behavior. It also could be passed down generations. No wonder I gravitated toward the wrong kind of men.

"What was the second part about?" Michael asked.

"The *Mademoiselle?* Oh, I wrote about Kent State and how that impacted my education." I said, then wondered if Kent State was such a good topic to talk about with a Vietnam vet. "It wasn't humorous."

"No. Kent State wasn't humorous. Bunch of guys avoiding the draft killing draft avoiders. I'd like to read it," he said.

"You sure?" It went over my head.

"Yeah, I'd like to. I used to think about becoming a writer. Still do. Part of the reason I went to Vietnam was to witness what was happening in my lifetime, I mean, we had a war going on. Why would I miss that?" Mike said.

That explained a lot.

He asked, "How was working for *Vogue?*"

"*Vogue* was tough; there was always someone crying in the ladies' room, and all too often, it was me," I said.

"How'd you end up there?" he asked.

"From the *Mademoiselle*. On the last day, we got to interview at Condé Nast, their publishing company," I said.

"Cool. Maybe I can read your writing before I go home?" Mike said.

"Sure," I said, but I wasn't. I tried to remember what I had said in the piece about the war. Would it offend him?

"What about Boston Conservatory?" Michael asked. "I don't think we spoke after you got accepted there,"

"I spent one year as a Drama major, Musical Theatre minor."

"When I was a senior at Marlboro High," he said.

"Yeah. My dorm room at 54 The Fenway was on the third floor, in a big old mansion with a huge bay window overlooking the gates to Hemenway Street. I shared it with two other girls, Debbie and Carol."

"When I came back from Africa to recover from malaria," Michael said casually.

"Malaria?" I cut in.

"Yeah, it was a regular occurrence over there. M-K sent me home for eight weeks. I used to hang out near The Fenway, at Michael's Pub. Ever hear of it? I heard some great jazz musicians when they were coming up through Berklee," Mike said. He swayed his head, remembering the music, feeling the rhythm.

"No, I was already in New York," I said.

"You left theatre, huh?" he asked.

"I loved acting, just wasn't sure I wanted that life," I said. "Besides, the Conservatory was in earshot of anti-war riots and tear-gas canisters going off at Northeastern."

"Musicians throwing rocks at the police?" Mike asked.

"*They* didn't, not from what I saw," I said. "Listen, a family that could manage music lessons could probably fight the draft. I never saw kids from the Conservatory or Berklee out with activists on the street."

Mike interjected, "Well, the US instituted the draft lottery in June that year, so guys in college still had their deferments. The year you graduated was the peak of the War. Tet Offensive scared the pants off Congress." He added, "They missed the whole point. We won. The media just reported it their way. Which is to say: We lost."

I said, "It was frightening, with all the protesting so close. My roommate went home to Cape Cod, brought in her record player. She played Judy Collins albums with whale calls to lull us to sleep. We needed lulling."

＊　＊　＊

I hadn't read about Tet in any detail, and I was concerned that what I wrote wasn't professional enough to share with Michael. I pulled out the Kent State piece and quickly read it, then to myself read, "*It would take another year and a half to bring us artist-types out. Kent State made protesters out of non-protesters; everybody got involved.*" Then I asked him, "You sure you want to read this?"

Michael said, "I was already in Vietnam, Kent State didn't make a big impact on me."

With that, I could see how our experiences failed to mesh—we were like 180-degree opposites. Kent State was massive for me; writing about it would win me a national competition, change my life. For Michael, it wasn't a big deal. I wondered how the Vietnam I wanted to know about would be compared to the Vietnam Michael had served in, that I *thought* I wanted him to tell me about. These were differences beyond semantics. Maybe it wouldn't matter; perhaps he'd still share a part of his experience.

"I left the Conservatory after a year; I made the dean's list, but I still had to repeat my freshman year, which was okay. I was at the end of my first year at Mass College of Art when Kent State happened in early May." I said, trying to avoid words like killing, and protest, and anti-war. "In my senior year, I wrote about how it altered my college experience. Here, this is Part II for *Mademoiselle's* Guest Editor Competition.[2]" I handed a copy of the manuscript to Michael, "You can read this. It's a little clumsy, I'll admit, but it got me here. They even considered publishing it. But, well, you'll see, it's a little all over

---

2   The Mademoiselle piece is found in Appendix ii.

the place." Talk about insecure!

Michael read while I made scratch cranberry sauce. After he finished, Michael walked to the counter between the open living room and the kitchen, "And they hired you from this?" he asked, not sounding too impressed.

"No, this wasn't a factor. (backpedal, backpedal) My editor had to go to bat for them to hire me." I said, "I didn't win on my good looks and trust fund."

"You've got the looks," he smiled. "Whaddya mean? You had to be rich to work there?"

"Thanks," I said. "They hired me anyway. Paid $135 a week, which is why I could have used a trust fund, I worked freelance nights. Illustrating for *Mademoiselle* would bring in an extra $200-$500 a month. But tell me about this." I held up a small brochure titled "*Welcome to the War, a Handbook from 173rd Airborne Battalion.*" Michael had sent it to me along with the copies of Zaire letters in his second letter.

Michael beamed, "Did you get the patch? I figured since you went to DC, I should make you an honorary member of The Herd."

✳ ✳ ✳

I started to read, "The 173rd was a guerilla-capable fighting unit. It was reconstituted on Okinawa in 1963 after a year-long service in WWII and became the first major unit of the US Army to serve in Vietnam.[3]"

"The Marines were in Nam first," Michael said. "Most guys from South Boston joined the Marines. By the time I graduated Marlboro, in 1969, the Marines were almost out."

---

3   Military advisors were first sent to Vietnam by JFK, followed by a detachment of Special Forces called the Green Berets. In one year US forces in Vietnam jumped from 600 to over 15,000. Johnson sent in the U.S. Marines in early 1965. Encyclopedia.com.

"South Boston?" I asked.

"I was born in Southie, and my parents moved to Marlboro when I was twelve. All our relatives still live there." Michael said.

"I didn't know that."

"Pissed me off. I had tested into Boston Latin for eighth grade, and then my mother said we were moving to the burbs. I hated that. Everyone who goes to Boston Latin comes out a doctor or a lawyer." Mike was agitated suddenly, "I will never forgive my mother for that. Never."

$*$ $*$ $*$

That didn't sound great. "I don't know Southie. Both my colleges were on the other side of Boston near Fenway. Are you a Red Sox fan?" I asked trying to tamp down the flare-up. "I used to skip school on opening day just to sit in the bleachers and get sunburned."

Michael didn't laugh. "I don't like sports much. But I tied the record for long jump your brother Stephen set at Marlboro High," he beamed.

"Really?" I laughed. "Stephen joined the Air Force, assigned to Korea. He did a supply stint in Vietnam during the war. He got up to Sergeant, married a Korean girl, brought her home, and they lived with my parents for a while. When I visited, the house would smell of kimchee."

I don't like kimchee," we said in unison.

Good, good, I thought. "You really went into the Army right out of high school?"

"Yep, on early enlistment, but my mother wouldn't sign for me, so I had to wait until I turned eighteen in October."

"Tell me about Vietnam," I said, knowing that groceries could wait if they had to.

"Well, for one, The Herd was famous for getting into places other units refused to go. Sky Soldiers—we were known as that—Sky Soldiers trusted Sky Soldiers, and we...well, I couldn't have served in a better unit. Tough to the core. I was very relieved when I got picked."

"What do you mean picked?" I asked.

"We didn't know until we arrived in-country which unit we were to serve with."

"Wow. That would bother me," I said.

"Didn't matter, I got The Herd, which is where I wanted to be. I didn't want to be with some grunt company. As a medic, I got assigned to their MASH unit: B Company. After five months, I won 'Herd Soldier of the Month' so they let me pick what I wanted to do next. I chose the LRRPs, stands for Long Range Reconnaissance Patrols. I stayed with the Rangers: Co. "N" 75th Rangers, even extended for a second tour. In '71, they said the war was winding down; "Peace Talk mumbo jumbo." Michael said, waving his arms, "They decided we should be part of the first troops sent home. With that, they decided to disband the 173rd."

"I was three-and-a-half months into my second tour—doing just what I always wanted to do—a LRRP medic, part of a six-man insertion team, and now, the other five guys were going home. I thought about staying in-country, but I'd come close to death a few times more than I cared to count," Mike breezed over that. "I even gave some serious thought to making the Army a career, but that didn't work out. After I'd dangled with my team from an EVAC chopper, I wasn't sure I could last without the 173rd."

Mike left it at that, and while story-wise, it was a good stopping point to run our errands, there seemed to be something left unsaid, something else dangling. Back then, Peace Talks dangled too.

✳ ✳ ✳

We ran out to do our errands, bought the turkey, and Michael and I stopped to catch a bite while out. When we returned, whatever edge either of us held began to melt away. Putting the groceries away was now a shared endeavor. We talked of meeting in DC and how we'd both been touched by it. Michael and I could still feel the impact of that vet/stranger/survivor who approached, then slipped away on the top of the knoll while the Memorial was dedicated just ten days before. (*Who was that masked man?*)

I wanted to ask him, "What did that mean to you?" But I didn't. Michael sat silently, probably still debating how much he could be open with me. "I only knew that I *had* to be there that day," I told him, "It was like I was compelled to go. I've been using that word when I tell people. Compelled. I was *compelled* to be there," as if some outside source had divined it.

Michael grew quiet, reminding me of the hot dog line, Steve McQueen and all. "You have to forgive me if I'm kind of quiet and awkward on the phone sometimes," he said. "Our phone is in such a location that there are usually two or three people within very close earshot, and I find that very inhibiting."

"Good to know." I said, "I thought maybe I was waking you up every time I called."

Michael sat, looking down a good while, trying to get his thoughts together. He wondered how to talk about suicide in the first place. And what would be my reaction? Perhaps it would turn her off, and she'll kick me out? Then slowly, he began: "I hadn't planned on telling you this, and not tonight certainly, but I must, well, it's like ... You brought me into your home, and you deserve to know that if I didn't go to DC for the dedication, I don't think I'd be alive now." He continued, "I was so tired of living, and Pete, Vinnie, Ron, all my friends, they were so tired of listening to me. I just wanted it to be over. I agreed to go to DC. It was the last thing I was going to do. I was going to see The Wall; and when I got back...I was going to kill myself."

Pin drop moment, I didn't move. I'd not come close to suicide before. Michael didn't move, not to drink, nothing. He just looked at me; I could sense it, though I avoided eye contact. It warranted some response, but I had none.

"I thought you should know where I was coming from," Michael said.

I sat looking. "Well, you're here, ten days later. And you didn't," I said, half asking if he was over it. I mean, it was evident for the time being, but what do you say? Not that I wanted him to answer me. "I'm glad that you can tell me that, Michael, I..." I said. And let it go.

Michael exhaled, then breathed a long sigh; he looked up with eyes forming tears, and I reached over and kissed him. Our eyes met. He returned the kiss and let the tears go. Sweet kiss. Lovely kiss. Not about passion kiss. Relief kiss.

"Are you okay?" Michael asked.

"I think so," I said in all seriousness. "Are you okay? is the question."

"You know," Michael said, "I consider you a friend because I feel that I can say things I really want to say from my heart and you won't think less of me for saying them. You may disagree with or dislike them and say so, but you'll still let me say them, and *listen* to them..."

Michael paused as he spoke, in what I'd called *staccato* back when we met. Now I saw that he was always thinking—of telling too much, of repercussions, of friends he'd lost, of missions. You'd read it in his letters too, lurking between the lines. Michael was a person who spoke his mind, which was broad and multidimensional. But there was nothing he could have said that would have caused me to send him away. Not even telling me subsequently that night that he had killed seven or eight of the enemy. I'd also never been this close to a soldier before, someone who had killed another human being. His honesty made me care for Michael even more.

He was strong, but he seemed fragile; I was independent but echoed inside from emptiness. Both of us had started the year behind us thinking we were finally on our way, then got punched in the face, forced to find new homes and to figure out who we were—or weren't. His tours of Nam still seemed to plague him. My 365 of celibacy took me down a new path. I believed him. In his words, his joking, and his stride Michael seemed okay, or on his way to being okay. By the size of his ruck, Michael carried his story on his back, and one day he'd get up and take it someplace else. That night he began to peel off remnants from the wrapped ball of his life, and if we cried, there were kisses, and as kisses accumulated, so too did the compassion, turning eventually to passion. And by morning, I was no longer celibate.

✳ ✳ ✳

If this were merely the tale of how I came to love again, or a story of how Michael Creamer found salvation in me and a miraculous soldier on the knoll, a messenger from God, I might finish this up and package these pages for the Hallmark Channel. We might entirely skip what happened over the fourteen years we'd been apart, the backstory stuff. But lives are formed by where we've been, not just by where we choose to go. My life was complicated enough; Michael's, having survived a war, was ten times more complex. Journalist Ann Jones writes about war from a newer perspective, from the Gulf Wars that America was yet to climb into. What I would have done with her insights then.

This one's central to Mike and Me—

> *"The violence of war does not end even when peace is declared. Often it merely recedes from public to private life.[4]"*

Mike had brought the War home with him.

---

4   Jones, Ann, They Were Soldiers/ How the Wounded Return from America's Wars—The Untold Story Haymarket Books Chicago 2013. p.111 (A Dispatch Books Project) p 5.

CHAPTER 14

Scared to Death

The next morning Diane knocked on my door like a dorm mother, "Martha?"

I could hear it in her voice; she was concerned about my soldier visiting, hoping not to find me gagged and bleeding in the corner. Instead, she found me trussing the turkey for the feast. I let her in.

"Diane, meet Michael," and because I had shared the humor of the Siberts, our plotting for Michael's early expulsion, and said, "I'm fine. He's fine. We're going to be fine." Gregg came from around the corner, and we all laughed. It was an open-door policy on the second floor all day long as we shared drinks and conversation, Scrabble, and rifle-range stories. Perfect for Mike. Perfect for me, letting go.

Thanksgiving with Diane and Gregg was delightful, with good food and company. Michael was raving all through the meal and dessert. He wasn't accustomed to sharing so openly or feeling good about Thanksgiving. He smiled throughout and thanked me often, especially that Night 2 of lovemaking.

On Friday, Michael and I slept in late then went to my studio. Outside, people milled around, on their way to Macy's five blocks north. I unlocked the door, and once inside the elevator, unlocked the floor, and we went up. The door opened straight onto the sixth floor.

"This is a really nice place you have," Michael said, walking around.

"I know. I love it here. I found the listing in *The New York Times* last February," I said.

"It's huge." And then he added, "I hate the Fucking *New York Times*."

I let it fly. "2,500 sq. ft.," I said. "I fell instantly for that complete openness." I said, spinning around. "I took a five-year lease." Photographers and several stock photo houses occupied about half the eleven-story building; MVP was the second small advertising agency.

"I opened my business when I was 26," I said, "and Perry Ellis became our client at the end of that year. As he grew, we grew. He insisted that all his licensees work with us."

"Licensees?" Michael asked.

"Like his sock manufacturer, coats, he has a knit kit line, (a Jeanswear line was coming). We do all the graphics and packaging and coordinate all the advertising."

Michael put down his coat, and I walked to the back to get the slide projector. I walked him around. I showed him the kitchen where I'd installed a counter, oak and antique metal stools, a refrigerator, a hot plate, a microwave, and a sink.

"I put a shower stall in the bathroom just in case I ever needed to move in," I said.

"Why don't you just live here?" Michael asked.

"Well," I said, "there aren't a lot of stores around. No pharmacy, no grocery stores. Nowhere to buy beer."

Mike moaned, "Enough said. I know what that's like."

"We moved because the staff got too big. Our old studio was on a super busy, cross-town street, East 23rd, at Park Avenue South. I started out in this neighborhood in 1978. It's so much better." Downstairs was the L subway train; it was a two-stop, ten-minute commute uptown to "Seventh Avenue," before the city tagged it The Fashion District.

"Most of my clients—Perry, Chaus, Drizzle raincoats, Bill Robinson, Carmelo Pomodoro—are on the subway line right downstairs." The same subway station opens on the north end to Times Square, where

Broadway and Seventh Avenue kissed, crossed, and parted. *Woman's Day* was just a hop across Broadway, in an elevated office tower. "We're under contract to redesign *WD's* entire editorial content—photography, illustration, graphics, fonts, layouts—we're on a six-month retainer. A friend of mine, the former Art Director of *Mlle*, Ann Shakeshaft, was called in to *WD*, and she asked me to co-creative direct with her."

Ellen Levine, *WD's* Editor-in-Chief, was happy to have Ann and me fill the all too often, male-dominated task of magazine redesign. We were near the end of that contract when I met Michael. Further uptown were other clients; I loved the proximity of our new studio. It was never just an "office."

"Come here, Michael," I said, hanging out the window on the W28th side. "The diagonal of our building provides a long look up Broadway, all the way to 34nd Street and Herald Square, where the parade was yesterday." Then I pointed out NYC's wholesale flower market that spanned two blocks west. "And right down there is one of Manhattan's remaining gay baths. You really can't see it, it's on this side, two doors over," I said. "It's where gay men meet up with sex partners, or whatever."

"Remarkably, they're still in existence," Mike said.

"It is." In those days of awakening awareness of AIDS, it would close not long afterward. "The 'morning' doves and foot traffic are pretty constant, which means you can catch taxis here into the wee hours. They wait to jockey the boys home from the baths."

"That's crazy shit," Michael said, "I saw some of the early cases of AIDS in Zaire. At least that's what *I've* determined it was." He walked over to the six-pack he'd brought, popped open a beer for him and one for me. "Okay, want to go to Vietnam?"

I walked back to the studio area with its big white wall. "Let's set up here," I said. I pulled over a desk by the low bookshelf and plugged in the projector while Michael began loading the slide carousels. Then I turned down the lights, and Vietnam filled the studio wall.

* * *

The first slide showed Mike as a scrawny soldier with an automatic rifle, an AR-15, almost half his height propped on his hipbone. "Wow," I said, "no, go back. How old were you then?" I asked.

"I was almost nineteen."

"When I was almost nineteen, I was in summer stock, playing Sandy in *The Prime of Miss Jean Brodie*. I had pleaded with the producer (he also chaired the Drama Department at Boston Conservatory of Music), to let me audition, not relegate me to what I was hired for, the Costume Mistress. I knew if I had that role, I could be outstanding. He let me audition; and after he had seen my first performance, I remember him approaching me, telling me I was excellent in the role, that I could be very successful in acting. It was the day I told him I was transferring to Mass Art, repeating my freshman year."

"That's when you left the theatre?" Michael asked.

"I did." I said. "Theatre left me feeling…I don't know, overly competitive. All alone." I hesitated. "Anyway, we didn't come here to discuss Drama, I'm sorry, let's see your slides."

"Okay fair 'nuf. These slides are from my Ranger days at LZ (Landing Zone) English, our firebase. Here, this is 'Golf' team ready to head out," Michael said, then moved to the next image, "this is 'Charlie' team."

"Which team was yours?" I asked.

"Well, they always needed a medic to go out with them, so I might go out with any of them. Here, here's 'Kilo' team waiting for the choppers."

"So, medics didn't fight?" I asked, not thinking about the A-K from before.

"Hell, I fought," he said proudly. "Had to. Too much could go wrong; lives depended on it. You go out with six men. You want all of them to be crack shots."

"What's that?" I said as the next few slides flashed on his buddies with their faces painted black. "You wore war paint?" One of the men was flashing a peace sign.

"Kind of; that's my friend Hubie," he laughed. "Camouflage. We needed to go in undetected. We're LRRPs. Choppers inserted us into the jungle where they suspected enemy action. We spied on troop movements and reported back so that others could attack," Mike said.

"Sort of like skulking?" I asked, referring to the goofy after-dark antics at Youth Theatre parties when guys would go out spying on couples necking and other behavior, in unlit cars parked by the reservoir.

"Yeah, like that," Mike said. "Only much more dangerous. LRRPs had instructions to avoid engaging with the enemy," he said. "Of course, that wasn't always possible. If we walked into an ambush, or someone sited us, we engaged." Mike lit a cigarette. He was fully engaged, reliving the sparks of terror he'd known. "Here." Mike showed a helicopter hovering high in the sky with a long rope ladder and six men on its rungs. "Here is an extraction."

"That's how you went in?" I asked.

"No, going in wasn't this dramatic, but occasionally, we had to get the hell *out* of there like that."

✳ ✳ ✳

I watched amazed: Six nineteen year-olds dangling with their guns and each other, high over a jungle valley hot with fear and no doubt death. I found it astounding that anyone could survive that...

"We were qualified in guerrilla survival training since there was never a guarantee we'd get out. Sometimes we were pursued, fought our way out, or had to hide out for five or six days. Lived off our rations."

I thought, how do you train for that? What job do you go home to? Maybe you don't. "Look at them," I said, "they're so serious." The Ranger team sat hunched against some sandbags, each one gazing out on the perimeter, with one young LRRP looking at the camera as if a fashion stylist had positioned him.

"That's 'Kilo' waiting to go in." Mike said and took a gulp of beer, "*That's the face of 'scared to death.'*"

I watched Michael in the light the projector threw off. When he drew on his cigarette, he'd wince; and I'd see traces of the warrior who'd gone to war. Mike pointed to a slide of a vet who hadn't made it home, his voice broke, and he swallowed it down with beer. I began to see a hurt that had no description, words that came out only so far, and got pushed down again. I think I first loved Mike in those moments, and I didn't ask for explanations. I trusted they might come, and I gave him space, the first of many times I'd do that. My curiosity for men who went to War brought Mike out and his chromes, and a hurt they captured deep within the film's emulsion, gave me a glimpse of Vietnam: the men and their faces and the danger they must have felt.

✴ ✴ ✴

After viewing Mike's slides, he and I walked quietly up Broadway; we had tickets to see *A Chorus Line*. My pal from the Conservatory, Thommie Walsh, was an original cast member; he got us into the matinee. Michael loved the show; I knew he would. Michael loved the Drama of *A Chorus Line*. He didn't dance, but he fit in well. (finally!) His flannel shirts were comfortable now. Afterward, we walked all the way home singing "Kiss Today Goodbye." But it cut a little too close to home. Another night of luscious sex and whispered sighs.

I didn't want him to leave. But he left for Massachusetts early Sunday when he could easily find a seat on Amtrak, anticipating correctly that returning college students would clog the train on its way back to Boston. Vietnam vets and college students were an on-going oil and water scenario.

Michael and I had just enough time to get close; enough time to begin to learn who the people we'd once been had become. And the

Michael I once knew introduced me to the Mike, who went to War.
They promised to return.

*One of Mike's
recon teams
waiting to go
out on patrol
from LZ
English.*

PHOTO: MICHAEL CREAMER

CHAPTER 15

Letters

With Thanksgiving behind us, Michael and I wrote as if we were long lost friends. We were both letter-writers. We were both starved for affection.

To hold a letter, to read it for the first time, to hear words spoken from a pen held in the hand of someone you love or admire is a waning wonder. My heart would tremble at finding a letter in my apartment mailbox. I'd race upstairs and rip it open to read words that contained the thoughts, notions, insights of a man so full of all those things, and who grew with every word in every paragraph, every letter. Best yet, I got to read them again and again. (Even decades later.) Michael spoke from his heart in letters, revealing lessons he'd learned or maybe never conveyed before...

The first letter from Michael since we'd become lovers.
December 1, 1982

> Martha—
> I feel like it's an anniversary—one week ago this morning,
> we woke up together for the first time. Hmm...So nice
> to snuggle up tight and hold you, feel your heartbeat and
> breathing and warmth. What a fine week! It was a long sigh
> of relief, a chance to be myself, to rediscover some better
> parts of myself that had been lost in a trunk someplace for

a while. Thank you for finding them for me. ... It's so nice to know that people like you still exist and to think that some of them are *women* on top of it all. Nothing like good news when one really needs it! You're so bright and talented and caring and alive. And so damned much a woman that it makes whirlpools in my blood!

Gawd! It had to be fate—had to...Two people each drawn hundreds of miles away from home for different and yet the same reasons, each lost in a crowd of 150,000 and their own thoughts, and Bang! A meeting...and a shared, deeply emotional experience...and all that's happened since... Whew! The mind boggles... You wouldn't believe the way I kicked myself for forgetting to take that lunch! The turkey was so good, and the pie...Is there anything you don't do well? The Amtrak cheeseburger, complete with that distinct microwave tang, just didn't cut it after all those good meals. I think I gained a couple of pounds, even dancing it off like that. Hey—we make a terrific dance couple. I love dancing just one-on-one at home—it gives one room to move. Hope we didn't make too much noise for your downstairs neighbors. (He chuckled fiendishly!)

I loved that letter. Loved Michael's acknowledgment of me, loved him talking about our fateful meeting, and the impact it had on his life. I felt the same way. I was unaccustomed to a man this articulate and thoughtful. He wrote so well.

And three days later, our responses were crossing in the mail.

December 4, 1982

Dear Martha...

5 AM, and missing you terribly. Just finished a long letter to a woman from Pepperell, MA.

Hmm... A week ago, at this time, we were sleeping after having seen *A Chorus Line*. I'm listening to the album now, lying in bed wondering how a futon that was always homey before could seem so empty now. It was a very special week for me... Hell, a special <u>month.</u>

Back some years ago, I kind of got into the habit (of necessity) of going through certain times entirely by instinct and action and leaving the absorption process, the integration of events into my psyche, until late-night moments sometime after the fact. My survival and that of others depended on that separation of the physical from the philosophical, and I guess it's why I got to be kind of a loner. Medics and team leaders needed to think, curse, and cry, too, but it had to be done where and when the people who depended on you couldn't see it.

So that's what I'm up to now, spending quiet time, reflecting on all manner of things, "Cabbages and Kings," but mostly about the last six months. That period seems to be a whopping, concentrated, straight-no-chaser slug of pure "elixir of Mike C.'s life." Rock bottom lows and soaring highs, old friends, new friends, departed friends, crouching insecurity, focused proud confidence, old places, new places, a lot to digest...Especially when much of it throws new light on past events, which also deserve consideration. And, of course, there's the future, too, something I hadn't seriously looked at until very recently.

Boy, something happened to me while I was in school. What was it? I don't know...financial considerations, the war, etc. ... But most of all, it was such a big change for me. Most of my fellow students just couldn't figure out the quiet blonde guy over in the corner. A few thought they had and thought he was too "insensitive" and "macho" to be in nursing school.

Sociology was bizarre…First time I'd taken it formally. I did all the reading, which mainly acted as a refresher. Still, the lectures were something else…Two hours of heavy shelling by every liberal cliché ever devised, augmented by bursts of selective statistics. (As the man said, there are three kinds of lies: lies, damned lies, and statistics.) Of course, I always had my hand up. There's one thing you should understand about me—I love to debate… to be ornery and contrary…Hey, some people bowl, some play backgammon, *I* debate. It sharpens the mind.

I finally developed the "Yellow Volvo Theory" of getting high grades on essay exams…All one had to do was close one's eyes, take a deep breath…then answer just as if you had a Master's Degree from Berkeley, did several years of social work but got out of it because you secretly thought that poor people were "tacky." You're going for another degree instead. You drive a yellow 1977 Volvo with any three of the following stickers: "No Nukes," "Save the Whales," "US Out of El Salvador," "Stop the Draft," "Ban Handguns," "Kennedy in '80," or anything with "Coalition" or "Collective" on it. You live either in Cambridge or Brookline, but are looking forward to Newton.

… I went through a class and an exam that way—as sort of a private joke—and was stunned that people were glad for it! They thought that I had either "seen the light" or was at least conforming! Whoa! What did this mean? Were they right? Should I try to change? I did try. And maybe when I did that, I lost a lot of things that kept me going at a time when I needed them most. After all, if you can't count on yourself, what do you have left? I stopped debating.

A lot of unfortunate breaks came along. Got stiffed by somebody who owed me money that I was counting on to pay for school. The VA led me down a rosy path of promises about the extension of time allowed to use my educational benefits, and then they turned it down flat... dorm fees went up...They changed half of the second-year curriculum to a place and schedule requiring a car. Those things and others just built up, and I guess the me that I was trying to be just wasn't up to dealing as effectively as the "regular" me would have. I lost confidence in myself as a medical person so severely that I left school and then proceeded down to lose confidence in the person person too. It was a very bad, black summer, the worst of my life. *Others I've had might appear to be worse, and perhaps were, but this time was different because I felt totally alone. There was nobody else going through the same thing.*

The fever seemed to break in DC, not 24 hours before we met. At least when I got to the Sheraton that Friday night, I felt an aura that maybe I could be myself again and have it all accepted. And I can't even describe the electricity, the sense of homecoming that filled all of us when The Herd formed up and marched on Saturday. Not the "homecoming" given by the civilians—a lot of us are still kind of hanging out on the front porch, not sure if we want to come back in—but the joy of us guys being together again! You met, thank God, a man who had been changed radically in less than a day. Well, more like *changed back*, really. We'll see where the "recovery" leads. —Mike C.

Re-reading Michael's letters reminded me that I threw the annual MVP Christmas party on December 7th, the first at the new studio. I didn't suggest Michael stay; there was a client I was interested in, and we dated a bit at that time. It was interesting to compare the two men; I'd later fix him up with a professional friend of mine, once I was clear he wasn't for me.

Michael's next letter came from the Marlboro Library, two plus miles from his home; he hiked there in a wind chill of zero degrees.

> Masochistic? No, just crazy… (his ellipses) and a bit on the outdoorsy side. Did a bit of research on this and that… Wrote a few letters to guys I met in DC…Found a new book called, *The Wounded Generation—America After Vietnam,* put out by the *Washington Post.* Looks interesting… Has excerpts from *Fields of Fire, Going After Cacciato, A Rumor of War, Dispatches, Chance and Circumstance,* and a Harris Poll on attitudes after Vietnam. There's also a symposium with Phillip Caputo, James Webb, Robert Muller, etc. on veterans. Looks like I've got tonight's reading!
>
> You know, I can't help but worry about the effects of all this on you. You mentioned "Sympathetic Vietnam Stress Syndrome"… God, I'd hate to see that! It's bad enough on us vets. I don't want to see it happen to you too! I felt somehow responsible when you said that it took you a while to get back into work after my visit…Hell, you don't want to end up like *me,* do you? Maybe that's why so many vets keep it in, withdraw, because we can deal (sometimes) with what war did to *us,* but seeing it affect ones we love is especially cruel. You know, almost any woman who's been involved with a Vietnam vet would advise you to steer far clear of us.

* * *

The warnings were clear. I'd been a sole-proprietor for five years now, and a freelancer before that. Every feeling I knew was bound in the over-riding stress of responsibility, of achievement. For Michael, his achievement, his accolades, the medals, and superlatives of his life were masked and made obsolete by cultures not socially acceptable at the time—the military, his soldier-of-fortune heroics with M-K. The US was just beginning to acknowledge Vietnam vets. Reagan himself did not attend the Dedication day ceremonies on the mall, which to me, was a demonstrable slap in the face by the Commander-in-chief.

Mike continued

> I know that I have a lot on my mind that I have to try to work out, and doing it alone is hard, but at least it spares the "Innocent Civilians."

> This place is closing soon! Gotta run. Love, M.C.

* * *

Dottie and Bernie's home was an hour away in New Jersey. Their home, with my two sweet nieces and their son Patrick, was my home away from home. When I first lived in New York City, *Vogue* didn't pay me enough to go to the laundromat, even if I could have found one in the Bloomingdale's neighborhood where I lived temporarily in a sublet belonging to photographer Debbie Turbeville. I'd take a suitcase of dirty clothes to work, catch a train at 6:00 PM, and haul it out to their house, their washer. That crisis having past, I still visited them often. For Christmas, I borrowed a car and drove to Massachusetts to visit my parents and Michael. I needed to see him on his turf.

December 28, two weeks later, Michael wrote to me:

"Thank you for listening so long, and so well this morning. I sure needed it…. (my ellipses) Guess it's the season: That year-end tendency to sum up and evaluate…Last year at this time, I was carrying a 98% average in a five-course curriculum, impressing the hell out of my teachers and the hospital staff. For three years before that, I was as happy as a rabbit in a root cellar working the tunnels, and for three years before that, I was really getting off on being Creamer of the Congo.[1]

And this year? Worst in my life, except for Nov. 12th on. And no warning… everything that could go wrong did, in classic Murphy mode. … think that I did it to myself, too. … I was always happy, competent, and highly confident as a medic, … Little did I realize that I was kind of an oddly shaped peg, rather elliptical. I fit perfectly into medical departments such as the Army's and M-K's, but could never fit into a hospital or civilian ambulance service. I was long and solid on the sides that called for preventative care, the perfection of basic skills, developing close bonds with a 'closed' patient population, and running 'my own show' with little supervision…. I was seriously short on being comfortable with people I'd never seen before, coping with and relying on delicate hi-tech equipment, and dealing with a rapidly expanding medico-legal bureaucracy. I admit to being an 'action junkie' too. A certain element of personal risk always added a needed spice… I've always been relatively non-competitive, preferring to challenge myself rather than others.

So, the hospital busted my ass. We talked about

---

1   A few of Michael's letters from Zaire are in the Appendix. There are too many to include all. (Another whole book).

'responsibility' on the phone. As infantry medic or head of a rescue squad in a tunnel or a bush medic in Zaire (I) almost always had the last word during a medical emergency. … It was my own show, and I could show you a drawer-full of medals and letters that prove it. But responsibility without authority is a time bomb that will do a person like me in.

The system just threw me … paperwork up the ass,
rules written with not the patient but the patient's lawyer
in mind, healing as a business rather than a calling. …
it was only a matter of time before Deep Shit and I made
acquaintance in some ward corridor. I did a really bright
thing and started to work part-time on a street ambulance

*A Long Range
Reconnaisance Patrol
(LRRP) out of LZ English;
by the looks of the raking
shadows, early morning
or late afternoon. Mike
is the second on the right.
Mysterious black blob
in center perfect for the
gutter.*

to have an 'outlet.' Big mistake. ... when I *did* sleep,
depression, anxiety, and loss of self-confidence: 'freezing
in the door,' they called it in Jump School. ... I didn't
know how to or even much *want* to do anything else. ...
You know the rest. So, what now? All I can say is 'Good
fucking question!' Enough of that, you must feel like
you've been locked in a room with a Doomsday freak.

CHAPTER 16

On the Home Front

Driving to and from Massachusetts that Christmas, I had a lot to think about. Being busy, I hadn't written any of what I hoped to. But driving gave me pause; 200 miles each way to think things out for myself. I loved to drive. I wondered how Michael would ever make a living; I asked him about writing, but he seemed stuck in the Nursing School mud.

I was certainly not happy with Michael's interaction with his family, especially with his mother, Dot, and the next oldest brother, Richard. How Richard got through Marlboro High was an enigma, Richard reminded me of a baby bird likely to fall out of a nest, and Michael was ruthless towards him. My sister Jean mentioned him; I don't remember ever seeing him around. At Christmas, he wanted so much for his big brother to acknowledge him, to be introduced to Michael's girlfriend from NYC, along with the rest of the family. The entire family barely regarded Richard; they ignored his long ghoulish face, one hand to his chin, the other wrapped around his emaciated waist, waiting for an opportunity to be heard. Michael discounted his mom almost as severely. At that first meeting, he corrected her pronunciation of their name as Cramer, not Creamer. The Creamer vs. Cramer thing upset the entire clan, and Michael wouldn't let it die. It was torturous to witness.

Michael and I would get together about every two or three weeks for connubial visits and talk about everything in the world. I was planning to lease a car, and he helped me decide on a Subaru. I'd drive to

Massachusetts to attend a (newly formed) Mass Art Foundation Board meeting, of which I was a member. We visited South Boston. Michael showed me where he grew up. I introduced him to my designer friends, Lee Doliber (Air Force vet) and wife Lyn, and they stuck like glue. We sang into the wee hours, drunk on wine or beer, singing as loudly as possible with Bette Midler, *The Rose* soundtrack. We overnighted with them. But we didn't have the comfort of our own place; it was left to Michael to travel to me.

He would write sexy things he couldn't say on the phone from home, "And why, whenever I think of the way you walk, do I get an erection?" And other long passages that went further than erections, but I've censored; you won't find them in the Appendix either...

Michael to me

> Jan. 20, 1983
>
> It's wintertime, snowy and wondering, why did I leave before I really had to last time? And when, if ever, do you feel like putting up with me again?

✵ ✵ ✵

Michael's friend Maryanne flew in from Swaziland during Christmas, and unbeknownst to me, he avoided her phone calls. After I returned to NYC, he wrote to me that he didn't know how to tell her about us. (or me about her!) I heard from Peter that their relationship had been on hold for a long time, but Mike reasoned his ignoring her, saying, "She wanted a more serious relationship with me than I was willing to give." She left half heartbroken and half pissed, according to Peter. Peter challenged Mike afterward. Maryanne had traveled all that way and had to line up an interim replacement as she hurried home. Man, all that way from Swaziland to Massachusetts? To talk a good friend out of suicide? Buck up, boy. I'd be pissed too. Ten years later, Maryanne shared with me that her trip was to talk Mike out of suicide.

Mike's same letter to me

> Walking for miles and miles in the 30-below wind chill and crashing my young ass out in the backyard in my winter sleeping bag. No tent, just me and the stars and the cat.
>
> Shit…The "Triple Whammy" hits next Thursday again, on the 27th. "Anniversary Reaction," they call it. On that day, it'll be twelve years since the siege of Hill 806[1], eleven years since my discharge, and ten years since the official end of US involvement in Vietnam. It hit me the first time just last year, and I didn't cope too well. Then I thought nobody cared. We'll see how it goes this time, now that I know at least one person does.

---

1   Hill 806 was fought in Vietnam by the Rakassans, the 187th of the 101st Airborne Division, a unit Michael would come into yet. Two-thirds of the 187th were lost fighting that battle.

CHAPTER 17

Uptown Girl

My life in fashion might have seemed fluky in contrast, but it was a natural evolution for me. I sewed for years, even before that dreaded Home Ec. class in junior high, making a cotton A-line skirt. (A Marlboro girl's rite of passage!) My mother always sewed. At ten, I made a box-pleated roller-skating skirt. I designed my Ursula Merkle costume for *Birdie*, a yellow pantsuit with a felt flower on my chest, its stem growing down one leg. I made a jumper cobbled in patch-work from different wools when I had no money for fabric. I made inventive clothing like a "Babes in Toyland" prom dress in a brown country print with an unbleached muslin apron, which was a bit goofy, admittedly. (I was named Most Artistic that night!)

When Michael Creamer was off at Fort Dix and Basic Training in '69, Boston Conservatory hired me to design the costumes for a student performance of *Cabaret;* I made an Independent Study out of it at Mass Art. That Woodstock/Moon-landing summer before, I worked as the costumer at Weston Playhouse in Vermont, where I cut, sewed, washed, rented, ironed, and worked my butt off on a ten-week stock season of eight plays while acting in four of them.

I landed at *Vogue* in 1973 when American fashion was coming into its own; Ralph Lauren, Diane von Furstenberg and Calvin Klein were relatively new, leaving Bill Blass, Oscar delaRenta, Geoffrey Beene, Mary McFadden, Halston, and Anne Klein a tier above, at a slightly higher price point. In 1976, I went on to Art Direct at the coolest retail shop in NYC, Geraldine Stutz's Henri Bendel, which featured the best fashion from Europe and America, including new young designers discovered through Bendel's Friday morning open-studio policy. I remember climbing up the stairs to the employee elevator at Henri Bendel, adroitly maneuvering around Friday hopefuls and their samples. Anyone who showed up with exceptional fashion to be discovered just might be. Stutz was a vital inspiration to my business, teaching an inclusion technique of weekly staff meetings. On Wednesday afternoon, every manager, from Security to Art Director, met in her office, bringing whatever verbal or physical specimen into a circle of grownup show and tell. All of us got a look at what was due in as merchandise, displayed on the floor mid-circle. Geraldine read us catchy copy she thought clever, or we'd hear about the latest shoplifting incident on the main floor. We got a fresh word on what was up. (My staff at MVP met altogether, on Monday mornings. It was greatly helpful.)

* * *

After Bendel's, I was wooed away to Art Direct a counter-culture fashion publication, *Rags*. That's where I met my friend Jean Butler (who'd put me up after the Thug beating). We photographed Gilda Radner (*Saturday Night Live* original cast member) on the top of a West Village brownstone. Gilda was clad in an enormous metallic parachute that almost flew her off the rooftop. Gold, Gilded, Gilda. Gold was fashionably hot; *Rags* was not.

At which point, I got poor again after depleting *Mlle* savings. When I hung out my shingle in March of 1978, I already had freelanced Tahari's logo. Then Elie Tahari called me to apply it to buttons, tags, order pads, and signage—23 pieces at $100 each. It was a veritable branding extravaganza before branding was a hot topic. That was enough to give my business a go. Why not? I worked at home; my rent was $215/month.

At the point I met Michael Creamer, MVP was billing a million dollars a year. Like Michael, I too was happier running my own show.

CHAPTER 18

Rotors Over Levittown

Michael was in New York again in February. It was the second or third day of his stay. As usual, I would go off during the day to work when he visited, then race home for very passionate love-making, discovery. Riding down Seventh Avenue in a taxi getting back from a client meeting, I first heard it: the sound of helicopter blades on the radio. I strained harder to listen. "Can you turn that up?" I asked the driver. It was haunting *and* beautiful, and when the deejay mentioned it was Billy Joel's new release, I asked the driver to drop me instead at Herald Square. I ran into a storefront record shop and bought the album, *Nylon Curtain*. I couldn't wait to get home and play it for Michael. After work, I burst into my apartment—

"You gotta hear this!" I said, psyched, holding up my album cover.

Rotors whirling, "Goodnight Saigon" was already playing on my turntable.

"You show me yours; I'll show you mine," Michael laughed, showing me his album cover. He had heard it earlier that day in Tower Records, where they still sold vinyl in 1983. We plunked down on the futon, cracked open some beer, and listened over and over until we memorized the words.

"Remember Charlie
Remember Baker
They left their childhood
On every acre...

94

(It was Michael we were singing about, I thought.) At first, we cried with each playing, then we made love sweetly, but I could see Michael was growing troubled. By that time in our relationship, I had read so much from the books Mike turned me onto *13th Valley, 365 Days, The Things They Carried,* but "Goodnight Saigon" was something else. It seemed to whip up Michael's personal sense of loss: He certainly had gone and left his childhood on every acre.

"Fucking Vietnam," Michael shouted.

I tried to engage; Mike needed to process all the hurt and anger of what it meant to be the guy holding dying men in his arms—it was heartbreaking to see him like this. Angry and crying. I couldn't console him. At first, I listened, but Mike was crying, "It had to be so hard, honey. I mean, you were the medic, what could you do? What did you do when you couldn't save someone?"

"You do what anyone else would do, you pick up your gun and help your teammates get out of deep shit and pray the EVAC chopper gets in to pick you up," Mike snapped back.

Billy Joel had accurately captured the sounds of Vietnam; my stupid questions were doing nothing but bringing him back there; they were agitating him. I never knew Mike not to finish off a six-pack a night—excuse the double negative, but it was one of those nights. Now, Mike didn't stop drinking. I was fearful for him.

Then it spilled out. "It was not what I envisioned flying east." Lost for a moment, then I figured: Mike was recounting his coming home from Vietnam. "At first, it was a relief, getting onto that plane, I was proud. But after the first two beers—you know," he broke to fill me in, "over there, they always handed you two beers when you made it back to the firebase, your reward for making it back alive. Didn't matter what went down out there, two beers." Mike continued, "I fell asleep until what must have been turbulence. We were landing in San Francisco, and it was morning. It was America, solid ground. I was overwhelmed, just started crying. I never thought I *wasn't* coming home; I was a crack shot; I was built like a guerrilla. I wasn't afraid of much," he went on, his pace quickened. "I loved going out on patrols; it's what my father did in the Pacific, only in rubber boats. F'n guerrilla warfare!!" Mike guzzled the rest of a beer, then crushed the can in his hand. "I remember running across the tarmac in Cisco; I couldn't wait to get home to see in my dad's eyes, what I'd come to know. To share that." He winced. "As soon as I picked up my bags, I planned to call, tell them I'd gotten off early, that I was on the west coast." Mike mimicked, "'No, I'm not injured again. Just had the rug pulled out from under me. They decommissioned The Herd.'"

* * *

Suddenly, as if he were there again, Mike grew repulsed, "I saw these signs in the distance—OUT OF VIETNAM. Friggin' war protestors, right where I had to walk. Not what I needed," Mike cried out. "Fine fucking homecoming. Gawd!"

"Did anyone warn you?" I asked. I don't know why.

"We'd been instructed that this might be our welcome h… yeah, right, our return. But I was a Sky Soldier. A medic. My job was saving lives."

"I'm so sorry, Michael." It was all I could say.

Mike's loathing hatred, "For the F'n anti-American chicken-shit liberal punks who spit on my Airborne uniform," was palpable. "Christ, I left Vietnam less than a day before, fighting for freedom, for America, fighting for them." Mike sucked in, trying not to cry. "Why did those Constitutional Rights Assholes allow that bullshit at airports? We didn't deserve that."

No. I worried that he thought that I one of those picketing assholes? I held my breath.

"'Hey, Baby Killer,' they screamed, 'You're not welcome.' That was my welcome home." Mike shouted, "Then two of them spit on me. Girls. Fucking girls."

He was crying. I tried to console him; my hands were shaking.

"Shit," he cried, "I yelled back, 'I've held dying men in my arms. Don't you know I saved my guys? Don't give me crap; this is a Combat Medic's Badge, for Christ's sake.'"

"I got my bags, then slipped into a john to change into civvies. I was over fighting. I needed a drink," Mike was trembling all over. Pacing now, a beer in his hand. Inconsolable. "I scouted the terminal until I found a dark corner of a quiet bar."

I pictured him hopping up on a stool where he could sit with a wall behind him, mapping out his whole area of operation, his A/O, as I'd already seen him do in restaurants. Mike continued, "I ordered a draft. It came in a frosted mug, and it brought me back to the last time I'd been home—the only other time I was old enough to buy booze at a bar." Mike was winding down a bit until, "It was the last time I got to see my father."

I didn't know where that was taking us, didn't feel that I could speak, but I did, "Michael, maybe we should try to get some sleep," I tried.

"You can sleep, I'm not going to sleep tonight, I know it," he said.

"Then I'll stay up too," I said. "Go on." I wanted to encourage him to get it out, but I was exhausted.

"My parents were dumbfounded that I was coming so soon; I caught a plane to Logan. I didn't use the military discount because I didn't want to fly in uniform. Didn't know if Boston had protesters. My Uncle Leo is a Boston cop; he picked me up from the airport and drove me out to Marlboro."

"Uncle Leo tells me, 'Your mother planned a homecoming of sorts. Just family. And she called a few friends of yours.'"

"I don't want a party." I said to Leo, "Why do you think I didn't give her notice?" I said, "I mean I'm just out of the jungle..." Mike lit another cigarette and drank a few more swigs.

"We arrive from Boston, and there was something wrong. 'Mike, where's your father?' Like I would know. I've been halfway around the world. 'Dot, where's John? When's he coming home?' I'd been up for a long time, I'm zonked. People keep hanging out because they don't want to miss my father greeting me. Leo leaves and goes back to Boston. And my father still isn't there, and everybody else goes home."

I ask, "He didn't come home?"

"He never came home," Mike just looked through me. "We never saw my father again. He ran away. Split."

"I didn't know that, Michael," I said. I didn't know any of this, no one told me.

"So now," Mike said, "it wasn't about me coming home from Vietnam *alive*. No, now it was about me and what I was going to do about him? What did they think I was gonna do? Recon? Search and Rescue?"

"I try not to think about What Ifs, but What If that didn't happen when I got home? What If my valiant WWII Recon Father said, 'Good job, Son.' What If he'd been there as the door opened, his son returning from war? Instead of the whole red-eyed lot of them sitting around weeping." Michael was woozy with words. "So, no, he chose that night—the night I come home from Vietnam—to abandon his family, to *not* greet his son, the Ranger Medic with a Distinguished Service Cross and two Purple Hearts!" Mike appeared to be winding down, "My father didn't give a rat's ass about what that might have said to me. Christ! He was a smart man. Went to friggin' St. John's."

Mike stopped suddenly; the exhaustion, the numbness, and the telling had surrounded him. He took a few beats. I must have closed my eyes for a moment. Then, "I would have done the same."

"Really?" I said, barely awake. There's a point in supporting someone so damaged, it's like the fringe area of the rug he's standing on starts pulling apart.

"My mother had never learned to drive a car. She hadn't worked since 1951 when I was born."

"How old was the baby in the family?" I asked.

"My sister Nell was eight," he replied.

I was going to fall asleep if I didn't talk. "What happened next?" I asked.

"When my mother called my dad's office the next day, they said, 'John quit, Mrs. Creamer. Didn't he tell you?' He left his car parked in the parking lot; his paycheck was in his desk drawer in an unsealed envelope, endorsed to her. It had a note: 'Don't come looking for me or you'll never see me again.' Welcome home, Son."

"That's what it said?" I said, "That's unbelievable."

"No, he didn't actually write 'Welcome home, Son,' but that's what I took it for. A fucking life sentence," Mike said. "I would have preferred to be captured by the VC (Viet Cong, the enemy)."

I was all caught up in Michael's father's story and Mike's words: "That's what I took it for." I thought for a long moment, imagining, dumbfounded. John Creamer had deserted his family on *the day*[1] his son came home from Vietnam. There it was. It was still haunting him. Mike's never-ending War. There would be no R+R for him, no chance to find the boy he'd left behind. No end to the mission, to the tour, to

---

1   This is what Michael presented to me. Only recently (mid 2022) did I find in Mike's documents, Mrs. Creamer's typed interview (Dec. 31, 1986) written for Mike to receive Disability. "2b)

When Michael was discharged from the Army in January 1972 he came home to a very unstable home life. Without explanation his father left the family for parts unknown less than a week before Michael's return. His younger brother was hospitalized suffering from a mental condition and (I, plus his) other brother and 2 sisters (were) in a state of shock (sic).

…Michael was very bitter and angry. … At this writing the family is still in a state of Limbo regarding his father's whereabouts."

The family obviously withheld John's departure from Mike as he was traveling home from Nam. So, for Mike, finding out his dad had left was the day of his return home.

the War. The end mechanism had disengaged.

My mind was reeling from lack of sleep, and Mike's ranting grew less coherent. Whatever we discussed—leaving, coming, going, arriving—Mike drank non-stop. He went out for replenishments to an all-night bodega over on Third. It was too late to knock on Gregg and Diane's door. I couldn't have walked with him; I was too exhausted and shut my eyes until he returned.

I knew about suicide, how Michael had contemplated it before we met, so it terrified me when he packed his rucksack at about 6:00 AM. "Don't sweat it," he said. I had stayed up all night with him, "You won't have to worry about me anymore," and he left to catch a train home.

Oh shit, I didn't know what to do. I was so exhausted. It wasn't like I pulled an all-nighter; I had been dragged through an all-nighter, and I didn't know how I felt about anything except this: what a horrible bad-dream-reality we'd just gone through, that Mike could never walk away from. And he just walked out of *my* door.

* * *

I had a breakfast meeting scheduled with Bruce Plotkin, a photographer friend who had worked with me on numerous jobs. I called him. Nervously, I relayed the long night's event, Michael's hasty departure, and how much I was worried. Bruce, who hadn't met Michael yet, said, "I don't know, Muff, maybe you need to stay away from that one." It was enough to make me realize I couldn't. Michael and I had met by miraculous fate. I wasn't giving up yet.

"I have to try. *I have to,*" I thought, and we canceled breakfast.

I searched frantically in a pile of papers for that newsprint handout I picked up in DC back in November and turned to an article in which I'd read about the emotional aftermath of veterans. I shakily dialed the number. On the other end, the person gave me the number of the nearest Vietnam Veterans of America counselor—in Levittown,

PA. I called, explained everything, racing as I did, "Can you help him?"

"Not if you can't bring him in. We can only help if you can get him here." He paused, "Can you do that?"

"I'll call you back if I'm successful." I said, hung up, pulled on some jeans, grabbed a cab over on Fifth, and turned it around for Penn Station. My heart was pounding, Billy Joel rotors swirling in my head; I wasn't sure if Michael had already boarded the train, or if, when I got there, he'd even listen to me. I bounded down the stairs where commuters, set in their morning routines, moved grudgingly out of my way. In the station, I ran from group to group, bench to bench, checking the obnoxiously turning, turning markers overhead for Amtrak and NJ Transit train departures. I circled the waiting area twice and had nearly given up, when there he was—sitting on a long wooden bench, staring at the floor. I kneeled in front of him, "Michael, I don't want you to go. I want you to come back with me. I found someone from the VVA who's going to help. Will you come with me?" I kept on, "I will take the day off." Michael smiled, a tear rolled down his cheek; he stood up, helped me to my feet, and silently we walked to Seventh Avenue and caught a cab down to West 21st.

Driving south and into Pennsylvania in the Subaru, in those days before mass market GPSs, in that morning of a leftover sleepless night, it was no doubt adrenaline that kept me awake. I was afraid. Michael and I didn't talk much; instead, I pondered some of what I'd learned since meeting him. The slogan for the Veterans' DC parade, "Marching Along Together Again," was a brilliant and ironic tagline, since most of the Vietnam vets had never marched *together*, even after they returned. Parades were generally community-based and many Vietnam vets in their rag-tag uniforms and long hair were not permitted nor invited to march. They made their own parades, at the end, or when they could.

They were boys when they landed in Vietnam, figuring it out as they went. At the height of the war, it was common that new recruits were shipped to Vietnam alone with no one they'd trained with. That seemed insane, and now I was deep into the insanity of such. It seemed *the* crucial mistake by US military: deploying troops (as in individuals) singularly and alone, without their troop (as in unit, regiment, etc.). Passing into Pennsylvania, I asked myself, were we *that* desperate to get boys into combat? I grew angry.

I became taken with the term DEROS. As once cohesive units would finish up, some of the troops would extend their tours and "Newbies" would join them. What was once a tight unit, melded into a block of men with varying "DEROS dates"—Date Estimated Return from Over Seas. It became the measure of trust, one soldier for another, based solely on when they "arrived in-country." A soldier, having completed his 365 days, was shipped home, as Michael had been. When a vet stepped off the plane, there was no accompanying comrade, only a vigilant set of anti-war demonstrators shouting, "Baby Killer" at them.

Afterward, I read how a soldier's welcome home (or lack thereof) would prove substantially to exacerbate the degree of delayed stress they suffered.[2] Delayed and deferred to me now, I wondered what I would do with Mike, since not even the Veterans Administration would acknowledge the suffering vets like him, dangerously close to suicide.

All I really knew of Levittown at that time was a derogatory little ditty, something about ticky tacky houses on hillsides. A theatrical touring company once visited our high school and performed it; Marlboro wasn't a politically aware community otherwise. I used the

---

2   Nicosia, p. 98. Research found "… a direct correlation between the amount of feeling a veteran may have suppressed during the war and the amount of delayed stress that lay somewhere in their cortex, ticking like a time bomb, waiting to wreak havoc not only on their own psyches, but on all those around them."

tune to keep me awake.

The Levittown veteran was just that. A veteran. Just that. He had been there—to the Nam—and was doing what he could to help. To listen. He was part of a growing network of Vietnam Veterans of America, founded in the summer of 1979, with *"Never Again Shall One Generation of Veterans Abandon Another."* Now they were walking the walk, catching their brothers like Mike Creamer, who were falling fast.

I remember sitting in the kitchen of that Levittown house, among all those cookie-cutter houses; how ironic it was that Levittown subdivisions of the late 1940s, early 1950s, were built to help veterans and their families coming home from John Creamer's war, WWII. Now we had come for help to Levittown, PA, victims of another war, veterans whom no one had helped transition home. I sat, exhausted, shocked from too much coffee, with the wife feeding her baby, wondering if she knew her husband before his service. I looked for signs of older children off at school. What had *she* dealt with? Did she "go" to war with him? Did she deal with rantings too? Should I expect it, the rantings? I wanted the questions to go away, but they persisted. They dragged me around the corner to ask what self-destructive path had I stumbled upon that my celibacy did nothing to remediate? What would my future be if Mike and I married. Had kids? Sitting there, surrounded by a backdrop of a seemingly messed-up lifestyle, the first Vietnam veteran's home I was aware of since meeting my vet, I tried not to judge. My life was nothing to write home about. They were trying to help. Behind a closed door, my boyfriend of fewer than four months, and the man/husband/dad/vet were hammering out the next steps of Michael's recovery. What about mine? The door opened: they asked me in; the room was stacked with books and papers. We all sat and just cried for a while.

"See, Martha, there's this syndrome called Post-Traumatic Stress

Disorder, or by its initials, PTSD." He went on, "Traumatic things happened in Vietnam, and vets like Mike witnessed them. For whatever reason, he's forced to act like nothing extraordinary happened. Sometime afterward, he's reminded of it, either by a flashback or a memory of something totally unrelated, and the old reality surfaces, PTSD sets in, and Mike loses control."

"I had to stuff a lot of crap," Michael added, "as a medic, there was a lot." He was crying openly, as I had never seen him. The other vet's words had pried him open.

"Eventually," said the counseling vet, "eventually the reaction he might have had, the *realistic* reaction Mike might have had, *if he could have*, comes up. PTSD is the result of having a realistic reaction to an unreal event. Sometime after the fact. It's the traumatic reaction he should have had in the first place." He added knowledgeably, "We see more and more of it. And we're trying to understand what triggers it." (The term PTSD wasn't *widely* used for Vietnam vets until 1980 when the DSM III, *The Diagnostic and Statistical Manual of Mental Disorders*, finally recognized it.)

"See, honey, I'm not weird," Michael laughed, "I'm normal."

"Can he get better?" I asked. I guess anyone would want to know that. No? I was worried about us now.

"He's going to have to come to grips with what he experienced in Vietnam," the vet counselor said, "and to understand what triggers his reactions before he can hope to control them. If he can control them." The vet went to look up the nearest vet center to Marlboro, Massachusetts, to find their address and phone. Mike and I sat speechless in the room, barely looking at each other.

I brazenly thought, not long before meeting Michael, that I had nothing left to learn. I honestly thought I knew it all. (I've since repented.) I recall the phone conversation in which I stated it; it was towards the end of my celibacy, in the MVP studio. I was standing, leaning against the half-wall of the financial office. I was talking to my sister Dottie, and it was late in the night. We had a new client, a friend, and his partner; who owned a small hi-tech company. It required me to learn a whole new tech language to write their copy. I caught on quite well, I thought. Got cocky. Now I was learning more than I knew what to do with, and it kept coming at me. The EVAC chopper needed to hurry the hell in and rescue me.

My fears separated me from Michael. Many fears, least of which was the fear of repeating my bad beau scenario. I needed to step back.

Emotionally spent, Mike and I thanked the vet and his wife. I hugged her and drove back up the New Jersey Turnpike to NYC. I do remember the ride back, if just the humbled expression on Michael's face. This person who'd become such an influence, who expanded my life by volumes, with his gigantic stories of courage and pride. He looked up at me from a head hung low, a look that asked, am I worthy of your love? Can you deal with what I've become? Silent questions. Unasked. Unanswerable. I didn't know.

I was exhausted, bewildered, hungry. We stopped at a drive-thru for junk-food; eaten as we rode home. Then Mike fell asleep. The day was a turning point in our relationship; I needed to look more clearly into what I wanted from a mate. I would go again to my therapist, Evelyn Nef, in Georgetown, DC. I needed a refresher course to deal with my erupting self-destructive tendencies. In pledging to do that for me, my passion for Michael dimmed. My race to the train station and subsequent trip to Levittown had superseded Mike walking out on me. He had his own work to do. PTSD was Mike's issue to follow up on.

Later he'd write this to me. I'll bring this passage to the fore now; it's what I imagine Michael saying as he humped his way from East 21st to Penn Station that long morning of a longer day.

I am listening to a piece of music by Mark Isham… "On

the Threshold of Liberty," from the *Vapor Drawings* album. … It never gets flashy or carried away; it just starts from nowhere and builds to a long burn then fades out again, much like the war.

The tone of it reminds me of how I'd feel some mornings on patrol, saddling up to move out from our night defensive position, damp and chilled and stiff from the night. Watching the backs of the Rangers ahead of me as they started to move, silently alert and determined, into the green mist of some choked and brooding valley.

I'd float on a weird tension, the constant, second-to-second self-reminders keeping me busier than I'd ever been in my life: scan this sector—place your foot here, *no, there,* watch not to snap that twig, shift your weight now so that the next step will glide you silently as you duck under the limb—keep your interval, scan that sector, pause, scan the sector again—make mental note of a good rally location in case we're hit—don't step in that soft spot that could hold a track—Scan again—I'm slack, so on a frontal contact I step to the left, and as the point man runs past me changing magazines I put out eighteen rounds on the arc from 10 to 12 o'clock, wheel, and run to the outside of the RTO while *I* change mags and he fires up 12 to 2.—Scan—Another step, all with the concentration and deliberation of a stalking cat.

It wasn't fear yet—fear would come in the ambush site as the doomed approached the kill zone, and I tried to guess which one, which now-an-individual-with-face-and-hair-and-sweat odors, would be in my sector of fire when the blast of the Claymore came to crack the world and swallow the silence? And then it would be *true* fear, sucking plummets of whirlpool nausea that would have

106

you vomit out the very marrow of your bones were it
not for the invisible steel cable that choked your throat
closed....and the dim, subconscious knowledge that the
other five men around you were feeling the same thing.
The trust that *they* would function, and then would come
the revelation that they were the best men you'd ever
known in your life and, so, when the eruption came, you'd
squeeze that trigger, and the fear would come under the
hand of purpose, and *you'd* function, too, rather than let
them down.

Music is so powerful. Michael suggested putting warning labels on the
backs of album jackets.

CHAPTER 19

Vomiting Fear

Vomiting fear? Vomiting fear. In 1968, the year before Michael enlisted, President Nixon sent Emmanual Tanay, a holocaust survivor, to Vietnam to investigate why our veterans were coming home to such severe psychological problems. Once back, Tanay informed Nixon that, "Guerrilla warfare was extremely dangerous to soldiers' mental as well as physical health; that these young men were in no way prepared for it, and that if the government insisted on sending them to engage in it, the least it could do would be to give them a thorough debriefing and plenty of counseling when they got back.[1]" Nope, Nixon never funded any debriefing, and whittled away at the budget for counseling as well. Mike's very first counseling was self-sought. He learned of it from a VVA handout I'd picked up, fittingly, on the dedication day for the memorial the vets had built for themselves. It was a service provided free, in a home office in Levittown, Pennsylvania, nearly twelve years after his return from guerrilla warfare. Then John Creamer's Exit Day happened. No warning. No debriefings. No father to greet him.

It was a difficult time for me. I never graduated from the notion that if I made love to a man, I would marry him. But I feared my friend Bruce might be right. (Maybe you need to leave this one alone, he said.) Michael refused to fully acknowledge the pain his father's de-

---

1   Nicosia, p. 180.

parture inflicted on him and never stopped blaming his mother as the reason he had left.

In the months that followed, we didn't discuss his father's disappearance once. I would find bits of details from Peter, or Mike's sisters. I was appalled at his father's behavior. It was worse than anything I'd heard of a parent's selfishness. It caused an emotional earthquake for Mike, ripping him, at twenty years of age from his patriotic pride of service, through which his brilliant military mind might have thrived. It left him on the other side of everything he'd recently learned, forever unable to assess his actions.

Mike's emotional instability loomed large. In early 1983, PTSD was seldom spoken of, not really understood. In my big family, I never was the child bringing home wounded animals; I brought home "The Closest Thing to God I Know," my wounded warrior.

PART II

CHAPTER 20

Spring Forward

If Mike took any steps to deal with his PTSD, he did them away from me. Mike was that guy who, once knowing the cause of a problem, pulled back and wondered what **he** could do to remedy the situation. Physician healing himself. Not me. I had to work it out. I remember while at *Vogue* when I moved into my tiny brownstone, penthouse apartment on W89th, my friend from Milton Glaser's class came over to visit. I ended up crying to him, saying, "Everybody thinks I must be the happiest person in the world (working at *Vogue*, getting an apartment with skylights and a roof terrace), and I'm miserable." He gave me his therapist's name, with whom I would consult and then stayed for two and a half years.

Previously I had therapy in college from a professor. (Sewed drapes for his office to pay for it). Both therapists were sexist; the second, upon hearing how I'd solved a tricky remuneration issue with *Rags*, sighed a deep sigh and said, "Why do you want to bust their balls? I'd be concerned if you were a MAN, Martha, but you're a WOMAN, and one day you'll get married and…" Good-bye. I had no plans for marrying soon, and when *Rags* folded, I started my own business.

Four years later, before I met Michael, I had a client, an older and thoughtfully brilliant woman, who gave me the name of her female therapist in DC. I flew down. Evelyn Nef, the therapist, conveyed two essential lessons to me in my very first session. One: that when a woman becomes pregnant, her attention turns inward, to herself. (That, in commenting on my mom's destructive behavior with her kids. And why she had so many pregnancies—eight before me.) Two: After seeing my portfolio, which she requested I bring along, she said, "We just have to figure out how to make your personal life as designed as your professional life." She blew me out of the water. Day one!

During that month or so, Michael and I still wrote, but we didn't get together, and his letters weren't passionate. In late March, he called me asking if I wanted to go with him to a Herd reunion in Virginia organized by the 173rd's Sigholtz Chapter. "Hell, yes," I said. We drove down together. It gave me the chance to meet Frank Baker, whom he spoke of often, and Sky Soldiers and their significant others who came for the three-day event. It provided great insight into why Michael was so attached to the Airborne, especially Rangers. In truth, I never met such a collection of sensitive, intelligent, real men assembled together in one place, even still. Michael had been corresponding with several of them since they met at the Washington Sheraton. Over non-stop drinking, he talked his heart out and enjoyed showing me off, the woman he'd met at The Wall, a New York entrepreneur. We made drunken love at the hotel.

At the business meeting on day two, members talked of creating a hard-cover yearbook to pay homage to the de-commissioned Herd, Michael sat intently. When they mentioned needing writers, Michael's hand went up—shades of Sociology class in nursing school—he was willing and available. It was then, with me knee-deep in MVP work, that I decided to support Michael's writing efforts and put mine aside. My private non-competition clause.

Michael's mind raced as we drove home from Virginia. He fully conceived the yearbook, paginating it in his head, pulling out scraps of paper, scribbling notes. I had never seen him as motivated except in bed, which I had missed during his two months away. He stayed a week in New York City, while he mapped out the whole Herd book. On April 5th, he sent eight pages of handwritten notes to the organizing committee.

Michael did most of that work at the NY Public Library. He would hike there each day. It was Fashion Week for me, so I was busy. He left to continue work in Marlboro, and I was glad to have patched the romance up a bit and sent him on his way. He sent his first piece for review.

Michael's essay of a particularly meaningful time:

The National Salute to Vietnam Veterans
November 10-14, 1982 • Washington, DC

> Some of the veterans wore 3-piece suits, others, jeans, and faded field jackets. Their ranks included former Generals and ex-PFCs. They were the Sky Soldiers of the 173rd Airborne Brigade, "The Herd." They had come to bear witness as the newest monument, (The Vietnam War [sic] Memorial) was to be dedicated in Washington, DC.
>
> All their lonely individual homecomings, years of sleepless nights, and sudden, sweaty awakenings might be forgotten now.
>
> I hooked up with them at the massive Sheraton-Washington Northwest Hotel, Room 1066, where the local Sigholtz-Capitol Chapter was sponsoring a hospitality suite. It became a gathering point for over 300 troopers and many guests, including retired General Westmoreland.
>
> It was Friday night, mid-point in a very special week. Long-lost buddies found each other over laughter and bear-hugs, shared photographs, and tears. Three Medal of Honor winners took the stage in the Sheraton's Main Ballroom and led a huge

crowd of veterans in an impromptu rendition of "God Bless America." But these were only lead-ins, preparation for the main events. Saturday, November 13th, was the day of the actual dedication and the day of the parade. At long last: "Our Parade."

The organizers set the parade up alphabetically, by state contingents. But many of the Herd troopers—me included—felt we wanted to be together, with our buddies, sharing the joys and sorrows as we had many years before.

So that morning, we linked up on a soggy corner of the Mall, the patches on our shoulders serving as beacons, signaling the assembly. There was only a handful at first, and then a dozen, and then a score. Our old rival, the 101st Airborne was gathering in its own small knot nearby, exchanging good-natured joshing with us, as always.

Wyoming, the last of the state contingents, stepped off and onto the parade route. "Okay, men," shouted a leader. *"We can take this one easy and just diddly-bop along like everyone else, or we can go for it. What do you say?"*

"Let's show 'em how it's done," said a voice.

"Yeah, we'll do it right," called out another.

"Hey, we're The Herd! We'll march!" I joined in.

Men who had been shivering in the bitter gray autumn snapped to and stood tall. In our assorted half-uniforms, the group looked a bit ragged. Most who had given no thought to a military formation in fifteen years discovered they could still remember to, *"Dress it right and cover down, forty inches all around."* The marching was rusty at first, but the old sense of discipline and rhythm grew. The ranks swelled to over a hundred now, and a uniformed, active-duty Major with large lungs of leather and an extended repertoire of Airborne cadence took the helm.

In that lusty Airborne growl of his, the words hit the

frigid air, amplified by the DC granite buildings. Onlookers strained to see where the words were coming from.

"Everywhere we go-oh,
People want to know-oh
Who we ah-are
Where we come from
So, we tell them
We are the Airborne!
Mighty, mighty Airborne!
Hard-charging' Airborne!
The One-Seventy-Third!
The HERD!
THE WORD!

More and more troopers joined in as we marched and turned onto Constitution Avenue. Now we were a unit: The sleeping giant of the 173rd Airborne Brigade was beginning to stir.

Then we heard it, a muffled muttering off in the distance, the most remembered of all Vietnam's sounds. It grew closer and louder. Eyes narrowed, ears strained, and heads swiveled up, searching...Then, there they were—the choppers! Four of them in diamond formation: Two Huey slicks, a Loach, and a Cobra gunship sweeping in low and fast over the Mall. Our entire parade stopped as every man watched, smiled, then cheered. The troopers hugged and back-slapped. Then a hundred stories, all different, all the same, spilled out as if a dam had burst, *"I remember that time we were hunkered down, said our farewells, and suddenly, there they were—the choppers!"*

The old warriors knew that it was our day. The years

melted away like ice in the Bien Hoa sun, and every man felt young again: Like a 19- or 20-year old Infantryman, Platoon Leader, Medic, or Artilleryman. We were ten-foot-tall and bulletproof! Again, we fell in line and began to march for the cheering crowds that lined the streets of the Capitol. Many in the formation limped or wore Purple Hearts, so the ranks were checked to confirm that a newly concocted plan could be pulled off, that nobody would be left behind. All agreed. We were ready. STAND IN THE DOOR! [1]

We waited for the Wyoming marchers ahead to pass several yards away. We'd arrived at the reviewing stand with its framework flying a massive Stars and Stripes. We needed a little room to operate—that's all the Herd ever wanted or needed, just room to operate. The command rang out:

"Brigade. Ten' sh…hut!"

A chill ran up the collective spines of we several hundred marchers.

"Double time…March!"

The Giant rose up to full height, faced the people for whom it had fought so long and so gallantly, and said, "Here I am, America. I'm the Herd, and I've come home!"

At that, the unit broke into the Airborne Shuffle, a short, heavy, quick-stepping jog. The paratroopers' own. The cadence rose, drowning out the ecstatic roar of the crowd. Above it, we could barely hear the announcer's voice, shouting into the microphone: *"Good Lord, what's this? They're double-timing! I don't believe it! This could only be the 173rd! Ladies, and gentlemen, these men saw some of the heaviest fighting of Vietnam; they were among the last to leave the country. I*

---

1   The vocal command prior to a paratrooper readying for the jump, with the jump zone in view.

understand that this is the first time the 173rd has ever marched on American soil. " The crowd roared louder. *"Will you just look at how they've chosen to do it? Folks, I give you the One Hundred and Seventy-Third Separate Airborne Brigade!"*

And so, the Red Bayonet borne by the White Wing, flashing from hundreds of squared shoulders, ended its long and proud hump, shuffling down Constitution Avenue… and into history.

Michael E. Creamer
N Co. Medic, 173rd Airborne Brigade [2]

2   Edited by Martha Voutas Creamer Donegan 11/18/2017.
Used by permission Turner Publishing, Paducah, Kentucky.

CHAPTER 21

On Assignment

To me, Michael Creamer was a fine, intelligent writer in the making; he struggled with things, but his words came out as beautifully sculpted imagery. Always his drafts were in all cap letters. It looked as if he never debated what he put to paper with barely a word crossed out. He could have written for any magazine I'd worked on.

I kept reading the long list of Vietnam books he'd given me; *13th Valley* by John del Vecchio kept me transfixed. I wasn't a fiction reader, but del Vecchio was a great writer. *Dispatches* by Michael Herr gave me the basic low-down. Mike and I would talk at length, usually over the phone late at night, to discuss what I was learning. He was my best teacher. But Michael felt frustrated by his writing; he wanted it perfect from the get-go, which is impossible to master. As good as he thought it was, he was unsure. When he visited, I'd edit his pieces, first the longhand versions, written in medium nib black Pentel® pens. Then Michael sat with a typewriter (the entire world wasn't on computers yet) and revised away. All I could do was encourage him to stay on task and work through his snags of no confidence. He managed his own money, but it had to be running low; he hadn't worked in over a year. I didn't ask, just picked up the tab when I could. Michael was grateful to be involved in something worthwhile. That was key for him, feeling worthwhile.

We didn't socialize much. When I tried to get him out, it went something like this—

"You want to go out tonight?" I asked.

"Not really," he answered.

* * *

My best friend in the city, Alene de la Houssaye, and her chef/husband, Abe, owned Texarkana, on West 10th Street in Greenwich Village. Tex was their second restaurant, opened after the success of La Louisiana, a small place on Lexington Ave, near to my studio. I had designed their logo.

"Come on, I made reservations at Texarkana," I said.

Texarkana had been an immediate hit upon opening, drawing hungry superstars eating up Roast Pig on Spit, and Gumbo as good as it got in Cajun country (Breaux Bridge, Abe's hometown in Louisiana). No other place served crawfish, flown in when it was in season. Wall Streeters claimed Tex for their own in the roaring 80s, when a good cut of beef was compensation for a bounding big board. I thought Mike would like Tex. Southern food was new to New York—it was tasty, and chances are you'd rub elbows with an up-and-coming personality, maybe sitting at the huge George Nakashima bar. One night a young Harry Connick Jr. set his keyboard at the end of the bar to generate pocket change. At that same bar, I would chat with Robin Wagner, the Tony-winning set designer. Calvin Klein was a regular, Whoopi Goldberg, David Halberstam and wife, Jean. I brought Perry and his design team out for dinner at both restaurants.

I was Dead Wrong with Tex; the place was the antithesis of Michael Creamer. After introducing him to Alene, who was managing the front of the house, she seated us at our table.

"Do you think we can have a table on the wall?" Michael asked me after she left.

"Sure," I said, wishing he'd asked Alene himself.

Combat vets like Mike could be ambushed in the middle of the floor; they needed an outside corner where they could scope out the whole A/O.

"Why don't you get Roast Pig? It's delicious?" I said.

"Too much," he said, "I don't want to pay that much for dinner; it's a lot. Look."

"Chicken Jolie Blonde is delicious," Alene said, swooping by. "It's much lighter."

"I love Chicken Jolie Blonde. My favorite," I said.

"What the heck is Chicken Jolie Blonde?" he asked me.

In truth, there were gay men at Tex—customers, and staff—and Michael claimed that gay guys were always checking him out. We stayed and had a drink; Michael wasn't going to order. "Too chic," he said. I took it more as pulling away, and I took it personally, since Alene was my best friend. I pulled in the other direction.

One last time I tried eating there with him, we were with my sister Dot and Bernie Glynn, my accountant, who was now an investor in Tex. Mike excused himself as we ordered, then split for my apartment. That was a hostile act; there was an unmistakably mean streak in Michael Creamer that could be downright lethal. I didn't want to marry him anyway, not with that open aggression; no telling how that would come back to bite me in the butt.

The energy at Texarkana was welcoming. I often worked late, alone, then cabbed the eighteen blocks and caught dinner. Alene was dear to me, always aware of what was happening and always good company. Originally from California, her Japanese/American ancestors were interred during WWII. Uncle George (Nakashima) was already an architect; he would move east during the forced interment, becoming known as a furniture designer. Alene's stories were fascinating to me, though not to Michael.

By the end of his last Herd assignments, The Battle for Hill 875,[1] the fighting side of Mike had reemerged, not just with me. The soldier was rekindled by the power of research and writing about those lives he could not save, of the hopelessness of their predicament, the valor that had emerged regardless. It was evident that Mike was eager to finish up, get out of New York City, and back to Massachusetts. There he stood in my office, his just-copied manuscripts in hand, typed, double-spaced, and stapled as if they were pieces of art. They were. He beamed.

Our relationship had grown less about romance and more about being that person Michael had introduced as "my friend" to the stranger on the DC knoll ten months before. I had hoped then I could be his friend. Right now, I vacillated. Mike was on his way, and I had helped the Vietnam survivor get there.

His trip to Marlboro was an ordeal of sorts: after five hours on Amtrak, Michael detrained in Boston, at South Station, where he boarded a local bus and traveled for two hours and forty minutes to City Hall, Marlboro. He often walked the 2.2 miles to his mom's. So, transportation was an all-day affair.

Back home, getting around took effort. The Creamer house was out in "The Old Rice Orchard" development. It was the first of many developments in Marlboro, a small city within commuting distance from techno-industrial Rte 128 to the east, and Worcester to the west. The development of single-story ranch and split-level houses brought an influx of urban exiles: Between 1960 and 1970, when John and Dot Creamer relocated there, Marlboro's population grew by 48.4%! The decade before, growth hit 19.4%. Bob Dylan had it right, *The Times They Are A'changin'*. We Marlboroites lamented the loss of our

---

1   The Fight for Dak To or The Battle for Hill 875 is in the Appendix

orchards. My grandparents' peach orchard on Hosmer Street was sold to make way for multiplex apartments where Michael's brother Steven and his family would live before moving into their new house.

Single-family houses went for $13,800 on average in Massachusetts in the 1960s, and Marlboro was by far not the most elite of cities. John and Dot put $5.00 down; John's G.I. Bill-paid education, his white-collar job at an established insurance firm, and his wartime service made them perfect mortgage candidates.

✳ ✳ ✳

After John Creamer's unexplained abandonment in 1971, Dot learned to drive and went off to her job at a non-profit agency near Main Street. Then she was hired at Raytheon, a company soon to be purchased by Michael's old employer, M-K, or Morrison-Knudsen. Raytheon manufactured American weapons of war, Patriot missiles.

On Michael's long walk, the same he'd made on Veterans Day in '82, around the lake, to the post office, this time to ship off his 173rd Airborne manuscripts, he thought about life. There wasn't any reason to stick around; his friends were all scattered. Peter was house-sitting in Walter Gropius'[2] house in Lincoln, prior to renovation. Vinnie was in New Hampshire, coming off a bad marriage. Yuoska (always called by his last name because he was the second Mike), newly married, was on the brink of busting out career-wise, same-same for Dave, working at the St. Regis in Boston, and Ron, still at home, was chipping away at his Master's Degree. Most were doing better than Michael, with no job and a waning affair with a girlfriend living far away.

✳ ✳ ✳

---

2   Gropius was a modernist architect, father of the modernist movement in America. Peter let Michael and I stay overnight once, since when I visited Massachusetts, we didn't have a place to stay except at one of our parents' homes, and we weren't married yet.

In documenting Herd history, Mike had become invigorated—vicariously reliving the power of the 173rd Airborne Brigade. "Hill 875" helped him regain the ammunition he needed to get out of the house and back into the world. Mike needed to take a stand, to move forward. That August day, he hiked with his completed essays addressed to The Herd Yearbook, shipped them off, and then feeling a rush of maybe machismo, Mike Creamer dropped in on the US Army recruiter, Main Street, Marlboro, Massachusetts.

Mike didn't plan to tell me of his reenlistment until I came to Massachusetts again, but he phoned to tell me anyway, "I'm going back in the Army. I leave October 26th."

Talk about pulling away.

"Great, you should go, Michael," I said, half stunned, half believing I didn't care. "You have an amazing military mind." If there was any accolade I could give him, it was this. He was always quoting Patton, or Charlemagne, or Shakespeare's warriors. I mean, what else do you do with that skill set? Let's face it.

"I think this will give me the closure I need, Muff." He was calling me Muff again, regressing perhaps?

"I hope so, Mike," I said. "I just reread your 'Hill 875'."

"What do you think?" he asked.

"First off, it's very well written," I said, "but man, what you all went through. To be so outnumbered. You had to survive even writing it."

Michael was silent.

"I'm sure it's difficult to move forward when you have unfinished business," I said as if Vietnam were an old girlfriend, and he was going back to her. He thanked me.

I knew that Michael was far from healed; I knew by now I certainly couldn't heal him, nor could I stand in the way of whatever it took for him to find his cure. I relied on a song I'd heard:

If You Love Somebody Set Them Free—by Sting.

In my journal, I found this: Obviously written to Michael, no date.

Parts of you come up every day for me. All day long. You have fed me so well on thoughts and time and images. I guess we had so much to know about one another, and we had so little time to get it right; you left me with all these things to remember you by. Now I need to watch you go away with love and respect enough to bring us to wherever we're going to surface next.

I'm not afraid of being alone. I can only be afraid if I forget the parts of me that you helped release that are true and real and fulfilling. I guess we bring a lot of crap with us from childhood. Baggage. Deadweight. And sometimes an opportunity comes to drop some of it. Just leave it behind. You have an opportunity. Use it.

We all tend to look at what's gone wrong in our pasts and use that to fuel the "that's why I didn't make it" fire. Lord knows childhood is rough even on those reared well. I've been looking at your life. It's a great study—full of curves. I always thought your father's leaving put massive screws to you, to your whole family. I never met him, and I hated him for leaving the lot of you, because he took from you your freedom of choice. The most physical result was that you left the Army; you have told me that you would have stayed. It probably saved the Army for you now.

CHAPTER 22

Into the Smokies

Okay, so on second thought, I wasn't totally willing to let *The Closest Thing to God* go. Who would? Michael was a handful; he was going off for three long years, but as I was packing up things he'd left behind, I found the response to his letter from Julie whom he'd met in DC.

She had written back to him: Michael, "I appreciate all the sources but most of all I am glad to be in contact with you. ... I tormented myself for not going back" (to the Sheraton) ...thinking she had lost her last chance to be with people who knew her husband. "I didn't want that weekend to be over. And now your letter has helped again ... Doug was one in a million." (Damn, I felt the same way about Michael.) Julie wrote, "I won't forget ...I'm glad I found you in the crowd." I remembered that she was partly responsible for holding Michael up just long enough for that perfectly timed hot dog line and snap! If I thought about that long enough, then I got that whole God-thing all over again.

I had vacation days coming, my client, Michael G. Abrams, was opening a shoe store in New Orleans. I'd been to NOLA once, Michael had never been. I thought a trip to New Orleans would be a great adventure. I devised a plan for Mike and Me to drive down through DC in September, stay a night with Frank Baker to pick up his camping gear, then Michael and I would drive further down the Blue Ridge Parkway.

"We can camp atop Mt. Mitchell in the Smokies," Mike suggested. "Then we could check out Ft. Benning in Georgia, home to Boot Camp." Having been out of the military so long, Michael couldn't keep his rank of E-5 and had to repeat training —a drag, but he said he didn't mind. "Don't have anything else to do," he said, overly noncommittal.

"Good, then it's a plan," I said, adding, "can we leave the car with someone at Benning?"

"Sure," Mike said.

"Then we can fly from Atlanta to New Orleans—on me—and stay at a B&B in the French Quarter—I have to check out the location for the new store, take some measurements for signage, and get a grasp of clientele at the new mall there at Canal Place."

"Okay," Mike said.

"I'll fly back to New York, and you can meet up with Frank in Atlanta, and you guys camp your way back to DC, then return the car to the city."

To Mike, it sounded like a good idea; to me, it would be a car ride with not much room for him to pull too far away. One can learn a lot about a person on a long car ride; I hoped the Smokies trip would be a leveling of our personalities. That is until the Night on Bald Mountain. (Cue in the Mussorgsky!)

I was a neophyte at camping. I'd camped a little bit in my life; I had a sleeping bag from somewhere. College students in the 70s ended up with sleeping bags—there was always someone crashing on the floor, stoned or seeking shelter from some storm. I packed my gear, Mike brought his from Massachusetts, and we drove off in my Subaru wagon. Michael was getting whatever else we'd need; he was an expert camper, though I didn't know he was a Spartan one.

If you've ever driven the Blue Ridge Parkway up into the aptly called Smokies, it takes your breath away. It also takes your vision away, as roads fall fast into steeply contrasting shadows, and before we had found our camping spot, night came on quickly. After parking, we had to hump an eighth of a mile or so to get to our campsite, on a ridge, and now it was getting terribly cold. I asked, "No tent?"

"It's nearly fall and clear; we won't need one," Mike said, adding, "though you know, Mt. Mitchell is the highest spot on the eastern seaboard. It can easily get down to below zero here. It's probably going to get that cold tonight."

"What?" I said. "It's not even the middle of September, I'm cold already, and hungry. Can we at least have some hot cocoa and start a fire?"

"You don't start fires anymore; I have this handy dandy little camp stove," he said, putting on his headlamp and pulling mica-thin sheets of metal out of a sack and configuring them into a stove. "Just take a tiny little flint, and there, we can heat some water for cocoa."

I was thinking warming embers, but, "Okay, what about food?"

"I have some Dinty Moore Beef Stew, and we can add this jerky I brought." Not what I'd envisioned, but I was freezing! I was dressed for the lowlands, and I couldn't stop shivering. I pulled my bag out of my sack, and Mike laughed, "Is that the bag you brought? That's a summer-weight bag." Then asked me incredulously, "Why'd you bring a summer-weight bag?"

"It's summer. I don't know from bag weights; a sleeping bag is a sleeping bag."

"You're gonna freeze your butt off," he forewarned too late. "Why don't you get into it and try to get your body heat going?"

"Yeah?" I asked.

"Go on, take off your jeans," he instructed.

"Take off my jeans? I'm freezing already. Why should I take off my clothes?"

Mike answered as if I were a child, "Because your body will give off

128

heat and warm the space between you and the bag. It will insulate you."

"I can't imagine," I said, slurping up the warm soup and waiting on the cocoa. There was no mention from Mr. Macho Survivalist of helping me out or changing bags with me, only that I was dumb to think I would survive in that bag. It kept getting colder, and now, sitting in my bag, half-naked, having drunk both soup and cocoa, I needed to pee badly. The facilities were about 50 yards down a rocky path. It was dark. I was miserable, I had to re-dress enough to make it, and whatever heat I had drummed up in that dumb old summer-weight bag would be wasted. I grabbed a flashlight and ran slowly for the head.

*　*　*

Back atop the ridge, I will never forget trying to get to sleep, shivering into the tensest state of unhappiness that ever existed. Mike was snoring blissfully, no concern for me. I fell asleep hating everything about this predicament—the bag, the stove, the Dinty Moore, which on top of everything else, was making me farty, the weather, Mike's holier than thou attitude, my car parked so far away. In the morning, all I wanted was a great breakfast, and I had peed my pants a little.

Benning was great for him, passable for me. He hooked up with friends he'd kept in touch with; we left the car and flew south. New Orleans was great for me, passable for him. (I live there now.) Michael didn't like the bed and breakfast on Royal Street, especially our front bedroom, close to people passing by. It by no means was the French Quarter of today with its bawdy drunkenness; it had a lesser version of bawdy drunkenness, sort of like TV violence then and TV violence now. Mike liked sitting outside a bar drinking beer. He sulked throughout the steamboat tour down the Mississippi on the Natchez. It cost so much even though I paid. He was not invited to the client meeting for fear that he would reveal his true disagreeable self, and my client might see I'd made a crappy choice of boyfriends and would lecture me to dump him before it got worse. So good, get over it, Mike; go into the Army. I'd just about had it. You want to get away, Mike? Get away; only don't come crying to me when the Army spits you back. And you should have traded that sleeping bag with me. (I would have, given the situation.)

When Michael returned the car, he trained home to Marlboro; we talked, but we didn't see each other for nearly a month.

Frank Baker, (left), former Ranger with the 173rd, who found Mike (right) at the dedication of The Wall; Frank went camping with Mike in the Smokies. I met Frank on this occasion, and snapped the photo. From Xerox.

CHAPTER 23

October '83

October was such an active month militaristically; Michael's reenlistment seemed pre-ordained:

- **OCTOBER 13th**, Grenada, a strategically placed, small island off South America, a territory of Great Britain, is seized by Grenadians

- **OCTOBER 19th**, the Prime Minister of Grenada is executed

- **OCTOBER 21st**, car bombings in Beirut bring down 239 US servicemen

- **OCTOBER 23rd**, 58 French paratroopers stationed in Beirut are killed

- **OCTOBER 23rd**, the 25th US Marines and Rangers invade Grenada, coming into criticism from the UN, which declares US in violation of International Law

I wrote in my journal that day: I almost called Michael, but it was 7:00 AM, and he sleeps so late. If he lived alone, I would have called, but that family's strange on the phone. So, I watched it alone. Watched and listened to the talk about Grenada. Remembering all that Mike had told me. I thought he would kill to be there. I wanted to know how they got in. How did the American Army land? Michael's a paratrooper, so obviously, I'm interested in the arrival process. ... I put the kettle on to boil. ... I wish I knew where we were headed (he and I)—what Michael knew and didn't know gets muddled in my opinion-making process with everything else. I live on the border of liberal and staunch conservative.

I start exercises the night before (the kind you undertake when you're turning a corner or changing a bad habit). One, two, three... I wonder if he's up? ... He'll be upset to have missed it...Four, five...They called it an invasion with multi-national forces. ... I feel so out of shape.

The whistle on the kettle blows me over to start the coffee. Some liberal R.'s and D.'s from Senate appear on screen to denounce our presence in Lebanon. "Bring 'em home." "Disgrace." I wonder if I'd not met Michael, would I be curling my lip now? Don't know. The outside world is encroaching too much on my private life these days.

And when Mike was in basic training, it would continue—

- **NOVEMBER 2nd**, the Grenada hostilities end
- **NOVEMBER 2nd**, a Palestinian truck bomb in South Lebanon kills 60 and wounds 30 American service members

All within a month. Mike was chomping at the bit.

At his friend Dave's prodding, I caved in and threw Mike and his buddies a combined-Libras-birthday/Mike-going-away-party at Dave's house outside Boston. Even at his party, after cooking all day, I didn't feel close. He didn't act grateful. He had all the regulars assembled, Pete, Ron, Yuoska, Vinnie, Dave, his wife, my sister Jean and a few other Libras I barely knew including a friend from nursing school. The last-minute timing sucked, Mike would leave for the airport right from Dave's, no time to be alone. Anyway, the message I got was not what

I wanted; it was however, what I expected. One of those times you're glad none of your pans were used to bake the lasagna! I left before most of the others.

I flew home from Boston; Mike went off to find closure. (Between you and me, can one really find closure when you're up to your neck in Boot Camp?) Afterward, I wrote in my journal

> "I am so afraid you'll misunderstand. But I love you, and I'm sitting on my bedroom floor crying at how much I miss you. I don't want you to think I'm not tough, but I miss you so much my head hurts. I am so sapped by loneliness that I could scream. Oh, Michael, Michael, your absence is a loss to me. I have put a vital part of me on hold. Postponed, put off, and I'm not sure that's in my best interest."

Michael's pulling away hurt me. It was a perpetual in and out. I had seen him do it before, but this time it would nearly extinguish the candle. I felt a need to get on with my life; I became more resentful that he never discussed his reenlistment beforehand. The re-up was immense, but in tandem with his detaching, cavernous. The more he pulled away, the less I cared, I convinced myself.

MVP had finished our six-month retainer to redesign *Woman's Day*. Still, later that same year, Ellen Levine attempted an impossible launch of a new publication for *WD* called *Traditions*: no budget, no time, very little content to work with, but no boyfriend to distract me either. I got to write some of the copy, as well as Creative Direct. After getting it to press in record-breaking time *WD* aborted *Traditions*.[1] Not sure anyone even knew of its existence, unless its sole purpose was to represent some intellectual property worth an inflated extra half mill or mill? I was immensely bummed.

---

1   Hachette, the French publisher who'd entered the US market with *Elle*, and looking to expand its holdings in the US, bought *WD* and all the titles held by Diamandis.

Ellen Levine, Woman's Day *Editor in chief, Ann Shakeshaft and me. A polaroid for Ellen's editor's column. This was the week after meeting Mike.*

CHAPTER 24

Cherry or The F'n New Guy

Michael wrote right away, seemingly oblivious to how hurtful he'd been, or that I had basically thrown in the towel on our romance. Abrupt changes in feelings we'd see again, and again.

> PV-2 Michael E. Creamer
> No address yet,
> Ft. Benning, GA United States Army
>
> Hello Hon,
> So far, it looks like the Army has changed some…Gotten rather lax. Been lying around since last night (the 28th), waiting to start in-processing. Did some introductory marching for about three hours, and got pulled for a detail—designing and lettering signs, if you can believe that. Otherwise, Nada! Very boring. Bad for the kids, cause they'll go into shock when the giant turds hit the propeller.
> Several other old-timers are coming back in, including a 101st Nam vet, two years older than me. All for the same reason too: The clouds gathering on the horizon. … We still don't have uniforms yet.
> I'm most assuredly missing you, especially since there's nothing to do to keep my mind off you. It's harder

after lights out when I know I can't reach over and touch you.

I love you, Mike C.

2 Nov 83
Hello Hon,
Love you. Miss you. Ain't got much time. Special testing today—They're screening out the bright ones.
Bye, Mike C.

4 Nov 83
Hello Hon,
As Tad predicted, I am trainee Platoon Sgt. My ass is being run ragged. I am moving like crazy 0400-2200 hours trying to babysit, cajole, coerce, coax, order, punish, reward, and otherwise control 43 kids through the most upside-down period in their lives. My arms are achin', my feet are smokin', and my head is spinning. Thinking of your love gives me strength. Martha mine, I remain…
Yours—Mike C.

★ ★ ★

It didn't sound much like the guy who'd left me two weeks before! As I'd discovered earlier, letters were a better means to communicate with Mike than speaking on the phone. Same, same, during Basic Training Redux. I could hear it through the phone: Mike, the good soldier, strutting, beaming, smiling, and making do with only a few minutes of phone time—the insecurity of a 5'5", balding, thin 31-year old becoming patrol leader. I felt a slight animosity home alone. His brilliant military mind had to go back in, I suppose.

Sometimes Mike would get to a phone with a hair across his ass, on some jag or another. He'd growl, "Why did I ever re-up?" and moan about "the f'n idiots in the Army now." Only Mike didn't abbreviate it. Every other word was the F word, and I found it best to hang up. Afterward, I felt great. I reveled in being single—I would never hang up on my husband. But single? I had latitude, agency.

I understood more fully that I was born into the Vietnam Generation: I had to be alone before meeting Michael, my doppelganger, my twin, my mirror image. If I'd never gone into my personal abyss, writing my many poems of aching aloneness, I wouldn't have asked where had my men gone, nor had my ear to the rails of what had become of my generation. I wouldn't have "solved" the gender gap (ha), I wouldn't have begun interviewing men who avoided the War but stepped into other battles because of their avoidance. I certainly would not have ventured to DC that day in November of '82, where I experienced an indelible real-time sense of God working through me. Of course, I wouldn't have re-met Michael, nor because of him, gone to Levittown to meet with PTSD firsthand. I sensed I was on a mission with Michael, and now with him gone, a different aloneness set in. Through all these shifts in viewpoint, I realized that ours was not just a romantic pairing. Michael was evolving into my significant other, a term Harry Stack Sullivan used, back in 1940, to define "one who directly socializes the person to whom they are significant." We were each critical enough to affect the other's emotions, behavior, and sense of self. "Self-concept is based largely on our perceptions—whether accurate or not—of who we are in the eyes of those whose opinions matter to us." Michael's opinion mattered to me.

With that realization, I decided to help Mike's enlisted *ennui* along; I asked him to list his Top 10 of many things—favorite Movies, Actors, Songs, Books, Foods, Places he'd been, People he'd met, and on and on. I sent him a few categories in one letter and a few in the next until

I stopped getting calls from a Michael so riled up over going through Basic again. This Top 10 meditation seemed to work: he wrote back keys to his passions, his influences, himself. Suddenly, I wasn't lonely, the man on the other end of the exchange was filling out, gaining dimension. And I had his letters. Best yet, I'd taken over directing our conversation. I found out much more than if I had left it to him. It was a hedge against Mike coming home to nothing all over again.

Mike was coming back to his senses about me, at least.

> 18 Nov 83
> Hello My Love,
> I think of you at all hours. I've pictured you walking to work while training at the nuclear-biological-chemical warfare range; (ha!) … you sleeping during 0430 runs… you driving around on weekends while I'm cleaning the barracks. We have old WWII buildings, so I'm sharing a room with 23 others. No dividers between shitters… heat is inadequate to non-existent. I've relived so many moments with you while standing locked in endless formations. …I especially like ones of our first weekend together, each beginning to realize that the other was a long-lost vital part that we had learned to do without, by hard and often disappointing improvisation…It's so much smoother now. Thanksgiving was a joy, the first lovemaking and all. It makes me happy when joy is rare, and tensions run high.
>
> We've covered cammo, map reading, military justice and courtesy, the gas chamber, marching, first aid, etc. My academic average is at 100%, and my platoon has the highest average in the company. Next week we start two weeks of marksmanship with the M-16, and we'll be

bivouacking at the range for most of it. No scarred floors to wax, if only for a while.

It's worse, I think than '69. Our Drill Sgt. is totally unpredictable, a real expert at head games. Whatever you've heard about the Army doing away with harassment is shit. They have stopped beatings, but they make up for it with things that must've been learned by de-briefing POWs. I'm glad that you can't see your man, shaven-headed, collapsing into ten inches of mud after endless pushups in driving, freezing rain. It isn't a pretty sight. They're stressing us to the max, the weak are being sent home in droves—about fifteen last week, close to 10% of the company.... Gotta go. I've written this in bed, under blankets, with a red-lensed flashlight.

I love you, Mike C.

PS Did you finish Fallows' book?

(*National Defense*) —Yes, I had.

It was letters like the next one that clued me in on the inherent differences between men and women, not gender gap stuff, but that Michael needed time to sort out his feelings. Years later he would say, "Can you give me time to process what you just said? You've thought about this for the last two hours driving up here (to our country home from NYC). You spring things on me; I can't think that fast." Unlike an Aboriginal walkabout, American boys of the Vietnam Generation weren't given time to form synapses to adulthood. Kerouac took his trip (literal and figurative) with the Beats. My generation lost their beats altogether. Brigham Young once said, "Give me patience to wait until I can understand it for myself."

I found a quote in *Chance and Circumstance* from the year Mike returned from Nam: "A 1971 Harris survey found that most Americans believed that those who went to Vietnam were 'suckers, having to risk their lives in the wrong war, in the wrong place, at the wrong time.'" Did this new enlistment make it more right? Would this be a better time for Michael, when he might be able to put his astute military mind to good service? Or had he become like an old boyfriend of mine getting two master's degrees to avoid the war. It remained to be seen if Michael would come out too overly educated that his re-up would become another blind alley?

From Mike to me

> 20 Nov 83
> I think back to a morning when I watched you walk off
> to work, umbrella in hand, and realized that I was in love
> with you. I was disturbed by it because my self-esteem was
> at a dangerous low, and I was sure that I didn't deserve the
> love of such a wonderful person. That feeling held for a
> long time, but the strength of your love beat it back and
> told me that I was worth something. It's fitting that you
> wear my jacket with the CMB because you did save my
> life in combat in a sinister war that sprang from the last
> one and was much harder to fight.

I couldn't have been happier with the next paragraph.

> Martha Mary, you are my love, my woman, the one that
> I waited so long for... And, like the rest of truly valuable
> things in life, you were worth the wait. There is no other
> for me. I adore you with a full heart and a full mind. I'll
> never let you go.
> Your man, Mike C.

* * *

We had both waited a long time for love, Mike and Me. I was plunked down in a postwar generation when potential mates were fewer, maybe were more hardened, or taken already. Perhaps in my mind, my life had been echoing Aunt Dot's, my mother's only sister, who spent her college classes without men. When the WWII vets returned in her senior year, Dot was quite used to dealing without men. Or a generation earlier, Mother's Aunt Ethel, who, until she was 32, tended her thrice-widowed aunt through The Great War and beyond. For years, I had been compared to them, as neither of them was married; all three of us made single by War. I was 33. At least I had hope that Michael's re-enlistment was serving a beneficial therapy.

Mike to Martha

24 Nov 83

So, on Thanksgiving, I'm grateful for living in the finest nation on earth, a country that sincerely desires peace and well-being and freedom for all the world. I'm thankful that every time this dream has been threatened, we've been able to find men who value principle more than their very lives. Ordinary individuals, who through moral strength and dedication, become the fiercest and fairest fighters the world has ever known. I'm thankful that I, myself, have had the honor of serving this country and knowing many of those men. And I am grateful that at last, I have found a true and good woman who shares my beliefs.

I think back to another Thanksgiving, 1970. After five vicious days in Suoi Ca Valley, which had included three heavy firefights and an NVA base camp destroyed, the chopper picked us up. I hit the rear, cleaned my rifle, repacked my ruck, knocked off my two beers, and headed

for B-Med to get a grenade fragment picked out of my
wrist. When I got back around noon, we had chow—
processed turkey loaf and instant potatoes with C-ration
fruitcake. It was a magnificent meal! I was alive to eat it. ...

For as much as I romanticized our relationship, Mr. Creamer put one
and one together and brought our relationship around from another
perspective.

> It occurs to me that perhaps things worked out for
> us this way so that we could be young again, starting from
> scratch, the way we might have years ago: With me in a
> barracks waiting for your mail, and you thinking of your
> boyfriend in the service. Strange…it makes me love you
> even more as if I was only off on a detour for years. Maybe
> the roads we took just led around back to the starting
> point, and this time we'll go up Frost's "Not Taken"
> road—together.
> Every last drop of my love,
> Mike C.

Things were changing at home; I could not watch war movies the same
as before I had met Michael. Alone at home, I cried watching *Gallipoli*
on HBO, seeing commanders in the rear, who did not know what was
going on in the front lines. The infantryman's fatal dilemma. It was all
too probable that it would happen again in the many conflicts around
the world—Grenada, Lebanon, the Sinai. As I transformed to sympa-
thizer, my wardrobe changed: I wore Michael's green Army shirt with
CREAMER over the pocket, his BDU jacket when it rained.

I wrote to Mike of my biggest challenge:

> Marlboro
> 25~27 Nov 1983
> It's tough being away from you—I know I'll settle into

the routine of it—heaven forbid you think I'm not strong enough (am I strong enough??)—The inability to speak to you on small matters is complicated. Michael, I just want to see you, talk to you, hear you, be with you.

Martha

It was Thanksgiving weekend, and my high school class was having its 15th-year reunion.

I wrote Michael the following

Sunday, 27 Nov

God, my head is very large this morning. I didn't sleep much last night—having stayed out till the wee ones. Some of my long-lost buddies were there. I talked about you a lot—you were there with me, so your presence was felt.

At the after-party, I talked with Mark, our old quarterback who attended Kent State during the shootings in 1970. I started talking about my *Mlle* entry, then Vietnam and my theory on how it changed us all. He grew increasingly annoyed at me. "Yeah, well, why doesn't anybody care about what it did to us at Kent State? What were we supposed to do? Just go back to school? Let me tell you; it uprooted us." I wanted to know more, but alcohol had taken his tongue, and my listening abilities were likewise impaired. I left not knowing his whole story, wanting to.

Yesterday Brenda, my best friend then, and I drove around; the skies were so beautiful. At lunch, she shared her own series of unfortunate life events—two still births, and a husband who left her—but she is now CFO for documentarian Ken Burns, so she's come out well. I'm glad.

Whenever I see beauty, I think of you, wonder where you are, what you're doing. It is a remarkable thing, love, huh, Michael? It grants you an absolute serenity, a space between you and your fears—an ability to see and possibly understand beyond what's on the surface. For a while, I have felt a sense that very little could throw me. That personal plateau I stood on allowed me to get through the early confusion and difficulties of our relationship. That stuff somewhat behind us, I have this enormous energy from the love we share. It makes it hard to imagine stopping, getting off this journey, and unimaginable that someone else could pick up on how much momentum you have contributed to my life.

Love, your sweetheart, Martha

And on the same day, Michael wrote to me:

27 Nov 83

Hello My Love,

… In response to your questions—Yes, the Army controls every minute, every second. No TVs, radios, Coke, candy, etc. We may get one or two cigarettes a day. I haven't even thought of beer in a month. … The time I spend without you is like purgatory, filled with activity but grey and death-like. You taught me what it was like to live and love again after years of numbness….

I live for the next glimpse of you.

Yours always, Mike C.

And he continued:

29 Nov 83

Yes, I was looking at the stars on that very night, at the same time. See? We made psycho-celestial love: Two stars, our own constellation.

Bad few days. Bio-rhythms must be fucked. Managed to flunk the PT test Sunday. Got 90 points for the run (2

miles in 15.07) and passed sit-ups, but blew pushups—I did 48 in 2 minutes, but the Drill Sgt. only gave me credit for 25. He was fucking with me to get me put on "remedial PT" (Doing everything with boots, helmet, web gear, and a 40-lb ruck.) Oh well, it will strengthen my ass up. He did it to over half the platoon. Cute, huh? Typical for a non-combat leg! ... am counting days [home for Christmas] ....20 and a wake-up!
Your other soul, Mike C.

More from Mike

3 Dec 83

Training is interesting. They're into the meat of it, training us to be what infantry-men ultimately are—skilled, efficient, professional killers. Hand-to-hand is rough and dirty; it leaves us sore. Broken bones are not unheard of. ...This week we spent a day with the M-203 over-under M-16/40mm grenade launcher, the one mentioned in *The 13th Valley*. I did well. I prefer the old M-79 "bloop tube," ...the 203 is awkward to aim.

Did I feel that way? That sure? I didn't know. I hadn't even been on an Army post except for that Smokies trip, dropping the car at Benning. I'd attended a reunion of The Herd, the Vietnam Veterans Memorial dedication, and lots and lots of fashion shows and ballet performances. I certainly loved Michael's letters, his love-making, his humor, his intelligence. I'll admit that the epic-ness of our romance was remarkable, or I'd not be writing about it. But marriage, was I ready? How could I be sure? ... I still found Mike's relationship with his family, troubling. Especially his behavior to his mother, Dot

Creamer, whom I found patient, kind and loving. Nor was he generous towards his brothers and sisters; he seemed not to acknowledge their father's terrible abandonment of them too. Mike and I didn't use the word abandonment. He spoke of his father's leaving, and even of how warranted, it was. To him.

Mike blamed his mother for having too many children, and he said to me, and in front of her more than once, "You should have stopped having kids after you had me." That comment probably arose because Richard was the next in the family, and Michael and Richard were like feuding Shakespearian brothers—princes about to do one another in.

It was a painful place to be—between the man I loved and the family I wished he loved. And only he was Mike Creamer as in Cramer. I would marry Mike Cramer, who adopted that tough name given him by some dog-faced sergeant in his first Basic Training, but his family all pronounced their name Creamer, as in Cream rising. Whenever we were all together, as when we were at a few weddings, it was awkward, what with introductions to others. Mike was relentless about it, too, correcting them.

It was at a family event that I heard a rumor of Mike getting into a fistfight at a wedding. I could see that attitude when he was with family. He was different with me; he'd stand and smirk and be ever so nice, but it was at weddings that he lost it, like a bad penny coming up.

My family wasn't great in the compassion department—some of us were with some of us, others of us weren't with others of us. One of us wasn't speaking to another, always, or from the time I was old enough to remember. I was the fourth girl in a long hand-me-down line, and there were two girls following me. It was excruciating. I once got sent home from third grade because the principal called me out and pointed to my see-through organza dress and said, "Go home and change. And don't let your mother put you in that dirty dress until it's washed." I was mortified; I had dressed myself that day. Not only was I "called out," but my mom was too. I refused to go back to school that afternoon. Big families suck.

Then this letter from Michael came. This was the letter that capsulized his dilemma into a pill I could swallow. It reminded me of the fragility surrounding the collective boys of *Chance and Circumstance* that enticed me to read further, and beckoned me to DC. I needed to find them. My boys. My men. I remembered how fragile Michael really was, and how necessary it is for all of us to feel worthwhile, or in a clean dress in third grade. Maybe I could help Michael through the rest of his issues, and maybe together we'd find and solve my issues.

My Dearest Martha Mary,

23 Jan 84

There are two incidents in my personal history where my life was saved by the merest chance, where I would have died had it not been for incidental moves made minutes or seconds before. Sometimes I wake up at night, nervous and sweaty, overwhelmed at what a thin thread there was between survival and oblivion at those moments, and terrified that it all came so close to going the other way.

The first was in the Suoi Ca Valley on the Tuesday morning before Thanksgiving, 1970. My team was set up in an L-shaped ambush on a trail junction. We opened fire on a column of NVA. I let off my first 20-round magazine until it went dry. I was partially covered by a six-inch diameter tree to my front and was semi-leaning against another of the same size to my rear—sitting, to get a better view of the kill zone through the foliage. I ducked my head down a matter of maybe eight inches, as I did my rapid reload, and a split-second later, even as my head was still moving, a stream of green AK-47 tracers came from my front and shattered the rearmost tree—literally blew it in half... At precisely the point where my head had been.

Years later, I was in Washington, DC, on 13 Nov 1982. I needed a drink because my throat was hoarse. I also needed to go to the bathroom. I decided to ignore the latter urge because the lines were too long. I stood in a concession stand line for several minutes and then spotted what seemed to be a shorter line at another concession stand. I moved to it. There, I met the woman who made my life over.

Hon, it frightens me how close we came to not finding each other that day. What would have become of me without you?

Words I can never say enough,

I love you—Mike C.

CHAPTER 25

Christmas Break

I rented a ski house in the winter of 1983. Ever since I was very young, I wanted a place in the country. Bernie, my accountant, told me in April that I needed to think about buying a house to offset some of the income taxes I was shelling out. The long weekend of my HS reunion, I drove with Mike's friend Vinnie and my sister Jeanie to find a Vermont rental, which was a straight shot up from New York City.

The ski house became where Michael and I would spend most of his Basic break; we invited the Marlboro crew up for a few nights, his friends and Jeanie. The gang was relieved to see him so alive again. We didn't ski much but cooked and built fires—to Vinnie's delight—and played a lot of *Trivial Pursuits*, which always ended with Michael winning. The rest of us occasionally made teams to compete against him, but Michael still won. He was so smart and even with a crew cut, was handsome, and sexy. Michael filled us in on what life was like in the Army, and where he hoped to get assigned, and what country the US was most likely to invade next.

Michael loved the country, even all the snow, but the five-hour drive from Manhattan was grueling for me. I often drove alone in the Subaru; Jeanie would meet me up there sometimes, driving west from Marlboro. I was not too fond of the ride back, having to leave by winter's early sundown to arrive home by 10:00. One snowstorm, I spun, almost off the road. The primary lesson that winter: Do not buy a house in Vermont. Massachusetts was too far, too. Often, I drove through Massachusetts, wishing I were already home. Connecticut is where I'd look for a home to buy.

Michael wrote when he returned to Georgia

>5 Jan 84
>
>Late-late, flashlight time
>
>My Dearest,
>
>God, leaving you Monday was one of the hardest things I've ever done in my life. I know now (as if I needed convincing) that you are the absolute love of my life, the woman who was meant to be mine. Our every action together proves that, and the acclaim is universal. Everyone is glad for us. We're a natural, kid. Shit, for a big tough ex-airborne Ranger and future Green Beret, I sure do a lot of sentimental weepy shit when I think of you. I miss you…I love you

Mike again

>9 Jan 84 Late.
>
>Dearest Lifemate…
>
>Gawd! They're running us ragged. Keeps me from going crazy missing you…. It's been rough, particularly those few minutes before I fall asleep in a bed that's missing you. I think of how you mold against my back, pressing close, your incredible softness keeping me safe and warm. Has it only been a week that I've been without you? It seems like ten years.
>
>I am somewhat of a minor hero. A kid from 3rd Platoon fell and dislocated his knee. Bizarre angles and lumps, lots of screaming; Drill Sgt.'s in a panic. They called for the Old Man. I arrived in a flash, took over,

issued orders, improvised splints from everyday items, astounded the masses with neuro and circulation checks, vital signs, and shock prevention. I summoned transport and proceeded to amaze the emergency room crew with down-to-the-last-detail diagnosis and suggestions for treatment (which they used). Now even the drills call me "Doc," and the 1st Sgt. is proud as punch of his Herdsman trainee. The legend lives on! (Yeah, right…dripping sarcasm.)

Your little warrior,

Mike C.

✶   ✶   ✶

He was sounding like his Africa letters—cocky and sure. I was lonely and depressed. (Probably from those 10-hour round-trips up north.) On 20 Jan, Michael wrote of his assignment to the 101st Airborne (Air Assault) in Fort Campbell, KY. "No beret, no jump pay, just choppers, a Screaming Eagles' patch on my shoulder, bloused jump boots with my greens." He was on a rapid deployment force that rotated with the 82nd Airborne for peacekeeping in the Sinai. The 82nd had gone into Grenada in '83; he was sure he'd be going somewhere.

Michael ends the letter—

The 101st is a first-rate outfit with a proud record from WWII to Vietnam. I'm going to a first-call combat unit that moves like greased lightning. I could phone you one night and be in a foxhole in Nicaragua before you get up the next morning. It's scary even for me (although I like that kind of scary, like a big roller-coaster), so I know it will be for you. Let's set a date. How's the summer or fall sound to you? My barrel is about to go over Niagara Falls, and I don't want anything to happen and not be your husband when it does. Shit, this spring!

I'm perhaps too much of a romantic, but I see our love as being set in this big background…that is described as "epic" or "sweeping" *a la The Winds of War* or *From Here to Eternity*, and I got the feeling with this assignment that the next chapter will be the point of can't-put-it-down.

Gotta go, I love you. I've never been surer of anything in my life.
Mike C.

CHAPTER 26

You'll Probably Never Understand

While Michael said that he was feeling better about the 101st, things got precarious before his Feb. 17th graduation from Basic. He wrote, "It will be so-o-o-o good to get the fuck outa this place!" Other companies were getting weekend passes, "We are getting shit." His Alpha company had the highest AWOL rate; Michael was looking forward to getting to Fort Campbell. "We should do something about picking out a wedding ring," but "let's wait till I'm settled to pick a time and place." Michael fessed up that maybe not getting assigned to Rangers was a good thing. He didn't think he could keep up; reality setting in.

> "The lure of being back with the 75th Rangers is immense—that outfit formed me, made me the man I am now, taught me about integrity and courage and comradeship and suffering and sacrifice." It was "the single most intense experience of my life in so many ways that you'll probably never understand no matter how much you try, or how much I try to tell you. You just had to be there."
>
> *War is an abomination. It took my love for you to bring that into high relief, even though I discovered and learned that fourteen years ago. To think that man aligns himself into separate blocs and leaves no real avenue for the settlement*

*of differences other than squandering his resources and
butchering his youth is terrifying.*

I loathe it. I'd like nothing other than to be with
you in peace, free of fear, safe from transgressions of
nations, ideologies, or individuals. You must know that
when the bottom line is reached, I'm a very live-and-let-
live individual. But the world isn't that way. Sometimes it
takes a soldier to keep madmen from shipping trainloads
of innocents to gas chambers. ... in today's world, events
move so fast that you can't raise an effective defense from
scratch in time to do any good. It needs to be sharpened,
polished, and ready to be drawn from the sheath at any
moment. And it must be able to win. There is something
worse than war. It's losing one. Ask the Jews, or the South
Vietnamese.

He asked if I'd come for graduation.

Party/awards ceremony the evening of the 16th,
graduation on the 17th; I'll probably get 3-days travel
time. We can rent a car or fly or whatever, just so long as
I can spend the three days with you. We can make love,
revel in the closeness of each other, and start to plan.... All
that I lack is your constant company.
Soon, my precious love, soon—Mike C.
Who loves you with all his heart, as he never thought
could ever be.

Three days later, a letter came with bad news: Mike would have to travel *en masse* to Fort Campbell right after graduation, and next, he told
me of his accident on the confidence course and the more significant
catastrophe of pushing himself while injured.

154

Friday, 3 Feb

There's one station, "The Belly Buster," a chest-high rack with an 18" diameter log. Two people roll it back and forth while you jump over it. I mistimed my jump. The log came back into me; I caught it full-on in my lower right ribcage, knocking the wind out of me. I finished the course, tried to ignore it.

Yesterday we ran the P+T (professional and tough), a 2 ½-mile cross-country run over hills, stream, and gullies. The sergeants got lost; we ran 6 miles in forty minutes. That afternoon we ran the bayonet assault course (one that killed the guy just before Christmas) twice, scrambling over log walls, under barbed wire, over ditches. The guys knew I was hurting—I finished P+T with the first group, but with hands locked on my side and in tears. They ordered me on sick call today.

I crushed the cartilage on the bottom three ribs and bruised the shit out of my liver. I'm on profile—no marching, running, PT, or lifting over 15 lbs. until re-check in 7 days. ... So, I may not graduate. Wouldn't bother with an extra few weeks, but afraid of losing 101st—getting some shit-bird outfit instead.

You know me—I'm the guy they coined "survivor" for. Shit, there's even some pride…you should hear the Drills, "That Creamer's one tough little bastard." See? You got a winner. A dumb shit, but a charger nevertheless.

✶ ✶ ✶

Of course, the Army didn't call me; we weren't married yet. Barely engaged. So when he arrived in Campbell, I flew to Nashville and drove up to see him, to check on the survivor. I hadn't received my military ID yet, and the car was a rental. Michael was waiting at the gate though, and hopped in the car. He had come less to meet me, but warn me of their seat belt law on post.

"It's mandatory," he said.

"That's okay, I'm buckled in," I replied.

"They'll take away our kids if they're not in a belt, or there's no car seat," Mike added.

"What?"

"They're very strict here. If our kids aren't protected in the car, they'll be taken from us."

"Oh, okay," I drove on. Oddball, I thought, worrying about kids we didn't even have.

It was the first in-person conversation we'd had since Christmas break from Basic. I felt immediately that we weren't going to live in Kentucky together.

Sister, Dottie Glynn and me, out at Texarkana, one of Abe and Alene delaHoussaye's restaurants.

CHAPTER 27

Fort Campbell, Kentucky

Michael's sentiment for warrior families was contagious; it was imbued in me. He was around military couples now, doing things other couples did. It wasn't foreign, not Marlboro, not New York City; they were out in the open now. I walked around New York City cloaked in it, unlike anyone around me.

> PV 2 Mike Creamer
> "A" Co. 3rd BN. 187th Inf.
> 101st ABN Div. (AASLT)
> Ft. Campbell, KY 42223
>
> 22 Feb 84
> My most valued person in the whole wide world…
> Wednesday night, and I'm up at the main PX complex
> doing laundry. Got my Walkman on and my pad in hand
> and two beers in my belly, rapidly working their inevitable
> way towards my bladder.
>   ZZZZIIIPPP—Time Warp! I am now in the Burger
> Bar; I skipped chow to get a jump on the washers… I went
> by the tailor and had all my Screaming Eagles patches sewn
> on my BDUs' left shoulders. I hung them in my locker, a
> whole row of little birds facing out to me (regulations have
> left sleeve showing) [A patch on right shoulder indicates unit

served during combat.] I thought about it…My Herd patch is hidden; but in the background, and the one-oh-one looks out at me. It's almost as if someone was telling me, "Remember the past—it's part of you and be proud of it, but foremost on your military mind should be this unit and how you can work to make it the best and proudest." The past will always be there for me… The future is something I'll have to keep earning by doing my dead level best each day of the present.

And that goes for my non-military mind too. The absolute brightest star in my life is you. I consider you a prize unequaled, a treasure to cherish. … to be loved with all my heart, with every stitch of my being.

Michael was changing, he spoke of marriage now, and it felt hurried. Could be his conscription in Rapid Deploy? Maybe he didn't want to be the lone, single 30-year old badass on the base. I didn't know. Didn't know the military, but MVP was overwhelming; I wasn't going to move away quickly.

Mike to Martha (continued)

Why do I want to marry you? Simple…each day of knowing you convinces me more and more that you are my life and the very breath of my soul. I can no longer imagine living without you. Things will work out fine for us because I'll always work to ensure your happiness.

In the laundromat and burger bar I was watching PFC-types and their young wives and babies. It made me think, there they are, a family together, putting time and love into making things work. The wife knows that one day the MPs might close the main gate, C-130s might start roaring off to an undisclosed destination, leaving her alone for a week, a year, perhaps forever. It's a very different and challenging life, and it takes a strong love to survive it. So, they grab every moment together, even if it's the laundromat. These are the people defending our country. I think we'll do alright.

And the Rapid Deploy factor was real:

Mike to me in a phone conversation

> "Hey honey, it's looking like we're going in. It's quick, I know, but that's what I signed up for," Mike called one night.
>
> "Are you kidding me?" I asked.
>
> "No, honey. You have to be prepared at any time," he said.
>
> "You just got to Fort Campbell. How can you be moving out so soon?" I said.
>
> "I'm part of Rapid Deploy. You know that," Mike said proudly.
>
> I knew that part, I didn't expect it would be within a month of getting situated. "Well, where to? Or can't you tell me?"
>
> "They don't say, only: Just get your gear in order, turn your paperwork in," he said.
>
> "Michael," my voice was petulant, reluctant. I was unwilling to go along with the absurdity the Army seemed to project.
>
> "This is what we signed up for," he said.

So now it was we. We signed up for this, don't you remember that day in August when he walked into the recruiter's storefront and *we* enlisted? I loved his newfound energy for life, I was grateful for it, but I sort of had bigger fish to fry.

In the same envelope with the 22 Feb. Mike to me

> 25 Feb 84
>
> Talked to you last night, let you know about Honduras....
> We're still not sure yet, but all indications point to it.

I think the following is the most telling self-awareness Michael had of himself, perhaps explaining his tendency to pullback, the coyness at his going away party. The Action Junkie:

> "I go bad without it; You've seen that.
>
> Honey, please listen. I think you fell in love because I was "an adventurer." Remember? You used to introduce me to people as such. The title is an active one—you use it, or you lose it. I'm addicted to it; now I'm into it again. I'll be challenged and, therefore, very happy here, aside from being away from you. There are risks and dangers, sure, but Vietnam, Africa, and the tunnels were the same; I took all of them on with a smile and a "let's go" attitude. It makes me feel special, proud.
>
> I know it's little comfort, but I'd like it if you could say to yourself and others, "My boyfriend is an Infantryman, a paratrooper with the 101st Airborne Division, Screaming Eagles. He's on the Rapid Deployment Force, and he's always ready to go and fight on short notice. He's in great physical shape and has the experience, training, and will to win against any odds. He's away a lot and I worry about his safety and because he worries that I'm worried, and he's the man I love, and I'm very, very proud of him."
>
> Small comfort, but it's all I can offer right now. That, and a love so real and so strong that it's the very driving energy of my life. Not an hour goes by without a vivid

picture of you pulling close in my arms and telling me that you love me too.

It's a difficult time for me too. I'm physically and mentally exhausted from Benning, the longest four months of my life. I'm overwhelmed by the move here— seeing you, the rush to in-process, drawing a ton of gear, getting to my new outfit, unpacking, packing, new places, new faces, a new life every day. It's been a monster, and I'm tired, confused, lonely, and not just a little scared. Please bear this out, Martha Darling. It's hard for both of us.

I love you so much.—Mike C.

Mike wrote of being homesick and his military life. His was a unique perspective: from one who went through the Army fourteen years before.

28 Feb 84

My Dearest,

Starting to settle in. The task isn't made any easier by the fact that I'm so homesick for you I could curl up and die. It's a snowy, sleety night; it reminds me of the evening we had to walk to the house in Vermont after not getting up the hill. Gawd, I would gladly give ten years off my life to spend tonight with you in front of a fire. The flicker of flames made you look so incredibly beautiful. I'm a lucky man to have had such a moment with such a woman. You are exquisite, a lady the likes of which I never dared hope I'd find. Darling, I hope you never get tired of hearing that I love you because I swear that I'll never, never stop saying it to you.

Monday…3:30 AM…

"Alert! Alert! Pack it up! Airfield time is zero-five-thirty! Nobody outside except to draw weapons! The phones are off-limits!" We're moving like crazy and speculating—Lebanon? Central America? It was over an hour before we knew it was a surprise drill, and that hour was taut. The rest of the morning was very hectic. Welcome to the one-oh-one, kid.

Do you know what frightened me? It wasn't the prospect of combat. That I welcome because it would vindicate the choice I made to re-enlist. It wasn't the possibility of death or injury; I've lived with that even as a civilian. I was arguably safer most times in Vietnam than I was in that California tunnel. It was the worry that something would happen to me that would leave you alone. The thought of you being that sad is upsetting to me. Honey, this is the real thing now. Some morning it may not be a drill. I promise you that I'll be as careful as I can be within the mission's demands and bring my ass back to you in one piece. You are the strongest reason to survive that any soldier ever had. …

The marches and PT are even harder here than at Benning—I'm a mask of pain during runs now; they're long and fast. We don't call as much cadence though, so it allows me to sing a song to myself that really gets me through. … *Turn on all the Christmas lights, baby's coming home tonight…* (Billy Joel)

Thank you for the perfumed letter. I keep it in my pillowcase to scent it. Please try to be less moody at the office, because those folks love you too. Do your Martha Voutas best for me, okay?

Please write and tell me you love me. —Mike C.

CHAPTER 28

Bulletproof

I didn't need slides; Mike sends vivid images of exactly how he stood on things. By March 16th, he was sure they would get orders to Central America within a few days. His unit had just completed will-writing; he was revved up, "...for years I've been sick of seeing those cocky, little commie motherfuckers playing Robin Hood for the goddamned CBS cameras... 'The Kissinger Report'[1] (says) the dominoes are all down—Southeast Asia, Iran, Africa...our trade routes are on a slender thread..." Classic Michael-with-a-few-beers. "We **have** to stand! The people of Central America want Marxist rule about as much as I want Herpes. It's being forced on them by a massive infusion of Soviet-made weaponry and a gaggle of knee-jerk dipshits in DC."

"Please help the kids that I'm with now, so they don't have to endure the same decade of outcast hell that I and all too many others did!"

I would hear that again.

Same letter, a little less raring to go

---

1   National Security Study Memorandum 200: Implications of Worldwide Population Growth for U.S. Security and Overseas Interests (NSSM200) "The Kissinger Report" was "initially classified for over a decade but was obtained by researchers in the early 1990s. The memorandum and policies developed from the report were observed as a way the US could use human population control to limit the political power of undeveloped nations, ensure the easy extraction of foreign natural resources... to protect American businesses abroad from interference from nations seeking to support their growing populations."—Source Wikipedia

It looks like I *might* end up as the Colonel's RTO/driver. Got called to the Sergeant Major's office today and offered the position. Of course, I was taken there by an escort of the Company Commander, two lieutenants, and the Platoon Sergeant, who stopped just short of the threat of death should I give *any* indication of desiring it. So, I politely declined, under duress. I'll most likely get pulled for it anyway. I got the impression a check went out on me, and it came back that I had that "cold motherfucker" reputation, according to some of my old N/75 Ranger peers. Makes me a good candidate as a combat bodyguard for a Lt. Col. who likes to command from upfront. And I had an RTO class this week—codes, call signs, etc.—and scored 100%... I'm a medic with experience at patching enemy-inflicted holes... And I'm a student of counterinsurgency. And blah, blah, blah. [He wrote it, I couldn't make this stuff up!] The more I think of it, the more I *want* it. It would challenge me. It would be like an unofficial Sergeant Major's Academy in many ways. But, if I stayed here, I'd probably get a squad within a year; I'd miss that in the driver's slot, miss all the grit-it-out responsibility. Ah, Martha, what the fuck to do? You know me, I'm a total *crazy*. I go in and kick ass at whatever. I'm at my first Army crossroads; the Libra in me wants to go both ways at once. ZZZZZZZZT!

How could you love such a maniac? I don't care if you even *try* to answer that. I'm just glad, incredibly, *ecstatically* glad, that you do. And I accept it all and return every bit of it.
I LOVE YOU—Mike C.

PS—Don't you worry 'bout *this* kid—he's ten feet tall, bulletproof, and has only used up four of his nine lives!

∗ ∗ ∗

Four of nine? Um... 1/Vietnam. 2/Angolan attack in Zaire. 3/Belly Buster? (Was he counting that, because that put the kibosh on the Rangers!) 4/Malaria that almost killed him in 1976, for which he returned home for a multi-month span.[2] (Then, of course, the 5/Boston and 6/California Tunnels?)...by my count.

In the next letter, Mike writes, "I'm not supposed to know, but I become a PFC (E-3) as of 1 Apr. They put me in for it here. The one from Benning 'disappeared,' as I thought it might. Fuck 'em. This kid will keep rising no matter *who* wants to squash it."

Work was always hectic for me in March, back in New York. The bi-annual fashion shows were in April and October, and clients were tense. I guess I was tense too, in 1984,

Michael writes me,

> "I wish I could be with you because I know that you're working your gorgeous, erotic ass off. Times are busy for you. I've seen you in those times, and know the way you come home late and exhausted, sometimes on the verge of tears, worn out from the day's demands. I want so much to hold you as you come through the door, squeeze you tight and rub the muscles on the back of your neck, kiss you, lead you to a soft seat, give you a Lite beer, and have you tell me how it went. ... You may have thought that the best thing you did for me was to restore my self-worth by making me remember valuable stuff in the past. Close, but wrong. The most important thing you've ever given me is yourself—a wonderful person to love and care for and try to make happy. Honey, no fucking badge, or

---

2   Interview with Ron Bucchino.

medal, or promotion will ever, *ever* mean so much to me as being able to make you smile that Martha smile, a smile made with your eyes and not just your mouth, the one that comes from your soul and lights up your whole face and makes you truly beautiful. …

I love you, Mike C.

Michael and I had seen *Uncommon Valor* in the movies but we arrived at the theatre late and missed the opening scenes. When it was playing at Campbell, he saw it again. He sat next to a guy his age. "Martha, we missed the best part. Incredible slow-motion scenes of a recon team trying to extract under fire in the face of an (enemy) assault. Chilling." The audience cheered when choppers appeared, or a fight broke out. When the MIAs were rescued, "The crowd went ape." He says of the guy next to him, "He and I were quiet. That's when I knew he'd been there. He was crying."

During the week, many of the enlistees asked Michael if that's what it was like. They showed respect for the Nam vets. "I have to set an example for them; do what I can to get them through that first bad month when it comes. The harder I work now, the more they'll listen to me then. That way, the shit that I went through will be worth something—it will help the kids out."

Same letter from Mike

The big gap in the Army right now is that there are very few *tested* officers and NCOs at the company level where it counts…. my decision was right. … Just let me help these guys get started right, let me get a few licks for myself and my buddies on The Wall, and then I'll be able to say that I did what I had to do. Then I'll settle down, at least get out of the Infantry. My body screams every day that I'm too old for this shit. It's flat-out *pain*. My knees, my ribs, my hip. That kind of pain is real, a warning. If I could get healed and do it without all the bone pain,[3] I'd stay with it forever. It's what I *should* have been doing all along."

While I never lived in military housing, or even close to a post, I was an Army Wife. That was oddball enough for the fashion folk in NYC, but I *was*. If Michael was figuring out what he simply "had to do," it was the ceremonial events that lit the flame in my chest; that's when I loved being a US Army wife. Growing up in the 1950s of Dwight D. Eisenhower, and the 60s with Massachusetts' own JFK as president, I cut my teeth on patriotism. We pledged our allegiances every morning at school, we sang "America the Beautiful" and learned all the verses, along with "The Star-Spangled Banner," and "America." We felt that God had 'shed His grace' on us. We learned reverence for veterans of Korea and both World Wars. They came to our assemblies at grammar school and shared, in broken voices, as they poked handkerchiefs into their eyes to dry their tears. I lead the Pledge of Allegiance over the intercom for four years of high school. All of that became politically un-correct in the late 60s and 70s. I missed it.

To be in a military family was to be surrounded by a love of country. It opened me to regional accents saying the same things: men and women, husbands, and wives telling how honored they were to serve America. We felt a tingle deep in our souls as drummers struck up the cadence, and colors were posted or lowered. We stood in silent attention and as I was wont to do, whistled between my fingers when we lauded some courageous act. We lauded. We honored. We felt pride and awareness—it was a beautiful internal thing; it was part of us, a spiritual center of what it meant to be American. I was an American; my husband served to keep us free.

---

3   Years later it would be discovered that bone pain was part of the after effects of Agent Orange toxic poisoning.

CHAPTER 29

The New Young Martha Voutas

MVP was in its seventh year in 1984, and for all that time, our client-base remained mainly fashion. Except for our few non-profit clients—the Ford Foundation, Girls Clubs of America, and intermittent work for Brooklyn Bureau of Community Service—more and more the Army Wife's role helped inform my choices. Perry Ellis had grown into a booming fashion house.

When I first met Perry in 1978, I was a young entrepreneur sent by his PR person, Rea Lubar, to design an invite for the Spring 1979 show. I met her in my first studio, rented for $100. a month, in a loft building on W 28th. I took the thirty-by-twenty-foot space that the elevator opened onto, between two gigantic artists' studios. In the right studio was my landlady and friends to whom she'd rented, and to the left, another tenant, a photographer who smoked weed and played Donna Summers' "Last Dance," over and over, as loud as the stereo would go. It was in this space where I hired my first employee.

Rea had come days late to see a pillow line my friend Phillip had designed; she was enticed by a flyer I wrote and threw together. (Phillip was counting on Rea doing it for him, but on the day before the collection opened, I hurriedly designed it for him.) Phillip introduced me as the flyer creator, and Rea asked if I wanted a job writing copy for her.

"No thank you, I'm a graphic designer," I said, "I just opened my business."

She laughed boisterously, "Graphic designers, ha," her voice crackled like gravel. "They're a dime a dozen."

Phillip interjected, "Not Martha. You really should see her portfolio."

Rea said, "Okay, show me." And after seeing my work, she sent me off to Perry. "I have this fashion client, Perry Ellis. He needs an invitation to his first show, it should be all pink and white, everything in the collection is all pink and white"—she barely stopped to breathe— "and the fee should be $600. and don't ask for a penny more." Rea gave me his phone number.

After unsuccessfully presenting my first pink and white design, Perry called me to meet him on the mezzanine of 575 Seventh Avenue. He had just signed the lease, and he wanted to convey how grand his new showroom would be. We walked together into a dusty, former bank. "We won't be totally ready, but we'll paint the ceiling," he said, pointing to massive chandeliers and peeling ceilings three stories overhead. "Maybe we'll have some cardboard boxes scattered around. Let people know it's in the works." I got it, designed an oddly sophisticated invite on frosted vellum, layered with 3-D packing matter, and a thick dark green die-cut folder they slid into. The copy read: "...inviting you to our new (not unpacked) home." Perry and I were a team from then on!

In 1984, after six-and-a-half years of designing all his graphics, and writing and creating press kits, ads, everything, Perry had expanded onto the entire floor that ran between Broadway and Seventh Avenue, a block below 42nd Street. His fall collection made for a beautiful show, but it hadn't shipped to the stores yet, where it wouldn't sell well. That wasn't the only big problem. Shortly, the epidemic AIDS would strangle the creative life out of the P.E. staff. Perry called me in for another meeting.

"Martha, we want you to come on staff; we'd like to offer you a job," Perry or Laughlin Barker, his romantic partner and lawyer, said. "We want you to oversee all graphics and advertising design. Work with our licensees to maintain the brand," Laughlin added.

"That's what I do now." I said.

"Right," said Perry, "but in-house."

Laughlin added, "We want to bring all that in-house."

"I don't think I can, Perry," I said. "I have commitments to my studio, my staff."

"You could keep your studio," Perry said, "some of your non-fashion clients."

"I don't know, but I think not," I said.

"We'll give you six figures and stock, of course," Perry said.

The changes in Perry and his company were the non-clincher for me. The Perry I'd met on the dusty stairs kept an open door for me. I wrote his quotes for press releases; I shaped and kept his identity consistent. There was no Internet, so when someone from the art or theatre world called him, and Perry didn't know who they were, he'd phone me because he knew that I probably would. Then Isaac Mizrahi joined the staff, and he knew everything. New staff surrounded Perry now; one of his licensees was Levi Strauss & Co., a west coast giant. Where once I fit in with all his team, now I didn't. It became difficult to gain access, even when I had deadlines to meet and needed the approvals that only he would grant. Besides, I wasn't fond of bustling, expensive-lunch Seventh Avenue itself.

As I was leaving the office, Perry and Laughlin threw in a clothing bonus.

I said no, as much for MVP and me as it was for Michael, my infantryman husband. The paradox of Michael on Rapid Deploy and me signed on to promote expensive clothing, didn't cut it. I didn't explain it outright to Perry and Laughlin; I just knew the incongruity of the situation was mind-boggling. I couldn't go back and tell my staff; the whole offer was a threat to their livelihoods. Michael was unreachable, I'd have to wait for him to call me. It was a conundrum.

Perry asked me a second time two weeks later; I declined again.

* * *

And they hit me with an irritating notion. "Well then, can you help us find the New, Young Martha Voutas?" Gosh, if I could find *her*, I'd be in Fat City. The big obstacle I had, being separated from Michael was this: I was a solo entrepreneur in an all-consuming service business. I took very little time off, and I wanted a weekend house. I toyed with the idea of writing but could find no downtime. Another Martha Voutas who worked so hard and learned so quickly, who moved and designed so fast? Bring her on; I'll hire her!

That year Perry found his Martha replacement—three women promoted from within—and as expected, my business began to dwindle. The IRS decided to audit me, investigate MVP; it lasted a month. Whoopee! It was tedious and time-consuming; it was a training audit. The older woman teacher/auditor was caustic and accusatory, asking first if we were in partnership with any firm listed on our Art Directors Club awards that were framed and hung around the office. "No, that's whose piece we entered in the competition. They and we 'win' mutually," I tried to explain. She saw a Drizzle ad, "Drizzle. Did Drizzle ever pay you with one of their fur-lined raincoats?" Vicious. The young male auditor/trainee apologized for her when she wasn't there. The IRS hit us with a $400. charge for insuring the Subaru for personal use. No fines. That in a million-dollar year.

CHAPTER 30

All in the Family

I visited Michael several times in Kentucky; I would rent a car at Nashville Airport, drive up to Ft. Campbell on the Kentucky/Tennessee border. Once we found a cheap motel, bought beer, and ordered a pizza or a sub, we'd hole up for the weekend. Michael was a combatant comforted, enveloped in the softness of my flesh. I was refreshed to feel loved, to be physical again, erotically aroused. Tears were not uncommon.

I remember it was a floating time for me; the two of us had met a year and a half ago. Still unmarried, we each lived suspended in choices we'd made. Michael brought up marriage in his letters, and after the passion we reawakened being together, I brought up parenthood.

I told Michael that I wanted to be a mother; my ticker was ticking. I was nearly 34, and I'd put my career first, switching midstream a few times—designer, actress, designer, now entrepreneur businesswoman. Michael said he didn't want to be a dad. I had come to the point of not *needing* to get married. I said, "I'm not going to marry you, if I can't be a mom." That weekend, we opted for more mad sex. I flew home, feeling somewhat sad, debating a need to move on.

Mid-week Michael called, "I have an idea. Do you want to move here? Start working for clients here?" Which was a whole other situation entirely.

"It doesn't make sense to leave NYC," I said. "I have a staff, great clients. Michael, I'd have to reestablish myself."

"Like me," Michael said. That seemed an odd comparison.

"Excuse me," I fired back, "you enlisted in the Army. You have a job, and I have a job in New York. I don't get it." Then we came to the parenting roadblock: "Please understand, I want a child, so I can raise her or him with real love, with no hesitations, with encouraging support. I want to see who that creates. Because that's not how I was raised. I want to make a difference in this little person's life. And I don't want to take anything away from you."

My life was MVP, my work and my days were not regimented. It was focused on creating new designs, writing proposals mapping out solutions for clients. Michael called for a *rendezvous*; he had something he wanted to say. It was a few weeks before I could get out again.

"You know," Michael started almost immediately after we checked into our motel, our ole Kentucky home. "I've been thinking about us and getting married and having kids. And I realize it wouldn't be just any baby; it would be *our* baby."

I remember the motel. I remember the moment. It was a sweet, un-coached, in-person declaration of Michael's confidence in our love. I believed he had overcome his objections to becoming a father. I wanted to believe he would be okay. I never doubted he was the *Closest Thing to God*, from first I heard it. Then, Michael shared something that opened my heart, "I just want you to understand what my hesitation at becoming a father is about. When I came home between my two tours of Nam in 1970, my father asked me to go out camping with him. I said, 'Camping? Dad, I've been *camping* all year! I want to go out and hear some live music; go to the Croft, to Boston, hear some jazz at Michael's Pub.'"

"I wanted to go out and get laid!" Michael leveled with me. "I turned my father down. It was the last time that break, outside of letters he wrote me in Vietnam that I would speak to him," Mike said. "You know, my father was in intelligence gathering in WWII. He was assigned to pre-landing ops in the Pacific, hitting the beaches in small, undercover recon teams."

As he spoke, I kept thinking about PTSD and about PTSD by its other names: Shell Shock and Battle Fatigue. I imagined John Creamer hunkered down in the steaming tropics, aware of what would happen to him should the torturous Japanese capture him. Maybe it never escaped his psyche. Does war ever escape one's mind? Did **he** get closure? By now, I had read enough to know that PTSD was a familial disease,[1] attaching to one generation after another, like an inherited propensity for cancer.

I put it together that John Creamer *had* to split when he did. Not that I condoned it. His timing pointed out he did not want to hear from Michael upon his return from overseas. Didn't want to talk to his son about tropical warfare, and he didn't want to explain things that—in all those 25 years since *his* war ended—he never could describe, explain, or talk about. So, John Creamer bolted, left his wife of 21 years, five children, and never said why.

Much later, I read a moving treatise on abandonment and how those left behind struggle to survive abandonment's profound impact on their lives. There it was: my Michael, clueing me in, his wife-to-be, of his potential stumbling block. I was deeply saddened by John Creamer's mindless run for his life, and how it branded Michael with the belief that he was not worthy of being welcomed home. There was nothing Michael could do to please his father; he missed the chance. The survivor of haunting recon missions in the Pacific, in whose uniform baby Michael posed at fourteen months old, with whom he sat and watched *Combat*; his father was the remaining holdout over Mike's sense of self-fulfillment. And he was nowhere to be found.

---

1   Veterans Affairs.gov: "But research now suggests that PTSD may not be an individual experience…it may be inherited. Studies have shown that experiencing trauma may leave a chemical mark on a person's genes, which is then passed down to future generations. (Pembrey: 2013)."

CHAPTER 31

Cornwall Bridge, CT

Michael and I had decided that I should look for a weekend house somewhere outside of New York City. In the late spring of 1984, MVP finished a huge fall advertising shoot for Zodiac Boots, on a drag-racing strip in New Jersey. We had a location van full of talent—models, makeup, hair, stylists, photographer, assistants, artists, plus boots and clothes to fit our "Fast Track Zodiac," an all-girl pit crew concept. After a very long day of work, heading back into the city, I was thrilled to have such a collection of people with me. I felt on top of the world—33 years-old, successful, and finally fully loved.

Days after the shoot, MVP threw preliminary layouts together. Next day I headed to their Maine headquarters to show Zodiac. Afterward, I planned to drive to a party in New York City for Bruce Plotkin and his new wife. I never made it. Too exhausted to fight weekend traffic on I-95, I checked into a Mystic, CT, motel, and crashed. I would awake the next day and look for a home in the country.

The next morning, I dug out my map and headed to the western part of the state, more accessible from NYC. It was nearly noon when I found my way across Connecticut Rte. 4. Along the way, I had written on the map several realtors' numbers and addresses of houses that looked appealing. In Cornwall, I soared around a curve to the right. Route 4 opened onto a long dirt drive with a sweet yellow Victorian farmhouse at its end. As I passed a blooming forsythia bush at the mouth of the driveway, I saw the sign: HOUSE FOR SALE.

I stopped, wrote the realtor's number, drove off, turned around, took a longer look, turned around again in the driveway, and streaked into Cornwall Bridge, a mile and a half down the road. There was a phone booth outside of Baird's Country Store, and I called Jonas Soltis Realty.

"Are you the woman from New York?" he asked.

"Yes, I am *a* woman from New York, but we haven't spoken," I replied.

"You're not here from the ad in the *Times?*"

"No, sir," I told him, "I was passing by. I'd like to see the yellow house on Rte. 4."

"Well, you better get up here right away," said the old voice. "There's someone scheduled to see that house; she'll be here shortly."

His house was past the firehouse. When I got up the ski slope of a driveway, a rather balding, eagle-looking man, tall, elegant and thin, came out to meet me. As I turned, looking out over the vista of pines and echoing hills, I thought what a beautiful nest he had built for himself. I entered, we talked quickly, he described the house for sale.

"Built in 1860 with additions in the 1930s," Jonas said, "it has three bedrooms, propane stove and heat (important fact in New England), a spring-fed well 25 yards up the backyard. Never gone dry in fifty years," he lied.

"It's got a working fireplace and sixteen acres."

I was smitten.

He wanted to know about me first. Who was I?

"Well, I own an advertising agency in NYC," I said. Is this an interview?

* * *

Soltis sat nodding. "It's a million-dollar company," I went on with names of the notable clients on my roster; didn't make a bean of difference. Then I began about Michael in Kentucky, "My fiancé is in the Army with the 101st..." and the old man got up off his tall-backed leather swivel chair and nearly did a jig. I continued about Mike's service in Vietnam and how we'd met. Now Soltis was breathing heavily.

From the word "Army" out of my mouth, the house was mine. There was no jig dancing; Jonas had risen to fetch a picture off the built-in bookshelves. He handed me the framed photograph, "This is my son."

"Air Force, huh?" I said; I'd gotten better at insignia reading myself.

"Yes," Soltis said with such sadness.

"Did he go to Vietnam?" I asked.

"No," Soltis said. "He was in during that era; he was a training pilot, and there was an accident. He was killed."

"I'm so sorry, Mr. Soltis," and I reached my hand over to comfort him.

Michael, the infantryman serving his country, became a top priority to Jonas Soltis. "If you like it, the house is yours," he said softly, "I hope you do. Let's go take a look." The woman from New York had only just pulled up his driveway; he ushered me out to his older-model Mercedes and tilted his cap at the woman from New York, "Hello, I'll be right back." It was angels again for Michael and Me.

Soltis, an ex-Connecticut State trooper, now retired, had come alive, eager to bring us under his wing. We drove back to the yellow Victorian. He knocked to assure the renters weren't at home, then turned the unlocked doorknob. "It's pretty safe up here," he said, "but you should lock the door, being right here on Rte. 4."

✳ ✳ ✳

From the hallway *cum* mudroom, with its muddy boots attesting of such, one stepped into the living room. I was doubly smitten: my dream house in the country. A huge fieldstone fireplace owned the far wall;

logs that had burned recently effused the room with smoky comfort. An off-white, wide-wale corduroy slipcover masked an old sofa that sat before the fireplace. Someone had painted the wide floorboards industrial grey. I crossed over to the bay window where outside draped ancient green swags of pine branches from century-old trees I somehow failed to notice on the first drive-by. I didn't need more convincing. The kitchen was antique, unaltered since the Depression perhaps, a bedroom beyond the kitchen was modern comparatively, with hardwood floors, a tiny closet, and windows letting in the afternoon light.

FRIDAY, MAY 18, 1984

Soldier of month named

The Hopkinsville Kiwanis Club has honored Pvt. Michael Edward Creamer, recently named ''Soldier of the Month'' at Fort Campbell.

Creamer is assigned to A Company, 187th Infantry, and the 101st Airborne Division (Air Assault).

PVT. CREAMER

Kiwanians, who honored Creamer Thursday, host each soldier of the month at one of their luncheon meetings.

Creamer, a native of Marlborough, Mass., is planning to attend Air Assault School and hopes to be accepted later for special forces training. He took his basic and advanced training at Fort Benning, Ga.

Creamer is a member of the Society of the 173rd Airborne Brigade, the Association of the United States Army and the 101st Airborne Division Association.

We talked about the details of my purchase on our drive back. I would buy to hasten the deal, and we could quit-claim Michael after the wedding. Soltis drew up the offer, and I signed off a check for $1,000. "You'd better register as a Republican up here," Jonas warned as I left his place, "that's the only way you'll get ahead in Cornwall." Little did I know of Litchfield County or Cornwall proper, the number of writers, artists, television and movie personalities living there. Madeleine L'Engle wrote *Wrinkle in Time* in Goshen, Thornton Wilder lived and wrote from his house overlooking Mohawk Mountain where they invented snowmaking, Tom Brokaw from NBC News. In our time, Whoopi Goldberg and Michael J. Fox both bought homes in Cornwall. Sam Waterston and his wife Lynn went to church with me. I introduced myself to N. Richard Nash; back in Youth Theatre in Marlboro, I played the Lucille Ball role in his *Wildcat*, Michael played the second male lead. I remember sitting in Nash's living room, where he explained how he made a lake out of swampland on his property. But I'm jumping ahead.

CHAPTER 32

The Knot

Over Memorial Day weekend, the week before our wedding, my four-and-a-half-year-old nephew, Patrick, Dottie and Bernie's son, drowned. It was a sad, sad accident; Patrick, born with Downs Syndrome, loved the water and snuck off at their country home. Up until his birth, we were a family prone to say, "You know, it's a wonder that among us, not one has any great malady." There were eight kids and nine grandchildren. Patrick was the first one not properly formed or fully functional. Such a sweet boy, Patrick taught us all about Downs, as Michael Creamer would teach us about PTSD.

Before Michael flew in from Campbell, I went out to New Jersey, staying to help Dottie, and delivering the eulogy I'd written loosely around Peter Pan. The funeral was standing-room-only with Kara and Kelly's classmates and the local ARC chapter, all showing up. Funerals for babies draw crowds. Several of our family members traveled down from Massachusetts to attend. Dottie wanted Mike and Me to go on with our wedding, June 7th.

✳   ✳   ✳

We had intended a minuscule wedding ceremony: my staff—and a few friends—Alene, Maryanne, in from overseas, Vinnie, Peter, Ron, Yuoska, Dave, our best man, and Dave's wife, Mona, plus Jean, my

180

sister, our maid of honor. But the news spread at the funeral… Martha was finally getting married! And to Mike Creamer!

So, our guest list grew: Michael's mom and sister Nell flew in because my parents, Greg and Ellie, were already in Jersey and coming, and Dottie, Bernie, Kara, and Kelly came. Before our ceremony, the whole bunch convened at my apartment for a champagne toast. I was nervous; Mike and his buds had already hit the Buds. *En masse*, we paraded, slightly buzzed, across Park Ave South to Calvary Episcopal Church, Mike in his dress greens bloused into his jump boots, and me in an antique white lace, mid-calf dress, wearing his garrison cap to top it off.

The reality of someone in 1984, from Gramercy Park Episcopal, marrying an active-duty soldier who happened to be a highly-decorated Vietnam veteran, was perhaps outside of that politically correct parish's purview. The Reverend Garmey seemed taken aback when we appeared, Mike in proud Army medals, and me in the 1930s, Pollyanna-all-grown-up turnout, curls circling my head. Mid-ceremony, at the blessing of rings, Garmey picked up the smaller ring from the presentation pillow, assumed it was the bride's, and handed it to Michael to begin his vows. I started shaking my head. "No, no."

Garmey eyed me, thinking that was his sign, ("Oh, thank heavens, we can call this mockery off.") to stop the ceremony.

I whispered to him, "I have the fatter finger." I pointed with one of them, "That's mine." At which, I broke out in bending-over giggles—nerves and champagne taking control. Garmey probably thought it was a sign that this marriage was doomed, but we got through it. Married. Whew.

After the ceremony, as we were signing documents, we were left without a key; Vinnie had to cab uptown from the reception on lower Bowery, so I could change my outfit. I hurriedly slipped on my new

Perry Ellis cable-front pink cotton sweater, poorly planned, because, in the anxiety and the 100-degree heat of the partially air-conditioned loft, I was melting. In my wedding pictures, cutting the cake, I wear a raggy T-shirt, borrowed for relief.

Michael and I stayed at Grammercy Park Hotel overnight. The next day we drove to Connecticut, where we stayed for only one night—in a dive, but the only motel in Cornwall Bridge. The musty floorboards in the bathroom bowed to wildlife beneath them. The mattress had springs breaking through. An ironic honeymoon, it was a relief to get out of bed.

The Vietnam Generation was an era of "sleeping" with someone—that's what we called it, "did you sleep with him?" as if sleeping didn't entail sex. When Michael and I were married, and we laid down together, it was as if I was bathed in newfound relief. I was married, yes, but that wasn't all. I was laying down gently with my husband with whom I had been legally, formally, joined together in the sight of God. I remember the sense of relief, of feeling safe, finally safe, of a worry that had followed me around since my precocious first sex as a teenager.

In Cornwall, I showed Michael the house we were buying and the sixteen acres of mainly steep woods. We parked, then walked around, peering in windows. The best part of our mini-honeymoon was renting a canoe on Lake Waramaug. It was a beautiful, hot, early June day in Litchfield County; we paddled around and jumped into the frigid lake to cool off. Mike had been reconstituted into a stripling eight-month-in warrior. He was so handsome and strong, and he loved Cornwall. "You found a great home for us. This has got to be one of the most beautiful places in America."

That night we drove back down Rte. 7, to NY Rte. 22, I-84, exited to the Sawmill, which dumped us onto the Henry Hudson, and into the city. Michael would fly to Fort Campbell early the next morning. I was 33, and Michael was 32. He had two more years to go in the Army. I cried soulfully at the airport, bereft and exhausted after burying Patrick, our wedding, and finally bonding with my husband after wondering for so long if it would ever happen. I was relieved, exhausted, but relieved.

Voutas-Creamer

NEW YORK — Martha M. Voutas, daughter of Gregory and Eleanor M. Voutas and formerly of Marlboro, Mass., was wed to Pfc. Michael E. Creamer, formerly of Marlboro, Mass., and son of Dorothy Creamer, by the Rev. Stephen Garmey in the Church of Calvary on Park Avenue South.

Witnesses for the couple were Jean Voutas of Hudson, Mass., and Mark Caney of Medford, Mass.

The bride is creative director of Martha Voutas Productions Inc., an advertising and graphic design studio in New York which she founded in 1978.

The groom is an infrantryman assigned to A Co., 3rd BN, 187th Infantry of the 101st Airborne (Air Assault) Division at Fort Campbell, Ken.

The couple will maintain residences in Kentucky, New York City and Cornwall Bridge, Conn.

We visited back and forth as we could.

Michael wrote from Campbell—

July 17th

My Darling…...

Over 24 hours now since you left, and I'm kind of glum. With each successive visit, you become so necessary to me. Being with you is my natural state, and when we're apart, it's *Koyanisquatsi,* "Life Out of Balance". … It was a wonderful, exquisite time of happiness and ease.

The 1st Sgt. told me today that I will get E-4 by September. By hook or crook. He's pissed I haven't gotten it already and says he plans to make a Sgt. out of me as soon as possible after that. Said the Company and Army need my expertise, insight, attitude, drive, and spirit. We have an ally, Hon. It's easier to be a good soldier when the effort is appreciated. Being a good soldier is beneficial to both of us—the passes I've had and promotions mean money. All my love, Mike C.

Wedding Day. Botton picture, Mike Yuoska, Mike, and Vinnie Fricault, friends who journeyed down to be with us.

CHAPTER 33

Rapid Deploy

As a new wife, the Army sent wills and contingency plans in case Michael went off, or war broke out. Army Wives pray a lot, and it was no wonder: we could live without word for days on end. This, in a time when the world was moving towards truck and suicide bombers. Mike wrote of training he was undergoing: "… I'm learning how to make incendiary devices out of bottles, plastic bags, gasoline, sugar, shit, and so forth. Very practical. … Next week comes squad tactics and hand grenades, among other things. Gee, I'll be just the boyfriend you need in NYC. Should be plenty of places I'll come in handy."

Michael took "the verge of war" seriously. Maybe too seriously; he heard sounding trumpets like Patton. He shared this with me based on his theory, "We need to work out a plan for when they attack Manhattan."

"They?" I asked.

"There are many people in the world who hate America," he said.

"They're not going to attack Manhattan," I said.

"That's where I would hit if I hated America." He said, "There are lots of countries who hate Wall Street."

My own husband hated Wall Street, so I stepped back a bit, "Right."

"If I'm not here, or if we get separated, put on boots—good ones—for hiking out, grab enough food, but especially water," he instructed, "and I would prefer you had a gun."

"I'm not gonna carry a gun," I said.

Michael continued with his exit strategy, "You need money in small denominations; you don't know if you'll have to buy your way out. Coins would be important if you find machines that still work, and maybe a foil rescue sheet." He kept at me, "Cross to the west side of Manhattan and sneak up parallel to the Hudson River, and work yourself through Yonkers until you get to Connecticut.

I took it all in. So, "they"-—those out to destroy the US—would take it out on New York City, where the money was.

"If I'm in Cornwall, I will work down Rte. 22, and find you." How, I didn't know, but then I remembered the 150,000 people in DC when we met. Mike would find me.

(Years later, in 2001, alone in Manhattan one August day, packing up a last load of things for a moving van going to my new home, in Belle Harbor, Queens. I prayed a little prayer. "Please, God, don't let the attack on New York City happen now, when I am separated as I am from my family."

Three weeks later, two airplanes flew into the World Trade towers. I watched their smoke from across the bay, and thought of Mike Creamer's astute political prescience.)

CHAPTER 34

Dottie Out, Reinforcements In

After Patrick's death, Bernie's brother offered him a job in Annapolis running his business. The Glynns would move by September of 1984, and I would lose my close-to-the-city family: my accountant in Bernie, my godchild Kara, her sister Kelly, and especially my Dottie.

Later that year, I was challenged to put together an NYC Alumni/ae chapter as the newly-elected Chair of Mass College of Art's Foundation Board. It was a task the Foundation Board hadn't completed in the previous three years. Artists are independent thinkers, especially those from Mass Art, the only freestanding state art school in the country. Most especially those who succeeded in escaping Boston, to the apex of the art world, NYC. Tough group to get together. I wasn't successful making it happen either, but in the process, I met alumnus painter Bob Barsamian and his wife, Katherine Snedeker. They lived and worked in a homey loftspace four blocks from MVP. Barsamian had this short answer for what Mass Art did: It taught us how to function, primarily, how to survive as artists. Artists' successes were tricky, individual. Many artists took ancillary jobs to get by. We tended to be less willing to join a group whether we'd succeeded or if we hadn't.

Snedeker was an artist, too, struggling to find which way to go. Most multi-talented people have a tough time finding out where their fortunes lie, and Snedeker was trying out fashion. When she heard that I had a fashion background, we snapped towards each other like those magnets back in Milton Glaser's class. She was from a large family, so we had a lot in common. Our friendship just grew and grew.[1] Katherine was unique from my other NYC friends; *Michael liked her.* Maybe because she was an "Army brat," and Barsamian was as antiwar as they came. He told me that her dad, Lt. Colonel Snedeker, back from duty in Korea, was called in to play an early command role in Vietnam. He carefully examined the Army's intent and said, "You're not getting me anywhere near that place." Michael, who strongly supported the Domino Theory [2] loved to debate with Bob endlessly.

Katherine became my pal; we planned a fashion show for her, thinking we could kick-start her business. It would be a private showing for existing and would-be clients. The long, narrow length of MVP served as a runway for models, with the audience seated in two rows on both sides. Models changed outfits behind the conference room partitions at the back. We were Judy Garland and Mickey Rooney, and as in their movies, we pulled it off. The show kept Katherine in commissions for the time being.

Barsamian, set on escaping the frustrating gallery scene in NYC, decided to start a new life for them in Dallas, where he already had gallery representation. Barsamian headed west to homestead, but Katherine wasn't hitching her cart to Dallas yet; her clients, like mine were also in NYC. She would wait for Barsamian's reconnaissance and more clarity, but eventually, she planned to move. For now, I had Katherine to myself.

---

1   Katherine Snedeker would own a successful furniture showroom, The Arrangement, in Dallas, with a Houston shop. She took on interior design assignments as well.

2   Domino Theory—the concept that if one country (as in Michael's case, South Vietnam) fell to Communism that the neighboring country would also fall, and on and on.

CHAPTER 35

1985 Arlington

On April 19th Michael was chosen among active-duty personnel as "Herd Soldier of the Year" by the 173rd Airborne Brigade alumni during their Annual Celebration outside of Washington, DC. Frank

Baker's Sigholtz Chapter hosted the event. Fort Campbell released Michael for the ceremony, and I flew to Washington, bringing with me a presentation, just in case I had a chance to pitch the 173rd's Yearbook design. As MVP's work was falling off without Perry Ellis, I needed to market myself continually. As a group, we toured the White House, and while there, George Bush invited Michael and other Herd dignitaries—not me—into his office. Michael received a pair of gold VP cufflinks and had a formal photograph taken with Bush, which his office later mailed to him. The next day, Michael laid a wreath at the Tomb of the Unknown(s) in Arlington National Cemetery.

On the bus ride out of Arlington, passing row upon row of white lozenge-topped graves, Michael whispered to me, "Unless one dies in batttle, The United States buries only Purple Heart recipients in Arlington now." Then he added, *"You know, I have two Purple Hearts."*

CHAPTER 36

Put Me Down Easy

In summer of 1985, Michael's platoon of the 503rd was sent to West Point to teach cadets, which meant that he could spend weekends in Cornwall Bridge. During his last two weeks on assignment, I took vacation to be with him as much as possible. Work was not going well.

I wrote Michael after he returned to Fort Campbell, on my birthday, 9/4/1985—

> Darling—
> I hate all this. I'm exhausted. I hate management. I don't savor telling people they're not working out; it's making me ill. I'm putting in hours to convince myself that I've given my all; if I work harder, I can win.
>
> Then I grow so angry and frustrated, feel ugly and mean and ready to burst. Not a tear in sight mind you— stone-cold, tight and stiff. I just turned 35, eighteen minutes ago, when I left work at midnight. Tomorrow I will start at 7:30 on a rush job for a presentation at 3:30 in New Jersey. I've got our first annual report riding on this, a $10,000. job, and boy, I need the relief—honestly.
>
> Please think lovely thoughts; send them my way. I need it all.
> Love, Martha

PS I love you, Michael. I'm okay. I just needed someone to talk to.

XOX MC

On the weekend, I wrote a 14-page letter, spitting it all out: Sat + Sun, Sept. 7, 8.

My Darling Michael,

Your first letter was like manna from Heaven. The mailbox glowed. I opened it and found your calming, loving words, your reassurance of our special love.

A tough week. Do you remember much of vacation we spent wondering what to say to A and N? When to say it? After I dropped you off, I went to the office (where has my *studio* gone?), and I found things N had been working on. It wasn't done. I got mad and worked on it.

Tuesday, Nancy had her last day. Everyone was surprised; I hadn't told them in advance. Wednesday, I had two presentations. N had been working on a logo, but she hadn't finished. I asked why she hadn't finished. N said she doesn't care about it.

Thursday morning, A called to say he doesn't feel well enough to come in, "Besides, there's nothing for me to do."

"A, yes, there is," I answered.

"What, Martha, what do you want me to do, babysit? Answer the phone?"

Well, I blew, "I'll tell you what to do; I want you to stop giving me such a hard time, and start supporting this *office* and stop being so difficult to talk to."

"Difficult? Me? All right, I'll come in right now, and we'll all talk about the problems," he said.

"No, A, *we* need to talk first, everyone doesn't need to be included," I said.

"Oh, that's what **you** think," A said; we set a Friday night dinner to talk.

That really riled me. I decided to talk with N. I told her I was having problems, and she said she was too. She hates work, coming in; she said, "It's impossible to talk to you, Martha." She said, "I think we've all changed. Maybe MVP should just cease to be. You seem to want to go live in the country full-time anyway."

I said it was implausible with a debt of $65,000.

Now I learn A is very fearful about AIDS. He apologized, said he was glad I yelled. That it took five and a half years for me to yell; he thanked me for making him grow up.

I got such mixed signals from you this summer, like your house-husband comment. I want a less complicated life; I tried to withdraw from work, and it didn't work. We could merge, or sell—but who would be interested unless I were on staff? I don't know what's realistic anymore; I almost want to talk to my therapist again. I worry about Cornwall Bridge clients supporting me... Maybe I'm so used to doing something so complicated that I don't know how to make simple assessments.

I loved your love letter. Purll[1] and I are fortunate to have such an eloquent, loving writer on our hands. Please find time to talk to me about our futures. (How telling, I pluralized them.) I need you to communicate. It was such a relief having you here this summer. I think maybe my attention was better placed on you *and* the company than on the company exclusively. I think of how difficult this MVP commitment sits with new priorities, and maybe

---

1   The cat Michael encouraged me to get when he re-upped. Mike was a cat person.

I should end it. I want to get on with my life and stop resenting my situation.

You are my life also. I need you to tell me what your hopes and dreams are so we can make them mesh. Take care of yourself. I love you dearly.

Your wife who loves you, Martha

And in two weeks, I write again:

September 22, 1985

My dearest husband and friend—

Your letter came on Saturday. I needed your softness to come through and touch me. To find me again. Help me locate those real parts inside me we so often leave behind. …Your words were vital for me; I took them to be true. I know that whatever happens to us, our commitment to each other to live in harmony and to share dreams is the essential aspect of our love.

I looked so long for you. …. I fell in love with you much sooner than you did me. Though I never was all that good at falling in love. I came to love you deeply in your most severe depression when I saw shimmering under your surface, a warm, tender, and boy-like presence. It was after our trip to Levittown Pennsylvania, that I came to love you fully. Then I met The Herd guys, and knew why. But I knew that I wanted to be a mother, to reach beyond this quasi-success and have some of what War must have been to you—a scope—and purpose to feel it for the rest of my life.

Your dreams must be met and honored and not set aside because of my plans for happiness. Sting says it well, the part about loving somebody—we "set them free." I think you are facing severe inner questions about coming out of the Army. Your letter was the first concrete evidence that you were dealing with that prospect. I hope you were honest with yourself when you say those things about being a house-husband and not necessarily the primary breadwinner. That was loving and generous, and I was relieved to have it on the table. Because if our *shared goal* is to have children—or a child—then that is like you say, "maybe just the ticket."

I need to know that you share that common goal: you don't have some deep trepidation that will ruin our lives, singular or plural. You have my eternal commitment to building a life together to take all your fears away about returning home. And to tell you this:

If having a child is so important to me, then I must work to find a way to afford that choice. I must address myself to it. For you to feel you have no options but to get a traditional, tedious, unfulfilling job is ludicrous. And no, it is not a problem that I would be the primary breadwinner. Just because I married you doesn't mean I can rest on my laurels. If *we* want to have a child, we have responsibilities that go beyond ourselves; anyway, we can work it out. Please, Michael, know I love you more each day. I am sorry if I have contributed to your anxiety. I miss you. I want you home.

Love, Your friend, Martha Mary

Sitting out a hurricane, I wrote Michael

September 27, 1985

It's better you're away; MVP is still socked into some heavy-duty financial problems. I had a chance to assess the situation, and I set up a new accounting system. Now, we were accruing bills daily so that I can see what comes in, while at the same time, billing more efficiently. I am resigned to a "we'll see" attitude. I debated seeing a head-hunter to find what was out there in the way of a job for me.

＊　＊　＊

Michael warned me that he might die young. I chose not to listen and I wrote, "I don't believe you will… too damn ornery. Maybe we could join the Peace Corps if we couldn't have a baby."

I wrote to him regarding our timing on pregnancy.

> Michael, don't you want a bit of a honeymoon? A trip to Europe, or Alaska, or Nova Scotia, or the Mediterranean, Egypt maybe? or Japan before we bear? Don't you think you could use a little private time? I know the biological constraints. But do you really want to go right into it? Or maybe have a honeymoon. I could even be pregnant early while on it, or I'd conceive in Ireland or Greece to honor the relatives. I want this in the mail before Hurricane Gloria's fury.
> XOX Martha.
> PS: I never loved you more than working out our future together. It gives me calm that nothing else can offer.

I wrote a day later,

> "We have caught up on taxes, but since looking more closely, I realize it costs me $22,000. /month to open MVP's doors. That's with payroll, insurance, utilities, on-going purchases, car, telephone, etc. federal corporate tax, NY corporate tax, employees' withholdings, disability insurance, rent tax, and sales tax. On an average of 22 working days a month, it cost me $1,000. to shut down for Gloria." In the previous three months—July, August,

and September—we had billed only $54,000. in fees and commissions, but $150,000. in gross (usually advertising space and printing would run that high). From the outside, we appeared to be doing fine; in reality we were $12,000. behind.

"Well, I'm going back to tax city. You're the best and least complicated aspect of my life. Don't let me put you down; I certainly don't mean it. I adore you."
Love, Your wife, Martha

An interesting turn of events. When we met in 1982, Michael was a complication— beyond all others that I had: PTSD, suicide, pulling away, and MVP was running like a spinning wheel. Business is like that. I remembered what I'd learned once, in a marketing course I took at The New School, that businesses go through cycles. I was at the end of the fourth and last stage in which I might simply fail without a rebirth of spirit. I had certainly changed; that was evident, but I was not sure I wanted to evolve forever.

Over the fifteen and a half years MVP was in business, we had 33 employees, including me. Many stayed for five years or more. Only three besides me were business thinkers: Katherine who was only transitory; another who was already retired and working to keep busy (I didn't like his style); and one whom I coached for years. (He'd go on to become an estimable marketer on his own.) In 1985, N and A were both coaxed out of the womb, Debbie Schuman MacRae, or Debra Fern as I called her, my college roommate, would come on as controller. She was a relief both from an accounting perspective and from a personal one. We also brought on a new production manager. And Lee and Lyn, my friends from Boston, were scheduled to visit in Cornwall for Columbus Day to start talks on a potential merger.

CHAPTER 37

Rakkasans

Michael was named "Rakkasan of the Year" by the 3/187th Infantry Regiment, part of the 101st Airborne, with whom he was serving at Fort Campbell. Rakkasans hold an amazing place in Vietnam history: Their heroic role in the battle named "Hamburger Hill," (May 10 to 20, 1969, on the steep, triple-canopied Hill 193), and for the grinding losses the Rakkasans endured fighting over ten days. While they were still fighting, news of their battle reached the Senate floor back in the states. It drew sharp criticism for US and allies' tactics to force a win in a grueling, heavy-loss, close-range infantry battle. It would mark a turning point in President Johnson's fervor to fuel the war with more troops.[1] For their 1986 Reunion, seventeen years later, Michael and I would fly to Fort Benning, GA, where the Rakkasans honored Michael. He sat at the head table with Gen. Westmoreland (ret), the commander of US troops in Vietnam, towards whom I harbored triple-canopied resentment. Michael introduced me in the reception line, I respectfully shook Westmoreland's hand. I was proud of Michael, who beamed.

In this letter, Michael writes the section I borrowed earlier to explain what he might have thought walking to the train station immediately before our Levittown/PTSD trip. (Page 107)

---

1   History.com July 28st 1965, This day in history.

Michael with General Westmoreland, commander of forces in Vietnam, pinning Mike's chest with medal.

Here was the evidence that Michael did find closure during his three-year, second-stint in the Army. I had new faith that our marriage and family would thrive.

Michael to Martha

> 3 June 86
>
> …Proposal—Can *I* get out of the Army and cool out for a while and relax and impregnate *you*, and proclaim the child as just a real special kid. Then, we put our efforts into remembering the important thing in life, even though it's more complicated than it sounds, is to love and create happiness for our family, and our adopted pets, and our extended families, and so on out to infinity?
>
> I think I've used up whatever stockpile of voluntary badass I seem to have acquired at birth. I've got a fair amount of self-confidence that could probably combine with a good dash of overall smarts and competence to make pretty good pot luck, so let's search the cupboards for ingredients and seasonings and start cooking something up, okay? We'll serve it up for two, and keep some extra plates ready to set.

I love you, Hon. You're the best a guy could ever find. Love, Mike C.

Michael writes of coming home for the summer; his unit will return to West Point.

22 June 86

My Hon...

Hopefully, I'll hit NY about the same time this does. I can't wait. I'd as soon spend two months in Hades as here (Fort Campbell). West Point will be a bit better than that. At least on weekends.

It'll be 120 days on the big countdown this Saturday. In July, I become a "two-digit midget." It's been hovering near 100 degrees here for a week with no break forecast. I hate it. Not a summer person. I like fall with its coolness and color and clarity and golden/amber light. Can't wait for it to arrive, complete with wood-smoke and Purrl romping camouflaged in leaves.

The summer solstice and full moon within 24 hours of each other started some long-buried Celtic/Druid kettle boiling deep inside (me). I've been yowling and hissing at the moon and wanting to kick some ass or sack a city or worship an oak tree. I'd settle for a good bed-bouncing session with you, some of that old M+M magic.

Got my nose buried in FM100-5, "Operations," the "How the Army Plans to Fight" manual. It's brilliantly conceived, amazingly well-written; it displays a remarkable perception of reality and draws the best lessons from military history. It damn near makes me cry that I don't see the least bit of attention paid to it beyond lip service. The demands it makes for an aggressive attitude, a hunger to train for nasty, independently cunning initiative, subordinates' trust, etc. doom it to oblivion. The "career" soldiers are petrified; an Army of freewheeling badasses—the Army that this country needs to survive—is as much a threat to them as a cocked pistol at their temple.

If only the Army had recognized the potential in Michael Creamer's brilliant military mind. Instead, Mike grew bitter and wanted out. He was "going bad" as he'd suggested he might, without enough action to engage in. West Point was exceedingly hard to bear. Mike's self-comparison to boys-on-the-way-to-officers brought up his lost opportunities as far back as Dot Creamer denying his enrollment in Boston Latin. He goes on.

> If there's any one thing this enlistment has done for me, it has been to drive home what a privilege it was to serve with November Rangers and the 173rd Airborne Brigade. … what a rarity it is in American military history to be with such an outfit at the pinnacle of its brief history. The Herd was born and bred to fight an Asian war. … throughout six years of combat, the quality and determination of its soldiers never failed. And when the 173rd did its job, it passed into history, never to be demeaned as a hollow, unmotivated bauble.[2]
>
> Well…I love you. I'm worn out, and so I'm gonna go. I'm always with you, Mike C.

I looked forward to Michael's return. He wrote to me

> 23 Aug 86
> Hello Hon….
> Sitting listening to *Prairie Home Companion* and nursing a four-star cold … Got two letters from you this week, the

---

2   173rd Airborne was reactivated in 2000 to serve in the mid-East.

first in I don't know how long. I'd almost forgotten how much I enjoy them. *Lake Wobegon Days* is a great read. The first hundred or so pages, the "history," was tedious, but then the book became an American classic. Possibly the finest nostalgia ever written.

"They" seem to have decided that I'm too short to fuck with. Yesterday I was given orders for a Good Conduct Medal (whoopee!) and told I have been put in for a third Army Commendation Medal. And they put me on permanent "special duty" to the clinic, which means that I go over there and do medical work all day, five days a week, and am not on the CQ or Detail Roster until I start my full-time "clearing." Of course, it may all be part of some sinister re-enlistment scheme.

Think I'm going to get a set of mounted miniature medals. It's my last chance to get it at a fair price. They'll be mostly for display, but I'd like to wear them at black tie functions such as reunions, banquets, and inaugural balls (who knows?). Don't you think I'd look classy in a tux with waterfalls of ribbons and bronze on the left lapel? Topped off by a little mini CMB and mini Jump Wings? I don't ever want to wear a uniform again because the uniform denotes rank, and these last three years have given me a startle-reaction to that. My "rank," as of 26 October, is simply "*Former Airborne Ranger Combat Medic*," with no stripes involved and no salutes except to the flag, and to those individuals who have earned it in *my* book. About the most demanding thing, these past three years has been "respecting my superiors." Wearing a tux with medals is an equitable way to thumb my nose at that. It makes me a *veteran*, not an ex-SP/4.

Michael wrote in July a blurb fitting of a New Yorker *article:*

I was really offended by a picture I saw: a group of corporate directors, starched and pressed, sitting in a high-tech boardroom with padded chairs and microphones and snazzy little name markers, listening to an up-and-coming middle manager giving a presentation with rear-projection graphics. But this wasn't Chase-Manhattan Bank in 1986; it was MAC-V Headquarters in Bien Hoa, Vietnam, in 1970, while I was in the bush country! From what's on the board and the looks on their faces, these people were swallowing a truckload of bullshit! These were the generals who were running the war, and they hadn't the slightest fucking idea of what was really going on over there!

Boy, did we grunts ever take it in the shorts for nothing! "The US Army, A Beatrice Company." If Lichtenstein declared war, I'd sweat because, by the time the career clowns checked to make sure that everyone's chinstraps were fastened, it would be all over. Honest to God, *this* time, I *am* going to write a book!

CHAPTER 38

Maryanne

Mike and his ex-girlfriend Maryanne went way back to his life in Africa. She and Michael had a relationship before we met. Black and white photographs of Maryanne and Mike show her as a young trooper working the cause of potable water for Africa. Mike loved that Starship Troopers ethic, even though his African experience was decidedly a "tearing down the forests for industry" mindset. Maryanne and I became friends too. Mike told her things he didn't tell me.

This is from Mike to Maryanne, which she gave to me.

> Ft. Campbell, KY
> 10 Jul 86
> Hello Maryanne…
> Cannot honestly recall when I last wrote…this is my
> "wind-down" assignment before getting out. …Am at West
> Point till 18 Aug, doing the same shit as last year. The only
> advantage is getting home on weekends. Otherwise, it's
> boring, frustrating, and chock full o'chickenshit. … I sure
> love Connecticut. I've spent time in about half the states,
> and only Vermont comes close. *Yankee* did an article on
> Cornwall entitled "Half-a-mile from Heaven." They were
> understated.
> I'm getting "civilized." I had a feeling that

this enlistment was a "make-or-break" one. It sorted
out certain things for me: although I loved the 173rd
Airborne, I always hated the Army... I've been reading a
lot of military history and theory, and the bulk of modern
battle theory points to one glaring, undeniable fact:
Nothing is worth risk of a nuclear exchange.

Start with that as dogma, and work back, examining
the "brinksmanship" and "limited nuclear employment,"
that forms so much of our strategy now, and you can't help
but think that a lot of the people with stars on their collars
have quite simply lost touch with reality. They seem to
think, "We may have to destroy the global village in order
to save it." Gwynne Dyer, the Canadian military analyst,
is probably right on the money with the postulation that
armies and even "war" itself have become obsolete.

Mike to Maryanne

17 Jul 86
Maryanne...
Martha and I got bikes for our anniversary. ... her bike
works fine. Mine did, until that ole' urge to fiddle and
dissect took hold, and what was a 10-speed a week ago is
now a 6 2/3 speed. (I'm better at surgery!)

I finally got around to replacing all that high-speed
expedition gear I had to ditch in Kolwezi.[1] No more
Army surplus camping. Got a Lowe ruck for myself, a
woman's Kelty for Martha, a Peak 1 stove and cook set, a
Timberline tent. (Yes, marriage has made me sell out! A
tent![2]) Hollofil II zip-together bags yay! a couple of self-

---

1   Both Maryanne and Mike did long ex-pat tours in Africa. Escaping M-K's enclave in Zaire,
Mike lost his gear.
2   So, I wasn't the first person to endure life without a tent! It seemed a game he played.

inflating mattresses, boots, raingear, daypacks, doo-dads, and the like. They've started delivering my Campmor catalog by chauffeured limo.

25 Aug 86
Hello Maryanne—
"Nostalgia Night" on the cassette recorder. "Average White Band" album, FLASHBACK to Mwene Ditu and the Main Tower Construction Camp with 150 linemen, early 1976. <u>Gawd</u>, talk about work! It was incredible... Three crazed Viet vet medics: Me, Walt from the 173rd, and Dan, a Marine, working 16-18 hour days to cope with a load of drunken, brawling, spoiled brat Americans and their huge Zairois crew and the crew's even huger families! ...soon as we got "off" some overly lubricated yahoo would pound on the door demanding that we call for immediate evacuation to Mayo Clinic for his buddy.... had to be the onset of the "Kasai Black Death." Right? I mean, he'd only had sixteen bottles of Primus...

"Whaddya mean, just drunk? You quack asshole pill-pusher. What *you* know anyhow? Why, I'll..." (He passes out, hits his head, and creates another hour of work sewing up his split skull.) Ah, Hemingway and Ruark only told the good parts!

Anyhow, just wanted to give you two more things to unass the Big "A" for.

The first is *Aliens*, the sequel to *Alien*. The only sequel I've ever seen that's worth its mettle. We're talking *serious* war movie here, *incredibly* done, with Ripley (Sigourney Weaver) emerging as perhaps the most convincing, independently feminist character ever seen on film. Max Blowout!
Love, and take care! Mike C.

PS—Yeah, you are neurotic and a bit hard to deal with at times, but given the tenor of the times, who the Hell isn't? … Think about two things. First, don't knock "The Mainstream" too hard. Now STOP! Think about it. Do it! The longer you're out of the mainstream, the harder to get back … Think again. What I'm saying is commentary, not advice; I know that you don't take advice any better than I do!

✳   ✳   ✳

In which Michael defines the essence of wanderlust that separately moved him and Maryanne to Africa. It's the force that pushed him to enlist early for Vietnam and get through tunnels and the Angolan uprising, and even his father's departure…. Like music with warning labels, these words should have been printed on Mike's jacket cover, warning those who fell for him and thought to hold on for very long.

> *… there'll always be a huge part of me that wants to*
> *kick loose in Somalia or wherever—running loose and*
> *eating dust, occasionally goosing danger's cute ass, and*
> *either ducking the slap or savoring the kiss.*

Michael wasn't always truthful with Maryanne; he avoided her in '82 when he was suicidal and she came to help. She told me, "I was prepared to do anything--quit my job, anything." Theirs was a roguish on/off relationship; they met after her stint in the Peace Corps. He wrote his "hard-knock buddy" these lines that I find cocky, this side of malicious. They must have been hard for Maryanne to swallow.

> *… there's probably a part of you that envies my having*
> *found a best friend who loves that in me and never tried to*
> *"tame" it—only offered an alternative that I could happily*
> *accept, and grew comfortable to let go of the tiger's tail.*

BILL STARKEY, MARYANNE LEBLANC,
MIKE CREAMER. SURVIVORS,
SECOND SHABA WAR. MAY 1978

It's such a close thing that ultimately, I can't even "wish you the same," for that would be presumptuous. Different people, different paths. As a hard-knock buddy, I wish you the best, whatever it is. Again, take care, and love, Mike C.

PPS. Remembered another reason to come back from Africa—You'd really like Linda Ellerbee's book, *And So It Goes—Adventures in Television*. She has a dry and acid tongue, hooked to a mind like a steel trap, which you'd probably know if you ever saw *NBC News Overnight*. (The show was the first network news show produced almost solely by women, so they called it *"Leave it to Beaver"* in the trade.) Your comments on Somali men remind me of her observation of Saudi Arabia— "The land where men are men, women are cattle, and goats are fun."

25 Nov 86 (Michael's postcard to Maryanne)

Hello!
Am up taking an Arctic warfare/survival school for a month (last two weeks: all fieldwork). We're about 150 miles SE of Fairbanks and can see the Brooks Range to the north and the Alaska Range to the south. Everyone else is learning to ski—I'm learning to fall down a lot. Write! Take care, Mike C.

CHAPTER 39

Civilized

I was anticipating that with Michael home, we would need to make changes. But finishing up his service as an armorer (gun handler in charge of arms of a military unit) and then assigned wind-down to a medical unit left Mike with few new skills on which to build his career; he was floundering again. I wondered what would keep him from merely surviving when he returned. (If he'd survive. If he returned.)

He wrote to me: 24 Aug 86

> ... so that you know I haven't retracted past
> pronouncements. I do intend to "demilitarize" once I get
> home. Everything'll get packed up and stashed except for
> the Sigholtz Plaque (From 173rd's Soldier of the Year),
> because I love it (and if I stored it, mildew would eat up
> the velvet), my black beret, and a "shadow box." I want
> to assemble a 3-D frame with ribbons, badges, patches,
> crests, etc., mounted on velvet under glass. And of course,
> the "Death Watch[1]" poster, if you want to hang it.
>
> All others I will pack away in storage. The Vietnam
> library will melt into the vast overall bookcase. AR-15 and
> the UZI will get sold or traded, but certainly disposed of

---

1   Photo by then PFC Paul Epley "The Agony of War" mistakenly called Death Watch by many. 173rd Medics were awaiting the extraction of a body on a stretcher.

somehow, along with associated paraphernalia. I'm going to keep the '03 Springfield. That's going to be my competition rifle. I may even end up with an M-1 Garand from the NRA match sales program as well, but those will be "civilized," with nice wood stocks. I promise no more high-tech mega-death 30-round magazine Rambo props in our house. Just the .22 rifle because it's versatile, and every family ought to have a shotgun. (That's just the Springfield now.)

I'm becoming civilized, Hon!!! Look! I haven't read *Soldier of Fortune* in five months or so; I read *Outside* and *Walking* and *Mother Earth News* instead! I bought a civilian blue winter coat, instead of an army arctic parka! I have civilian camping gear in blue and green and orange instead of Army combat gear in OD and Camo! I read more books on wildlife than I do on the military now! I got a tennis racket and Reeboks!!!!!!

I still may yet actually manage to fit into some little corner of the everyday world!! I'm not even going to join the SF Reserves or anything! I'm just going to say: "When time demanded it of me, I was an Airborne Ranger in Vietnam. I did one of the toughest jobs ever asked of a young American during one of the toughest periods in our history. I did it well, and I'm proud of it. It taught me a lot; it had both good and bad effects on my life. I survived the aftermath, too, which was the hardest, bitterest burden this country ever put on its sons, *much harder than the impossible war they asked us to fight.* I may not have a lot of material things, but I have much more—a fine, loving wife, a nice house, true and tested friends, a sense of realistic values, and a soul that's been fired to a temper and quenched; won't find that even in the finest steel. And I have the right to look myself in the eye and smile because I've always had the courage to be myself."

You're right. I only feel down when I try to measure myself by the scale set by those who put money, status, and possessions at the top of the heap. I never felt comfortable going along with that. Perhaps I screwed up by actively rebelling against it, which meant that I did acknowledge it. Now I'm coming to where I know it's there, nod, and just get on with my own business in my own way.

Let's do it, Hon... Let's build a life with our house and our cat and our future child, and some sort of work we can do that gives us time to be together and enjoy our bikes and tennis rackets and camping gear and friends. We can do it.

I love you, Mike C.

I felt with that I had an influence on him. And maybe he on me. Some letter, some discussion I can't remember. Phone calls were rare, there were no cell phones then, and we had busy lives. His time wasn't his own. He continued to show me how far he'd come from when we met.

25 Aug 86
My Hon....
For some reason—maybe it's because I got my ETS.[2] orders today—I played *Nylon Curtain*, an album that has lain untouched in the cassette rack for a long, long time. It brought back moments from years ago when we were first starting to know one another.

I'm glad we did. I'm glad that you were pretty sure and patient and persistent. I'm glad that I was absolutely

---

2 Separation typically occurs when someone reaches their Expiration of Term of Service (ETS) and is released from active duty.

last-drop burned out that I was laid wide open to feelings of love and the support that I'd categorically denied for so long. There was plenty of pain back then for both of us. More than enough …Too much, probably, for either one of us to have handled alone, and we learned to cope together, two survivors on the same little island. "Birth pangs" wouldn't be too far off the mark. Think of it… Two people, a man, and a woman, come together attracted by an inexplicable force…The inevitable happens. There follows a long period of growth, and yet of burden, washed with emotion, uncertainty, and fear for the future.

Then it climaxes, in a welter of fear and hurt and lashed but indomitable hope—and a new life—a

wondrous love opens its eyes on the world and begins its own unique voyage of struggle and discovery… And, if luck holds, fulfillment.

This kid will never doubt the "miracle" theory, believe-you-me! And soon I'll be back, and we can get down to some serious work on our second child. Is there a better word than love? If not, we'll have to invent it for ourselves.

In the meantime, I love you, Mike C.

PART III

HOME (NOT SO) SWEET HOME

CHAPTER 40

Winning

The Army was over. Mike and his friends liked to winter camp when no one else was around, and the bugs didn't bother as much. Since that frigid night atop Mt. Mitchell we spent in 1983, I didn't care how many frigging bugs bothered me camping. He and friends Peter and Vinnie went off together in late 1986, got stranded in a snowstorm at a trail lodge and had a great time.

At MVP, we were working to find some new clients. In late January of 1987, I was asked by Allen McNeary, who served on the Board of Brooklyn Bureau of Community Services (for whom we'd just completed an anniversary gala at BAM, Brooklyn Academy of Music), to present to Liz Claiborne Corporation, where he was a vice president. They were looking for a creative surrogate to make decisions that Liz usually made, while she took every other month off, her segue towards retirement. The presentation would be to Liz, her husband, Art Ortenberg, their other partners, Allen, and a few key managers heading up divisions.

MVP planned its presentation around a slide portfolio, which I carried with me on an earlier appointment with my OBGYN to determine if I was pregnant. I found out I was. I was glowing as I cabbed over from Second to Seventh Avenue, with my little secret. My new marketing director, J., was coming twelve blocks uptown from the studio.

As I sat waiting for J., I saw our competition exiting the conference room: a buttoned-up group of three. Allen came out, "Ready?" he asked.

"I'm waiting for my marketing director, but I have slides." I handed off my ring of slides for Allen to set up. He came back, said, "Well, we're four minutes late already, and this is one group you don't want to keep waiting. Please, don't even mention that someone else was coming." He turned to a woman behind the desk, "Just keep her out here."

✶　✶　✶

Once inside, I got the nod, and all the partners of Liz Claiborne Corp. looked up from an enormous mahogany table. I began. "Hello, I'm Martha Voutas," and I was off. I felt powerful and strong, knew the industry, knew design, knew I had a baby inside me. I was in my element, a perpetual performer again on stage; showing our work gave me confidence.

When I finished, J. was waiting outside. I took the leave-behinds she'd brought and handed them to Allen who walked us to the elevator, shushing J. as he did.

"I wouldn't even let her talk in the elevator—too many industry people."

Once out on the street I asked, "Where were you?"

She defended herself, saying, "I got there right after you went in; that &%#*-head wouldn't let me in!"

"What happened?" I walked quickly, hailing a cab downtown at the curb.

J. said, "I got into a cab, and the traffic was so bad on Sixth Avenue, I told him how he should go." She was whining.

I was high on the presentation, the baby. "So….?"

"And he didn't listen and that's when I had to bop him on the head," she said.

"What?" I asked.

"I bopped him…" She needn't go further.

"J., you hit your cab driver?" Our taxi driver who'd taken in the conversation looked back through the thick Plexiglas partition, checking who she was in case he ever picked her up. "J., you can't just hit someone," I said.

"He wouldn't do what I wanted him to do," J. said. "And then he pulled over and said he was going to get a cop."

"Oh great," I said.

"I got out and ran, and that's why I was late. He made me late." She finished.

She was already finished in my mind, especially when Allen called later that day and told us we'd won.

When I saw J. start to calculate her commission—I kid you not—I interrupted, "I don't think so, J. You weren't there. You didn't win that client, I did. You didn't even get to bat."

"But I got there right after they closed the door. I told you that woman wouldn't let me in!" She was ready to bop me.

I replied, "Right, that's how I was instructed; you would have been noticeably tardy."

J. packed up her stuff right then and there; I didn't need J. I knew just who to call. My best buddy, Snedeker, came right over. I gave her the news. She drove a tough bargain, setting terms for salary and bonuses, and I think she may have thrown in a round-trip ticket or two to Dallas. But she agreed to come on board as Claiborne's Account Manager to get us through.

CHAPTER 41

Losing

I drove up to Cornwall that night to tell Mike of our winning double-hitter. I told him about our baby first. "This is fast, Martha. Don't you think it's too fast?" he said.

"No, Honey, this is what we talked about." He'd been home three and a half months.

"Yeah, but not recently."

"Well, it always was part of the big picture, nothing changed," I said, momentarily lost in his tone. What was Michael thinking? I was more than ready; I was pregnant. "Besides, now we have a saving grace," I said. "MVP's on retainer with Liz Claiborne for six months, and renewable for another six. We're getting $35,000 per month," I said. "We'll be pretty well off for a while."

"What about the merger with Lee and Lyn and Boston?" Mike asked.

"We're working on it; we'll see." (It was still a desire, but it would be postponed by the Liz contract.)

Over the next months, Mike went in and out of emotions, lining them up, shooting them down. He was collecting separation pay from the Army, but nearing its end, he started interviewing. I cheered from the sidelines—backward, forward, fight, fight, fight—an emotional tug of war.

Suddenly Mike talked about calling our marriage off. "I would leave," he said to me, "let you have your baby," (Oh, I see, he saw it as my child, just as he'd blamed his mother, 'She should have stopped after me,') "but I don't want to be like my father."

My heart stopped; what could he mean? That's not what he wrote to me about. "I waited, Michael," I said. "I waited, unlike other women who have children out of wedlock." I tried not to attack him, but I didn't understand. He knew I never wanted to be a single mother. My hormones went haywire, not just because of the situation he was suggesting, but because it came from Michael, *my* Michael, who wanted nothing more than to get on with having our little family.

Mike got a job; the Job Corps in Torrington hired him when he went to apply for other jobs. He managed their veterans' desk, which seemed a perfect fit, I thought. It meant that he'd stay in Connecticut, and I'd come up on weekends whenever work allowed. As for the marriage? He stuck it out, but he seemed rueful.

One weekend, in Cornwall, after finding a yellowed newspaper clipping, I showed it to him. "You sent this to me in a letter from Fort Campbell." Mike read the title about how much safer it had become for older couples to have children. Not speaking, he put it on the end table.

"See what you wrote on it? 'We're gonna be okay, Hon, exclamation point, exclamation point.'" I left the room and went in to sleep.

[In findings, after-the-fact to us, in 1971, Sarah Haley, a counselor in Boston's VA, in breaking research "found Vietnam vets having trouble with wives and children, many having difficulty with intimacy, or their wife's pregnancy, or especially with the vulnerability of a newborn baby."][1]

---

1   Nicosia, p. 201.

I had my work cut out: I served as Creative Director on all the new business at Liz Claiborne. MVP worked with middle managers heading various divisions; it was difficult. Most of our existing clients had been newborns themselves; we'd grown up with them. Claiborne was full-blown when we entered the picture with earnings of $850,000,000, and would become a billion-dollar entity during our tenure.

We had huge assignments:

1. Launching Dana Buchman, who for years had been Liz's sweater designer. With this, the Claiborne Corp. sought to diversify into the "Better" or "Designer" market.

2. Designing packaging, marketing tools, and displays for Claiborne Menswear': a new division of accessories: dress shirts, ties, socks, underwear, and belts.

3. Working up concepts for a new Claiborne-owned retail store, aimed at eliminating the middleman. Tasks included naming it "First Issue," branding it, employing old US Postal graphics in the public domain. Its proposed turn-around time was nearly impossible, and

4. Simultaneously working on the many Liz Claiborne divisions, everything and anything that needed communicating.

The very first month, with no notice, Liz was gone; off on her segue. Into the frying pan. We'd survived a retainer much like that at *Woman's Day*. It was challenging for existing staff, forced to deal with, and sometimes take instruction from outsiders like us. I was pregnant, challenged to the max at business, and dealing with Mike in real time.

CHAPTER 42

The Pregnancy

I'd been making choices, "moving forward choices," the "finally we'll be a family" choices—to buy a washer and dryer for the Cornwall house—these were massive obstacles for Michael, 'Belly-Buster' obstacles. Tiny sparks left untended, unspoken, now ignited a firestorm.

"You know, if you install a washer, you're going to blow out the plumbing here," Michael said. "I'm telling you, whatever we have for a septic system is ancient!" (He was right; the septic would go and need replacing when years later, the washer was finally installed.)

"We need a laundry here, not 13 miles over the hill in Torrington!" I reasoned to myself. "I want to use cloth diapers; I don't want to dump disposable diapers in landfills." So naïve of me.

The differences in who Michael and I were when we met back in DC's parallel lines were so evident now with the baby coming. We had never lived together, except on vacations. From beneath the patina that coated our marriage when we lived apart, the hard part of marriage, living together, crept in.

Michael was feeling the pressure of doing it my way; it brought up old Marlboro crap. "This is as bad as my mother yanking us out of Southie. Why did it have to be her way?" The old concern of whether Michael liked his family, and how much he blamed Dot Creamer, had risen to the top. And as he'd felt about his mother's choices all along, he laid the new blame on me, "It was going so good," Mike thought.

"Why did *you* have to go and screw it up with a baby? I don't need a baby to feel good." Michael said, "We have a great sex life. We were happy without a baby." It stabbed me deeply. Crushed me. We had a great sex life: passionate, ardent and winsome all at once. It wasn't just *your* sex life you lost!

Over time, I stopped answering to avoid conflict. I'm sure it seemed to Michael that I simply wasn't listening anymore, but I had a baby inside me. I needed to protect it. Mike kept on, "With a baby, we will never walk the length of the Appalachian Trail. Never be thru-hikers[1], toughening up and melting off pounds, growing long, lean muscles."

It was a dream of Michael's to hike the Appalachian Trail. I wanted it too, either both of us all the way, or the both of us through parts. I realized the belly-buster accident smashed his dream. He walked with a slight limp and complained of pain in most of his lower body. I thought to myself that surely there must be something wrong with Michael or something troubling him that he wasn't telling me about. How could such a loving, intelligent man react this way? What was driving him? If he had a bigger fear of Agent Orange, and the damage it might cause, I remained uninformed. What could be the matter?

Then one day, Michael pulled down his rucksack from the top shelf of the closet in the front upstairs bedroom. It was the room he'd set up as his writing room, his small Smith Corona typewriter on what had been my college art desk, his papers neatly stacked on that side of the bed. He began to pack essentials that he would need when he left. He sat down on the far side of the bed, where, looking out, the vegetable garden that he and Peter had dug was perfectly framed in the eyelash window. The Appalachian Trail was only a mile away. Michael lit a cigarette and watched the sun sink beyond the tree line. Vietnam vets hated fucking tree lines. An ambush was waiting behind the tree line.

Michael wept.

---

1   Thru-hikers on the AT made or attempted the trek from Georgia to Mt. Katahdin in Maine.

When I got to Cornwall that weekend, I could see Mike's ruck was packed. I telephoned Peter, a good friend to both of us; asked him to come down from Newburyport, where he lived now. His home was in a partly defunct Airstream trailer on a property belonging to New England Antiquities. I explained the situation, and in the middle of telling it, I broke down. I never wanted to go it alone. I'd seen such unhappiness in single-parent families. I waited for Mike to start our family, and now I'm not going to have a family anymore; I'm going to have <u>a baby</u>.

In his patched-up car, Peter barely made it from northern Massachusetts. "Are you talking about leaving?" Pete asked Mike. The three of us sat in the afternoon of an otherwise beautiful, late spring day, under a grand maple tree, one that Mike wanted to take down because it was only ten feet from the house. It was our shade from afternoon sun; Peter and I had tapped it for syrup-making the previous spring when Mike was in Kentucky. Once you tap a tree and it gives you something as valuable as maple syrup, it's hard to imagine cutting it down, of walking away.

Pete took out his knife and whittled to take his mind off what he needed to say. By choice, Pete wasn't often the guy in charge. He simply started: "You are the two smartest people I know, and if you can't work this baby thing out, I give up on mankind." Michael heard enogh truth in Peter's words. The three of us cried, cradling each other, just as Michael and I had five years earlier with the, "Do you know who you're with?" vet.

"You need to get help if you can't work it out yourselves," Peter finished.

That week, Mike and I went together for counseling at the Hartford Vet Center with Mike's counselor, a combat veteran, and a nurse. And there it was again, Mike began, "I don't know why she has to go through with it..."

"Through with it? Don't you understand?" I pleaded, "You had to go to Vietnam. You wanted to be there more than anything else in the world; that's why you became a medic. They needed medics, you told me so." I kept going; it was more comfortable to speak up with someone there to mediate, "And three years ago you went back in the Army. You didn't ask me before you enlisted. You wanted to see if you could make it 'all right,' if maybe this time you'd come out a hero, not spit on in San Francisco or ridiculed in class. Can't you see?" I let the tears come with words I needed to say: "This is important for *me*. To have this baby, to see if love can make it better, to take away all the remorse, and chase away failure." Then I reminded him, "I never would have married you if we hadn't decided together on having a child."

They were quiet, then the counselor said, "So this is kind of like your Vietnam, is that right, Martha?" I could hardly look up, like Michael that day riding home from Levittown, where he'd first looked PTSD in the eye.

"I guess. I guess you could say that," I said.

CHAPTER 43

Turn, Turn, Turn Around

I felt better for meeting with his therapist. I wanted to believe we were on the right path. I wrote this afterward, that day in May 1987 to our baby, the child we had already named, Merrill.

* * *

Dear Merry,

Today, maybe, I feel that Michael might get the help he needs to get healthy. Today, I think maybe Michael might accept the nurturing of family that we have ahead of us. For you will be born in two-and-one-half months, and your mom and dad love each other very much. Today, the acknowledgment that Michael needed, which might enable him the freedom to love openly and genuinely, was given to him. So tonight, I have hope. Tonight, you and I and your dad do not have to live with fears of not being listened to, for today, your dad received confirmation from someone in whom he had staked so much.

Merry, I love you so. I look so forward to sharing a life with you, Little Thing. I can't wait to see your face and feel you suckle at my breast.

We will learn to love and deal daily with our pains.

We will teach as best we can, the daily lessons of love, and sharing with your dad. Together, we will grow and become a family each of us is happy to belong to. We'll do that for one another. I have new faith tonight.

I love you. I'm off to bed. You are kicking so hard. You must be hearing all of this. Good-night. Good night. Love, Your mom

I thought Michael understood from that session; for about three weeks, he seemed to. Then Michael abruptly changed his mind. In the mornings, I found him sleeping on the couch in the living room. He now read a book when I was around; he did not want to have a child. At first, he hid that from me. But I knew too well Mike's jolts; I was used to his transitions from sleeping soundly to not sleeping—insomnia taking hold. When I arrived in Connecticut, I recognized in his sweat-soaked pillowcases, evidence that the stressors had visited him during the week. I worried, was Michael any better now than before his re-up in the Army? He was doing that same pulling away, separating himself from me.

We barely used our bikes in the cellar; I suggested, "Let's do something. Let's go for a bike ride and a picnic." Michael agreed to a ride; he nixed the picnic. We headed east out Rte 4, then north beyond the landfill. I worked out with other pregnant women in New York City; thought I was in shape.

I didn't plan for the ride to go so long; we ended up pedaling three to four miles to West Cornwall, the sun was fading. When we were on Rte 7, Mike just wanted to get home, away from me, away from the baby. Home was at least 3 ½ miles farther. He took point while I, exhausted, tried to steady my bike. He sped up, his anger driving his pace. I fretted over how safe it was to get so heated. We barely spoke.

I walked my bike up the last hill to home. He was already inside. I locked my bike in the cellar; Michael left his out. That night someone stole it. We never rode again. It was Sunday; I left early. I didn't blame him; I was the one trying to do something, go for a ride. But he was so self-centered, and that whole second half of the ride, I felt him trying to kill our baby, already seven and a half months inside me.

I said, "Listen, if you don't want to do Lamaze with me, don't. I'll get Alene. I'm sure she'll coach the delivery. But would you come to the city when I go into labor, please?"

Mike didn't answer, but popped open a beer and walked outside. He wasn't rude; the pregnancy made me averse to the smell of beer—I got so nauseous. Mike bought himself some space with that. The odor on Mike's breath was the most troublesome; it reeked like a rotting liver or how I imagined a rotting liver might smell. In MVP's small studio elevator, I had the worst time. Once after an unusually slow ride down, I couldn't hold my breath any longer, and I got the heaves. Mike said, "You really can't stand my guts, can you?" Exactly, that must be where that term came from.

"No. It's the same with messengers who drink." I said, "Don't take it personally."

But he did, it was apparent. On the Friday I started my maternity leave, Mike came to New York to be with me. We were headed out to an evening movie with friends, and I was lagging at the door to the apartment. The three of them were already on the stairs. Mike stepped back to the door and said, "Will you ever weigh less than 200 pounds?"

I could barely think for trying to breathe. I staggered backward, into the apartment and closed the bathroom door behind me. I sat on the toilet, collected myself to the degree that one could, having heard that. I came out and said, "I'm not going. Go without me." Then I said, "That is the meanest thing I ever heard anyone say."

Michael responded "Oh, okay," in that innocent boyish way, that placed blame somewhere in the never-land of his pre-pubescence. He closed the door and left.

I lay down on the sofa, crying from deep within, and fell asleep as children do, snot wetting the pillow. I woke two hours later in crippling waves of labor, got up, crossed with difficulty to the wall phone in the kitchen. The movie should be over. Mike answered the beeper he carried and called back. "Mike?" I looked down at a hugely bloody thing that just dropped from between my legs and plopped onto the kitchen floor. Was it the "plug" or what remained of it, an ominous brownish muck. Was it my baby? I cried out, "Come quick, I think my water may have broken, but something else is wrong." I then called Alene, who reached me first.

When Michael arrived, no apologies were forthcoming. He was all business. This wasn't how it's supposed to be... From that moment, as he whisked me to the hospital in a cab, until Merrill's birth, it played over and over in my head: This isn't how it's supposed to be.

CHAPTER 44

NYU Medical

(Tense change. This will always be Present in my mind.) I want to deliver natural, no meds, but after several visits to my pre-birthing stall, my OBGYN begins reprimanding, "You're not working hard enough."

I'm working very hard, I think. I made it clear, something I learned in birthing class: "I don't want an enema."

She has the nurse give me an enema. Scolds me again. Comes back, looking haggard (she's in her first trimester of pregnancy and doesn't know it yet) and says, "We're going to have to induce you. It's past the witching hour." She would know!

Mike is feeding me ice chips in pre-delivery, alternating with Alene. While we are all together, Alene says, "You know, this is probably going to be your only child, Michael. I won't be offended in the least if you want to be in the delivery room with your wife." Michael only looks. "You still have time; think about it." Alene has the generosity of the world within her.

Michael decides to go in with me to deliver. When Merrill crests to the outside world, her face blue, she clocks an Apgar[1] score of 1.5 (out of a possible 10). STAT. Mike gets it, ER, ED kind of talk. "*STAT. Get neonatal down here right away,*" the OBGYN hollers to her nurse. A flurry of white coats descends from the floor above. She points to

---

1   APGAR Score: A means of measuring a newborn's health at the time of birth. Ten is excellent.

Merrill, screams, "Intubate her!" She walks over to me, ripped open from birthing, I am bleeding. Michael stands at the foot of the bed looking pale, then takes my hand, holds it tightly. In the corner of the delivery room, Michael watches from the corner of his eye. He is on the far side of my bed. He's moved as far as possible from the embodiment of his fears. Not a sound from Merry; the doctors huddle. I crane my neck as they wheel her away, up the elevator to the Neonatal ICU.

Michael steps back. He is afraid to look at my face; I see him, avoiding me. Then I stop looking at him and close my eyes. My Merry's not well! Can they fix her?

The doctor is sewing me up. I remember the delivery room from nightmares since, from being there too long. There is only a foggy sense of eight long months of knowing she is with me. Time spent waiting to meet my child inside. Who does she look like? Does she have long dark hair like mine as a baby? Will she take my nipple? Does she look intelligent? Is she long? Who will she be like? Mike or Me? Things we can tell just looking at her. But I can't look at her; I didn't have the chance.

It's past. Tense. They, whoever they are, wheel me out to the hallway. Alene is waiting; she has figured out most of what's happened. The three of us cluster. I have been so wrapped, muffled in my own emotions that I barely hear Michael.

"I knew this would happen," Mike says.

Alene tries to say nothing but the pain on her beautiful Kabuki-like face is beyond words: for Merrill, for Michael, for being there to see this turn of events. It carves furrows in her brow.

I wanted to ask Michael why, if he knew, why didn't he tell me? But I can't get the words through my teeth. (Or maybe I asked him, and he answered, "Because you wouldn't listen.") I think that is possibly true. I owe that truth to come out now, like my baby already out and upstairs. They'll save her, I think, praying. They'll save her, Michael envisions, cursing. Whatever worried Michael about Agent Orange—the stuff he hadn't told me—that he and his vet counselor or the group therapy members discussed—-people who already knew—began sloshing in his brain. But I did not know. Like warnings from the past, from the VA: We have determined that your unit fought in areas contaminated by Agent Orange, which he never mentioned to me. Michael never went to get tested. Not even during his re-up. *Nada.* I did not know.

In the hospital hallway, just outside the delivery room, there are spent beds on which babies were born that evening. Healthy babies, I'll later learn. They've jacked the beds up, lining the corridor; I sit on mine with its side down in a chair-like position. I am numb down there. The stitches hurt, I smell of Betadine, my legs are shaky, exhausted beyond any reality. It flashes to me: Michael is going to kill himself. I only wonder when.

It changed my life instantly; part of me was gone—the hoping part, my Merry, the part I believed could make everything all right. I thought nothing of the meanness of Mike's 200 pound words as they wheeled me to recovery. (Ha! Recovery.) What happened before the birth had split so far away, as we spun off in a new dimension. Together we sailed silently in a capsule of doom, he, in control now to steer us to a new planet—Saturn perhaps. I held no power except to hold myself upright, cry silent tears to honor them, the suffering father and daughter.

What did I do wrong? Was I too old? —almost 37? A bad egg? Stripping lead paint during pregnancy? The pre-natal exercise class? The food poisoning I retched through? An oddity of coming together, the two of us? Overheating on that ludicrously long bicycle trip? Residue anger? Sinful behavior? Or was it exposure to Agent Orange as Michael thought?

Too late, he told me, "I knew something was wrong." Later his vet rep would say that Michael spoke of it mid-pregnancy, "If anything happens to that baby, I don't know what I'll do." All the while, not telling me. Not helping me see into and beyond his fear. He could not share it—maybe it was connected to that, "*You'll never know, Martha, no matter how many times I tell you.*" Or that stare I first saw in DC, that blocked others on the other side.

And Michael, what were his thoughts as he cabbed home that early morning with Alene? He would never tell me about his uniforms in Nam, soaked with Agent Orange defoliant that his recon team had crawled around in for days. Years later, Ron told me that officers instructed Mike, a LRRP coming in, wet with the stuff from the field— "Just throw your uniforms on the fire. You can never clean that shit out." (Or Mike's VA notices back in 1978 and '79, warnings to come in for testing.)

CHAPTER 45

Wakeup

When your DEROS date approached in Vietnam, heck, even before that, soldiers counted down to the night before they would board a plane for their -ROS—their Return from Over Seas. It wasn't unheard of that the day a Newbie reported in-country for their year of fear, he/she counted the remainder of a tour as "364 days and a WAKEUP." Once a soldier approached a wakeup—if you could survive the last days without some significant shit going down—a wakeup signified a joyous thing. You were going home. My 42-week wakeup was defeating.

All the babies in NICU were either BGs or BBs; my Baby Girl was a BG. Maybe it was a privacy measure, to call the babies such, and label all their test tubes with BG or BB. Perhaps not give them names to keep them distant, just in case. … I didn't want to go there. They said the vials for little babies' blood samples were small, and the spaces for their names were smaller, so it was easier to write BB or BG.

That first night as a NICU baby, Beegee Creamer had her blood drawn; it was required to test and see if her mother was on drugs. A mother was not asked first, just checked through her kid's blood. Beegee Creamer was not a crack baby; NYU didn't take my word for it—didn't ask. It was offensive to me that my struggling infant had blood drawn for a drug check.

When I went upstairs to see her, Merrill had tubes all over her body, one up her nose, sensors on her chest, a line out a blood vessel at her temple. I was alone, thought I might collapse. Later that morning, the same doctor who sucked Merry away from me— "*STAT.* **Get neonatal down here right away**," came to sit on my bed as I was ordering a machine to help me pump my breasts. "I don't think you should pump milk," she sneered it seemed, "I wouldn't get close to that baby. Not at all."

The 4-bed room where they wheeled me was empty after I delivered, a huge relief. I could cry in peace. I was working, and I still was, contrary to what that witch doctor said—my baby couldn't move, she couldn't help. Merrill's birth was finished and a new trauma about to begin—yes, this was my Vietnam, I'll tell that to Michael's VA shrink if I ever see her again. And what's this for Mike, his third Vietnam tour?

One by one, the new mothers started to fill the other beds, and within a day, they filled my room. At first, it was fine—mothers being there. But then the babies came in, babies who moved and cried and goo'ed and broke my heart so much so that I would escape to the BG-filled NICU. I hated my room and the joy just walking in, with those presents and their smiles. I had not learned grace yet, I'm sorry. A new mom in maternity and no baby? Error. Not processing. What's wrong with *that* one? I couldn't bear their suffocating happiness closing in. Staying in University Hospital to be near my baby was not what I needed right now. I needed to be home.

Or did I? Going home, I found a room filled with lost hope—baby furniture and a beautiful quilt my sister Barbara had given her—and stuffed animals, physical reminders that Merrill was probably never coming home. Oh, God, Michael went home alone to all of this while I was in the hospital!

Michael was cautious, forming his thoughts first. He had no friends in town; his buddy Tom went back to Fort Campbell, though he wrangled a few days to stay with Michael while I was in the hospital. Friends sent cards and fruit baskets. Michael went outside to smoke his cigarettes or maybe to get air. My stitches hurt, and Michael, the medic, checked on me to see that I was okay at least down there.

We—or rather, me—I hoped that Merrill's medical issues would be solved, and he carefully couched his informed opinion.

"We have to get the crib out," I said.

"I didn't want to mention it to you. I can take it apart," Michael responded.

"Dottie says someone in her old neighborhood will take it," I said. I half resented that our baby problems were common knowledge. Heck, everything annoyed me.

And I confess, at times, I just broke down sobbing to Michael. He held me, mainly on the open futon that once was our couch. Sitting up or lying down and weeping together.

"Do you think we'll end up losing our house?" Michael queried quietly. I had thought of that myself. We just didn't know what would happen on top of our baby in the hospital. It was a terrible place to be.

How I missed her:

> August 7th, 1987
> 5 Days Old
> Dear Merry,
> I needed to talk to you this morning. I'm here, and you're there, in the hospital—NYU Medical Center—uptown and east of me. I hope you're not hurting right now, not lonely, and not afraid. Whatever else is ailing you, I pray it's not fear that you aren't loved and watched over and cared for.
>
> We got so close, you and I, all those months together. All those talks in the shower each morning. I have a hard time showering now. I cry because you're not with me. I can't talk to you quite the same way, and I can't bring you back in *vitro* to a safe, protected stage inside of me.

Was it safe? Were you as healthy and kicking as I remember? I called you my soccer player. I knew you'd come out and be like your mom—active and rough and ready for all this—I knew nothing of you. In my liberalness to not mold you, and in all my conservation of those things necessary to do while you were still in me, I didn't ever imagine that you would have such a hard time...I thought to do everything I could to care for you before you came out, for us to see your pretty face. And now, well, Merrill, I'm so scared and missing you and needing badly for all of us to be together. I want you to get well, please.

Your dad's asleep on the couch where we've slept together since I left the hospital. He sweats at night. This whole thing has been hard on him too. He never knew real love, to recognize it, and trust it lying there in NICU. He loves you very much. I see it in him—deep and sad, and rich like a chord he found within himself.

We are blessed by your presence here with us. Blessed because every day, our love for you and our love for each other grows and grows. And it has picked up where the belly stopped.

Aw, Merry, I don't know what to do to make it all go away. I'm not at my best right now. I'm driven by stress and the urge to always be with you, but I lack that clarity that at times I possess when I'm able to wade through extraordinary situations. I think of your birth as an extraordinary situation—one we came through together— doubts and fears and sheer delight with you inside me. Dad too. His undulations of finding his way—in and out—joining up with us in the very end, to share what meant the world to us—your coming.

I guess, to some degree, I'm numb with the turn

of events. I—like all those good doctors working so diligently on you—I don't have an answer. I keep holding out for some chord within me that will keep me sane and still believing that you will recover, without building up false hopes that inevitably will eat away at me and everything I've dreamed of.

You are all I dreamt of. For months we shared our lives, and I somehow expected to keep on doing that. I'm sorry I cry—I haven't lost my faith. I'm trying to build it against the knowledge that all my dreams and expectations didn't help make it any better. Didn't give me what I really wanted, and I sit here, so afraid to want anything I can't have.

Thank you for your father. You brought his love back where it belonged, and I'll forever thank you for that. Whatever else, Mer, thank you. I love you so.
Please wake up. Mom

Right away, the hospital assigned us a social worker. Dennis was great, explaining that most likely, our baby could never live at home. She would need constant care. He explained the policy of making her a ward of the state to manage costs. It was a huge relief. Then he laid on me the new reality of *Advocacy*. "You're going to have to be your baby's Advocate now." I remember he told me alone, outside on the front lawn before they built new buildings on First Avenue.

I flashed to remember what I knew of Advocacy. "But if anybody does sin, we have an advocate with the Father—Jesus Christ, the Righteous"—1 John 2:1. I felt like a sinner. I felt that I had done something wrong. I was still a practicing Episcopalian; we were married in St. George's Church. Mike was a fallen Catholic. Now I was in the hands of Dennis, our social worker, to bring us the communion of the liberal and holy state of New York into which Merrill was born. One of a handful of states that would guide us through our Hell, lessen the financial burden on parents of kids born into inexplicable lives. It would be okay, but we only knew that after the fact. The early stress of losing everything, on top of having a sick baby, hung over us like the proverbial axe in the cellar. I prayed that Merrill would miraculously recover.

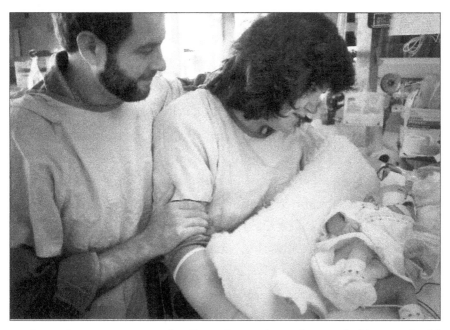

Mike and Me in NYU Medical's NICU with BeeGee, probably a week old.

CHAPTER 46

Waking Up

Waking up was Hell. No social worker there to sign away the morning, to fill out forms to avoid the reality of waking from a nightmare that wasn't a nightmare, was it? Merrill and Michael filled my dreams as well as my daytime hours: What now? Over and over, I woke in night sweats, sometimes in tears; would there ever be an end to worry? For weeks, the doctors searched for something to go on, some treatment, some similar case reported to the Network of Terrible Cases to be on the lookout for. We called Ellen Levine, then Editor-in-Chief of *Good Housekeeping*, she was always so smart about facts, and her husband was an obstetrician. A Honcho. High up. Ellen asked for facts; she and her husband looked into it. Two or three instances of hope from the hospital: "Come in, we want to talk to you about a new finding we have. Michael and I would respond together, go in. Maybe…." Nope. Then repeat. And repeat again.

Michael aptly put it, "It's a practice. That's why they call it Medical Practice." I don't mean to make light of it, because Agent Orange poisoning, which Merrill most likely was impaired by, was happening worldwide and in Vietnam, but, again, like PTSD, it had not been widely diagnosed. The hospitals were not aware of these cases. Ellen's husband contacted Cornell Medical Center, one of the most prominent neurological research institutes globally. I remember rushing fresh blood samples to the 168th Street Center, Michael and I speeding up the West Side

Highway with this little ice chest. No one had any findings to compare it to, probably because the government certainly didn't want the families of these tiny poisoned kids to hit them up for compensation. Many of the children died in the delivery room (as Michael wished Merrill had— "The doctor should never have resuscitated her"). But Merry had her parents' tenacity; she would linger for ten and a half months.

Wishing and praying were hurtful. Over the first few weeks, I watched as parents came through that NICU. I watched if their kids got better. Many did. I also observed a stream of quick deaths when they would ask me to leave the tiny NICU so that parents could have time alone. I was there on days when they executed DNR (Do Not Resuscitate) orders, and the parents might stay and be there for their child's end.

I thought August would never end.

CHAPTER 47

After Birth

The long week after Merrill's birth, Michael asked for a leave of absence from the Job Service and drove down to New York with more clothes. It was painful for him to stay for extended visits since the waiting room for the small 4-6 baby NICU was on the same level as the Medivac pad. The helicopters brought Mike back to the boonies. I understood. I remembered our Billy Joel/Levittown encounter. What I probably didn't acknowledge—going through my private Hell—was that his new trauma got heaped atop the old one. I thought he thought it was Agent Orange doing this to his baby. But he knew that this was Agent Orange that had done this to Merrill. Mike's war just kept keeping on. When would it stop coming back? We were enduring a combined trauma, living in our separate ones.

I wrote to Maryanne more than a month after Beegee's birth.

> September 12, '87
>
> Maryanne—
>
> Got your letter a while ago, and events have prevented
> an early response. Mike and I are now in NYC, awaiting
> word from a vast staff of doctors on whether our daughter
> Merrill, born August 2nd will survive, should survive, or
> anything at all.

After a reasonably normal birth labor, Merrill came out unconscious and had aspirated meconium[1]. However, many babies are born with meconium poisoning. In this case, standard revival methods failed. They intubated her and have basically kept her alive since birth. (Note: it wasn't meconium—MVD)

All efforts to locate (another baby with) her illness have failed thus far. She's basically neurologically asleep without normal reflexes such as swallowing, sucking, and blinking of eyes. She's otherwise a beautiful baby—perfectly formed and looks a bit like both of us.

We're pretty bummed out, as you might imagine. I just felt you should know even though there's nothing but prayers you can help with. Maybe from your side of the world (Swaziland), it might re-balance things here.

We're both on leave—me for the past month—Michael's missed three weeks. We go up north weekly to collect mail, etc. Otherwise, we're in NY. I'll leave now for Mike to write. Take care. Keep in touch, Martha.

Hello Maryanne—
Short update on Martha's letter. It's been hard for me to write, as you can imagine. We had a conference with the doctors, who have said that they've run out of good options. Merrill will never come home—she will, at best, be institutionalized for a much-shortened life span, and will never improve neurologically beyond what we see now, which is nil... Cause: Inadequate brain stem formation + function...Reason: Unknown... Maybe we'll know someday after an autopsy, maybe not.

---

1   No one had discovered her cleft palate yet. What else was hidden?

(Here, I questioned Michael's strict blame-setting on Agent Orange at this point. Wouldn't he have been more adamant?)

One-in-a-million happening, and we drew the short straw. They counseled not being aggressive on life support measures... I agree. But it's hard. Puts our lives, all three of us, in near-total limbo. I'm on a leave of absence, but have to go back the 18th to at least finish out my "Trial Period."

Don't know what will happen from there, but we'll cope... I'll write more later. Don't get down—I try not to. I'm just resigned, that's all. Write and tell me tales of The Murky Green! Love, Mike C.

If Michael's portion seems upbeat, it did to me too. He took on the role of guiding me through my blinding motherhood, especially considering my delivery room revelation that Michael would kill himself. I wonder if this is how Michael behaved when his father left the family? Did he assume the kind of control he was exhibiting now? He had written before when we met: "...*Years ago, I got into the habit of going through certain times entirely by instinct, leaving the absorption process, the integration of events into my psyche, until late-night...sometime after the fact. My survival ... depended on that separation of the physical from the philosophical... Medics needed to think, curse, and cry, too, but it had to be done where and when the people who depended on you couldn't see it.*"

Somebody told me that Steven, the youngest brother who went on to become a Captain in one of Boston's firehouses, took on most of the Creamer family care. Mike moved to South Boston for some of that time.

✱　✱　✱

Michael again returned to work; there was little he could do. It was bad timing for him; it was then that the Veteran's Administration realized that job retention needed addressing. Michael's vet desk needed to treat the whole person. When a veteran came in, Mike needed to assess: Did the vet have a house to live in, or clean clothes to wear for an interview? Did her teeth need fixing before sending her out? etc. Michael trained in those new aspects; his crucial and challenging role was moved within the Disabled Veterans Outreach Program (DVOP). As a DVOP specialist, Mike was "providing intensive services to meet the employment needs of disabled veterans and other eligible veterans, with the maximum emphasis directed toward serving those who are economically or educationally disadvantaged, including homeless veterans.²"

Michael's day was complicated by the crisscrossing details of vets' lives, and Vietnam vets were complicated. Tom "Sully" Sullivan, one vet who became a good friend of ours, told me Michael found him living in the woods in a lean-to because his wife had kicked him out of the house. ("Oh, but that was warranted," Tom said.) Tom was the product of a single-parent, alcoholic home. As a boy, he cleaned up his mother regularly. After serving with the US Marines in Vietnam, Sully became an alcoholic and crept into a cesspool of worthlessness. Tom, for a time, lived as a sad remnant of what the era left behind. He rode in patriotic parades around New England in a holding-pen, portraying POWs and MIAs whose unsettled whereabouts left cankers on the war's already ugly face.

Michael Creamer literally went into the woods, pulled Sully out, and got him functioning.

2　Department of Veterans Affairs website.

CHAPTER 48

The AT

A month or so into Merrill's life, Mike asked me to come to the country one weekend and join him for a hike on the Appalachian Trail. "Come, it will be good for you. You need some exercise." (Shades of the "ever weigh less than 200-lbs?") "You can't run to the hospital every chance you get," he said. Michael was right, but it was hard to admit.

We belonged to the Appalachian Mountain Club. To hike, you didn't have to be a member. Mike, Vinnie, and Pete had hiked parts of it many times. The Trail traversed north aside Cornwall, on the Kent and Sharon side, crossed Rte 4 just west of where Rte 7 intersected.[1] On our side of the bridge, Richard Bramley's Cornwall Package Store offered a free beer to any thru-hiker making it up from Georgia. There were 99 different brands from which to choose.

The summer before my pregnancy, Michael was home often. We met a thru-hiker at the package store, picking up his free beer. After chatting, Michael asked me if he could invite him home. I wondered why not? "Would you like to come to our house and maybe take a shower? You could have a home-cooked meal, spend the night," Michael asked.

"Sure," said the man, not long on words.

'What's your name?" Michael asked in the car.

---

1   Later, the Appalachian Trial was rerouted around Cornwall, up the Sharon side of Rte. 7.

"Oh, we all have 'handles' on the Trail; they call me Hiker. That's what I go by, Hiker."

"Alright, Hiker. Say, we're just debating picking up a couple of lobsters over in Sharon, is that something you'd like?" Mike asked.

"Don't know. Never had lobster," Hiker replied.

✱ ✱ ✱

Hikers on the Trail smell a lot like smoke from sitting around campfires; this one looked like smoke as well. The Trail fires covered Hiker in a sooty blackness reminiscent of the slides from Mike's LRRP team. Michael drove us home and stayed with Hiker as he showered; I went over to Sharon to pick up three lobsters; it was our Fourth of July celebration. When I got back, Hiker cleaned up good, and Michael and I went about trying to solve lobster cooking, which, if you haven't cooked one, can be rough.

✱ ✱ ✱

We ate the lobsters, as the sun was getting low before losing it behind the tree line. Afterward, I ran out with garbage to dump in our compost pile. As I turned the corner of the house and onto the patio, there was Hiker, one hand leaning against the house, the other holding onto his whizzer, whizzing a stream of urine just where I was going to walk. Had it been brighter, or had I any notion of what becomes of one living so long in the wilderness, I would have made an abrupt about-face. But I was tired, and racing as I usually did, I nearly walked into it, causing Whizzer, I mean Hiker and his whizzer, to turn and almost spatter me. He was embarrassed. I was embarrassed. I ran inside and told Michael, who laughed hysterically. Hiker walked in all embarrassed; we all laughed. He opted to spend the night outside. By morning Hiker was gone.

(I remembered that comic relief from back when it happened and thought we might need it right now to get us through.) Before Merrill's birth Michael and I, thespians at heart, acted out scenes of a family in conflict—an Albee play or better yet, a Sam Shephard. Michael was keeping his distance from my protruding belly, me lamenting whatever would become of me. Then the curtain rose again, and there was Merrill. Michael became more attentive to me, kept whatever dread he felt from penetrating our perimeter. He found things for us to do.

Merrill introduced new characters on stage. Significant among them, a bespectacled neonatologist, Dr. Wasserman, who by the luck of our draw, became Merrill's doctor. Randi Wasserman stepped forward from a wall of doctors with no answers, a Greek chorus that mumbled to move the action ahead. Randi shared her personal story of loss with us at a time we really needed it. I really needed it; to know that choices people make can turn deadly on them. Her doctor-husband died of an incurable illness he extracted while in the tropics on a trip he needed to go on, alone, before becoming a father, which he deemed, likely to tie him down. He passed within days of their baby's birth. Randi became a close friend; she encouraged me to get out and hike.

With Merrill in the hospital and no new findings (there never would be any, but I hadn't given up on miracles), Michael and I day-hiked with a local Appalachian Trail club. I remember wearing sunglasses and not smiling. I hadn't relearned how to smile yet. Michael was trying with all his might to prod me along. I had lost most of the pregnancy bulk, but I was still overweight. I walked as close to the back of the hikers as Michael would allow and then fell back, leaning against a tree so no one could see my shoulders rising and falling, sobbing away. I hated hiking then. Hated hiking with them, with him. Hating that I even said that. (About him.) Hated Connecticut. But what I truly hated was being 100 miles away from New York University Hospital, not seeing Merrill all weekend.

And I hated people calling now, months later, well into the fall, maybe at the office even, and saying, "I'm so sorry, Martha, that I haven't reached out before, but I didn't know what to say,"… and them crying unstoppably on the phone. I wished that I didn't have to console them.

"It's okay. Really, it's okay. I'm over the worst." With Merry in the hospital, I wasn't yet. "How are you otherwise?"

I was so sorry I put those words close to their mouths. Don't anyone dare ask, 'How are you otherwise?' There was no otherwise.

Sorrow was perfectly fine, and people could share in that. They might often take big chunks of the heavy, tacky stuff of sadness away when they hung up, left the table, or closed the door, but only if, and when they did it at an appropriate time near the loss. What hurt most was to be dragged through morass again, months later, and the scab would come off, pain deep inside would resurface, and nightmares too.

CHAPTER 49

Disabled

I went back to speed-walking, an exercise I preferred vs. jogging or power-walking, which the supermarket *Vogues* called it. (I remember when *Vogue* wasn't sold in the supermarket when homogeneous media wasn't rampant.) I would walk four miles in an hour. It was cathartic.

Mike's hips were giving out from jumps he'd made from airplanes and helicopters. The Belly-Buster injury that Mike sustained in Boot Camp never fully healed, and of course, new emotional wounds were substantial; they too layered on. In a more comprehensive, under-published truth, muscle and joint pain were stacking up as chronic complaints by those suffering from Agent Orange[1] exposure. Agent Orange caused other significant ailments: depression, anxiety, insomnia, and lethargy, all the maladies Mike Creamer suffered.[2] Mike tried to jog the loping inclines on Rte 4 but scrapped that plan when pain consumed him. Mike didn't have catharsis.

He sought out a weekly group-therapy session at the Vet Center in Hartford. It was farther than he wanted to drive, but it was all that was available. He encouraged Sully to drive with him from Litchfield, about half-way. Gary Millard, a navy pilot from West Hartford, was also in that group. Cornwall was in the remote NW corner of Connecticut amid

---

1   Nicosia, p. 458.
2   Jones, "Countless disabled infantrymen (from the Gulf War and Afghanistan) seek relief from the aches and pains of bodies broken down by the weight of their equipment.

rolling hills and spent mountains, making for dark winding roads where stag-leaping deer were prone to crash into speeding cars. Three seasons of the year, the slightest snowstorm turned to whiteout conditions on that piece of the road up over the back of Mohawk Mountain on the way to Hartford; so more than once, we had to wait for sanding plows to forge a path, and get us down. At night, when the vets' group met, Mike would have preferred the comforts of his Camels, a blazing fire, and a pack of beer. Nights he didn't have to venture out, Mike sat home, patted his cat, Tiger, and when he could wrangle it, smoked some weed to soothe the pain and sorrow. As he opened to the empathy of vets' sorrows—*he wasn't the only one hurting*—Mike decided to file for disability from the VA.

Mike's VVA rep was a kind and handsome vet named Jim Tackett, who drove a small pickup truck with a similarly small shack built atop the back. Jim told me that the whole setup was, "Perfect for someone like me who loves to fish," but his eyes betrayed a certain sadness that was also a dead giveaway for a Vietnam veteran. Jim would drive out to our house and give us instructions on what needed to be done next, always ready to help.

Applying for disability was an obnoxiously lengthy process requiring Michael's personal letter-writing, an accounting of how his life had changed, my accounting of the same, two or three testimonies of people who knew him before and after the war, his mother included, and doctors' letters from the VA shrink and medical side. Charts had to be filled out, letters copied and sent in triplicate and such. Busy work. But it paid off: Mike was declared 50% disabled for PTSD and osteoarthritis, as well as for emotional issues. Michael's non-taxable monthly income grew close to $700 and would allow him to work less or take a less stressful job. I don't think he would have bowed to such a "lowly" thing on his own; he was South Boston Irish. To him, this disability was the dole. But now he had the support of the other vets in the group, many of whom were also filing. "Hey, it's America," Gary, the Nam navy pilot shot down twice, said. "We fought to keep it free."

✳ ✳ ✳

The disability check was due compensation for Michael, not just for the injuries he sustained in Vietnam but also for his baby girl. While I was unwilling for a while to admit it, Michael came to understand that Beegee's neurological malformation was all about the Agent Orange that his LRRP team took cover in. The brass were aware of the toxic contaminant in the field; now, the VA was doing what it could to downplay complications from Agent Orange. The VA's way was to avoid responsibility—provide minimal services.

That outreach mandated by Congress from the Department of Defense alerting Mike to "probable exposure to the toxin Agent Orange," and asking him to come in for a blood screening probably wouldn't have changed a thing, even if he'd gone in. The alert came as findings were released following a ten-year hush-up by Dow Chemical revealing staggering facts about Dioxin, the main component of Agent Orange. Testing veterans would prove inadequate as it consisted of only a urinalysis and simple blood test. Vets with Agent Orange exposure should have received "full blood workup, chest X-ray, liver and renal function profiles, sperm count, and a referral to a dermatologist.[3]

✳ ✳ ✳

Manufacturers of Dioxin hid evidence that it was "the most powerful carcinogen known.[4] "After an explosion in a European manufacturing plant revealed its volatility, Dioxin brewers discovered a safer way of mixing its batches. In 1960, years before ground troops were dispatched to Vietnam, Dow Chemical US paid $33,000 (a substantial amount in those days) for that deadly formula from the European

---

3   Nicosia, p. 459.
4   Nicosia, p. 440.

manufacturer who slapped a 10-year non-disclosure on Dow US. In April of 1970, when the gag order was finally up, the US Surgeon General issued a warning to put an immediate stop to the use of Agent Orange in Vietnam. The first VVA newsletter in the Spring of 1979 reported: "Dioxin was 100,000 to one million times more potent than Thalidomide,[5]" a drug used in the late 1950-60s on women to prevent miscarriages. Thalidomide disfigured babies; now, similar babies were born in America of Vietnam-vet spouses, not to mention mothers in Vietnam.

The US Government didn't want the onus on them and tried to stop the truth of Dioxin from making it into the mainstream press. In testimony before a Senate Veterans Affairs Committee hearing in 1979, Maureen Ryan, a mother of a severely disabled Agent Orange child testified. "Agent Orange has come home from those battlefields with our men…what the United States and what our Vietnam veterans did not know was that they carried home a tremendous legacy with them." When she was interrupted, she lost her syntax, but she still delivered this message, "They (the men) did not know that genetically on those battlefields were (the future of) their children.[6]

Of course, this is all latent information. Back then, I would tell people that Beegee was "neurologically not hooked up right."

---

5   Nicosia, p. 447.
6   Ibid.

CHAPTER 50

Rescue Op

Katherine Snedeker stayed at MVP, postponing her move to Dallas. With Beegee still in the hospital, Katherine saved my life, choosing to support me when a dark cloud followed me like Charlie Brown's Linus character. I went back to work. Back in the saddle, ha! I was readying for my first Monday morning organizational meeting, and one of my staff asked, "Are you okay?"

"I am," I said. "I am, I think."

Then another asked, "Are you okay?" "How are you?"

MVP Staff around this time. Clockwise from left: Gregg Lipman, Katherine Snedeker, Norico Kanai, Heidi (from Mass Art), Michelle, and a pregnant Martha. Notice my mini jump wings. Norico had been with us nearly since the beginning.

Then I started the meeting, only to stop. And I told my staff, "Already three of you have asked if I'm okay today. I'm okay. And I'm not okay. It's going to change all the time. And one day will be more okay than another day, and maybe months from now," I said, honking into a tissue, "I won't be okay. I'll start crying, and you'll be worried. I want you to know that it's okay not to be okay because it's really sucky that this has happened, and it's what we got. And it is time to get to work, so, okay?"

They laughed. I cried. We all cried. I laughed. By the time we ended the meeting, we were all okay. Or not okay.

CHAPTER 51

Tell Me a Story

It is said we all live "the story of our lives." This story stays with us; it becomes a factor in shaping our outlook until a new story comes along, which supplants "the old story of our lives." This book opens with a picture of baby Michael posing atop an ottoman, beaming brightly, wearing his father's Army jacket. All you can see is his head and the jacket, which covers his entire body, and a Christmas tree in the background. That would make it Christmas 1952; Michael is fourteen months old.

Other people can impact the story of our lives. Whoever clothed Michael as a soldier helped shape his life, and the photograph itself plays its part. I learned about this story concept studying with the late graphic design guru Milton Glaser that first autumn of 1973, in New York City. Glaser wanted each of us to explore our memories and illustrate "The Story of Our Lives." I recognized mine stuck back when I was six when my mother mindlessly left me outside of my aunt's locked, quasi-suburban house, fourteen miles from home. I remember thinking something significant: I alone would have to take care of myself. I knew immediately as Glaser assigned it that it was the story of my life. I was stuck; the magnitude of being left was weighty.

I finally got unstuck 26 years later when I met Michael Creamer on Saturday, November 13, 1982, in Washington, DC. That story lasted about five years and ended five years later when Merrill was born and the story evolved into this: I gave birth to a sick little girl with an Apgar score of 1.5. She probably shouldn't have lived. Her brain was not hooked up right. A team of doctors labored to save her. She lived in Neonatal Intensive Care at New York University Medical Center.

Looking back at Michael, I wonder if the story of his life ever changed. From seventeen, his story whirred around like this:

- I signed up to go into the military right out of high school.

- I trained to jump out of airplanes; I became a paratrooper.

- I served with the 173rd Airborne Brigade in Vietnam.

- I was awarded Soldier of the Month in my medical unit in Vietnam; the battalion commander let me pick where I would serve next.

- I chose the N/75 Rangers; I became a LRRP and went into Vietnam's jungles in six-man teams to hunt down the enemy.

- I returned home from Vietnam alive.

Then

- I became a Vietnam Veteran on the day I got home, and my father abandoned our family.

- I went to Africa as a bush medic, a skill I learned in Vietnam.

- I survived Zaire's jungles, though I had to fight an enemy to get home alive, as in Vietnam.

- I hooked up with the 173rd Airborne in Washington, DC, at the Vietnam Veterans Memorial Dedication. That saved my life.

- I met a woman I knew at the dedication who wanted to know about Vietnam.[1]

---

1 "Falling in love was Mike's R&R for years while he was fighting the war in his mind between Vietnam, Zaire, his father, and his hunt for purpose...no one keeps a suicidal person alive; they keep themselves alive and do it because someone else is their purpose for living."--S. Brignoli.

- I went back into the Army to get closure for Vietnam.

- I survived that. (It wasn't like Vietnam.) Still, I got injured; came out alive.

- I have a baby, neurologically impaired, from wading through Agent Orange in Vietnam.

- She probably shouldn't have come out alive. A team of doctors fought to save her. She lives in the Neonatal Intensive Care Unit at New York University Medical Center.

Mike kept leaving pieces of his Vietnam story, morsel by morsel, like Hansel who had to find his way home, all the while moving deeper and deeper into the woods—

CHAPTER 52

Beegee and Me

Little by little, life got better for me, right after it was the worst. Three months into her life, a nurse dropped her in NICU, and though the consequences of Merrill being dropped were probably nothing—given her Quality of Life—some baby under that nurse's care might have suffered a much grosser result. It was a traumatic moment.

It reminded me of my obstetrician's advice the day she was born, "I wouldn't get close to that baby." Instead, I grew as close to my Merrill as I could, knowing that there would be no further opportunity to be a mother with Michael. This was it. No-brainer. In Merrill's ten and a half months, I made a full swing (not Kübler-Ross' list, mine): Disbelieving, Angry, Lost, Guilty (what had I done to her?) Caring, Accepting, Loving.[1]

By crippling coincidence, my oldest brother John and I became close in the early months of Merrill's life. He and I were embedded ICU parents—me with Merrill, and he in Oregon, with Joseph, his oldest boy, who placed a bullet between his eyes with John's .22 caliber rifle. Joe was a 21-year-old when he attempted suicide. He'd enlisted in the Navy wanting to become a corpsman, influenced of course, by his Uncle Mike Creamer. But the school was full and had a waiting list, so

---

1 On Merrill: Merrill was my mother Eleanor's maiden name. Merrill's middle name was Donovan, Micael's mother's maiden name. Merrill was motherhood to me. I loved being her mother.

the eager recruiter signed Joe to train as a sonar operator. Sonar training was nerve-wracking and caused Joe's epilepsy to flare up, which
the recruiter was aware of but hadn't passed that info on up. The Navy
canned my nephew (just as the Army blew off his dad twenty-three
years before, sending him home because of nerve deafness). In a series
of mindless moves by the Navy, Joe came out on the short end. Sadder
still, Joe had married during his truncated time in service, and by the
time they booted him, his wife was already pregnant. So, she turned
around and did what a girl married to a guy on the verge of a nervous
breakdown did: She threw him out. By the time Joe got back to John's
in Oregon, he was suicidal.

During those nights, when Michael stayed in Cornwall for work,
John and I lived on parallel planes, four time zones apart. We talked
for hours on the phone. Whatever differences we held—primarily age
and musical tastes—were wiped away by our transcontinental duet of
our children in jeopardy.

Beegee stayed for three and a half months in NICU before they moved
her to a double room with a window overlooking the East River. For a
short while, Merrill was the only patient in her room; she had the crib by
the window. I took more freedom to hold her. We would sit, the two of
us; I would watch the boats and the barges going up and down the East
River, north towards West Point and Albany beyond, or south towards
the Statue of Liberty, past Rockaway and out to sea. I could see the traffic
on the FDR, the elevated highway between us and the river. Watch it
swell, becoming red and thick with brake lights: go, stop, go, stop, go,
stop. I counted on my fingers in runs of six, or four, how many times
it took to come out to the starting pinky again. I air-typed my fingers,
always keeping the touch-type skills of high school Typing I. Someday, I
would have to write this all down, for someone, somewhere who needed

to know what people go through, how they endure THIS. Not like those *When Bad Things Happen to Good People* books, given as gifts, then left in hospital waiting rooms on critical care floors. I received two.

I found things to fill my mind, like trying to remember military code words for the alphabet, things that Mike and I could share: *Alpha, Bravo, Charlie, Delta, Echo, Foxtrot, Golf (I'd always forget golf), Hotel, Indigo, Juliet, Kilo (thought it was drug-related), Lima, Mike (**Mike, Mike, Mike, what are we going to do?**), November, O, I would always forget and have blanked at this moment too, P, the same, Quebec, Romeo, Sierra, Tango, Umbrella, Victor (I often spell my name on the phone: V as in Victor, O-U-T-A-_____), W, who cares. It's Whiskey. Repeat...* mindless meditation games to get me through life.

I developed this over-the-top ability to sense pain; it came the night they yanked Merrill out of my body nearly lifeless. I see violence on TV or big screens, and I will feel it intensely— buzzing, triggering through my nerves—as though I was rewired in that ghoulish delivery room, stitched back together with some dollop of the pains of the world. Is it my sins? I list them in my mind.

Finally, I let Merry teach me What on Earth she came here to teach. She taught me patience, before which I had none. She taught me to meditate. She taught me to listen to her deep, relieved, inhale, inhale, exhale breath when I calmed down enough to comfort her. She taught me about what was best—given the circumstances: This was the best she could do, and all I had to do was the best I could do. When she moved out of ICU and into that room, she taught me to be brave and take her off her beepers. I walked around the pediatric floor, Merrill in my arms, showing her the wonders outside of her crib that the hospital had to offer. I sang her "Somewhere Out There." She was out there.

Occasionally the two of us would sleep together on the pull-out Naugahyde parent's chair with its wide Mission-like arms. First, I'd stuff some of her soft plush toys onto the crack where the cushion met the arm, nest my arm atop that, nest Merrill inside that, and we would doze off. She would sigh her deep, relieved inhale, inhale, exhale breath when she thought I needed it. I was her distraught mom; I needed it.

I became nurse-quality-good at suctioning Merrill, removing the thick mucus from her throat, though I only bathed her twice. It was terrifying to place her in a bath with that open tracheostomy; I was sure I was going to lose my grasp on her soapy behind, and she would slip down and drown. It became my new nightmare. Aroused by bathing, Merrill would move the most then, turning her head from left to right as though she didn't like it. Bathing wasn't comfortable for either of us. I left it to her nurses.

* * *

Michael came down from Cornwall when I had to stay in town or when Merrill's health was faltering. Now Michael and I were about to learn the meaning of putting your child on a DNR order. Do Not Resuscitate was obviously something Michael knew about, having gone through medic training and nursing school. Putting your own child on a DNR order was a whole other thing. University Hospital never asked us for such an option while there was still a chance, a hope, while "the (medical) practice" was still in play. Now a month out of NICU, they asked. Merrill could hardly breathe with a sinus infection. Mike and I sat holding hands in Merry's room; we'd brought in a small radio/cassette player to play her music, and we waited. After a long while, with nurses checking in every fifteen minutes, we went home to 21st Street.

I honestly thought we had signed up for some cinematic scene where our daughter would die before us. I knew these special babies died; I witnessed that in NICU. Even going home, I thought they would call us in the middle of the night to tell of her passing. The next day Merrill was better, and the DNR, null and void. We did sign a second one in the hospital. Again, she was sick with a fever, and we signed. Then they asked if she could receive fever reducers.

"It's to fight the pain; we don't want her to be in pain unless, of course, you don't want her to receive pain medication," the administering nurse said.

"I thought they said Merrill couldn't feel pain; that's what they told me when they dropped her," I said. Michael said nothing.

The nurse kept on, "It's your call, Mrs. Creamer."

My call, my call; I am so sick of my call.

It was complicated. That night of the DNR2, Michael and I had tickets to "Prairie Home Companion," a live show at Radio City Music Hall.

Garrison Keillor was in the habit of doing Farewell Concerts; this was one of them. We had great seats up front for the early show, where we watched in wonder as Keillor, script in hand, barely, if ever, glanced at it. We laughed and had such fun, despite the DNR, then we cabbed back to the hospital to check in on Merrill. She was still hanging on. We decided to listen again on the radio in her room to the second performance of PHC. Hardly a word was different; we were astonished, becoming even bigger Keillor fans than the big fans we already were. Again, Merrill got better, maybe due to Mom and Dad's rare laughter.

Merrill did get a roommate, an Orthodox Jewish baby boy, who stayed for quite some time with her. There were plenty of Orthodox Jews in the hospital; it was an excellent hospital and close to the lower east side, where historically Jewish neighborhoods remained. Hassidic Jews don't name their boys until after their bris; thus, the baby remained a BB for some time. They thought it was funny that I called my baby Beegee. Their BB needed to get strong enough to operate into his lower brain for a stent. It was a long time coming, and when he received the stent, it didn't take. Then they had to wait until he was strong enough to withstand another operation. Eventually, over months, BB got his second operation and his stent and went home. Merrill never did go home.

Obviously, after two DNR's, the hospital caught on to her resiliency; they informed us that they needed Beegee's bed. They were a hospital, after all, not a babies' home. Dennis, our social worker, and I began to search for a critical care facility for babies. One was being built on Sixth Avenue just south of the flower market; still a residential no-man's land before the high-rises went in, but it wouldn't be ready. One on Long Island, but maybe not the right place. One in the Bronx, but with a long waiting list. Finally, Dennis found St. Margaret's Home for

Babies and Children, up the Hudson in Albany. It was far, but in truth, Cornwall Bridge was halfway up to Albany, on the other side of the Hudson. Mike and I agreed to visit.

A note from Dennis to me: 10/27/87

> Martha,
>
> Here is some material on St. Margaret's. The baby is on their waiting list. They have 30 other children on the list, and they average one admission per month. (*Criminy!*) It will be some time before they are ready to admit her. They are sending an application; once they review it, you can call to see the facility.
>
> Call me if you have any questions. I'll speak to you soon. We will still make phone calls to see if there are any other facilities closer. —Dennis.

CHAPTER 53

Quality of Whose Life?

Merry was about five months old when Mike and I visited St. Margaret's. At first, I was frightened even to cross the threshold, to go inside. We were escorted through rooms where the best of St. Margaret's patients received what might politely be called Activity Time. Merrill was not destined to hold up her head nor sit up; she would not be a candidate for Activity Time. University Hospital had determined she was blind and deaf—blind I'll give you, deaf? I don't think so; she loved me singing to her, I would watch on the monitor as her heart rate went down. But Merrill wasn't educable like my nephew Patrick had been; she wasn't going to thrive in any sense of that word.

I had never heard the term "Quality of Life," but it had been bandied about to where it was a mainstay in our lexicon. Then our tour guide brought us in to see the other Merrills of St. Mag's, the Merrills grown up to eight or ten. The boy Merrills and girl Merrills, and just as one could discern a Downs Syndrome child by their appearance, these were undoubtedly Merrills. I could see in their faces the look that Merrill had, a look I had never witnessed in a person, except perhaps a character in a horror movie. There was a limpness to these children's bodies like the limpness in Merrill. I could tell that Michael saw those similarities too, which was all the more frightening because until then, I hoped maybe we could still try for another child. But it was clear: here at St. Margaret's, this was the best we could hope for. This would be her quality of life (lower case intended). She would live and die in a vegetative state. She would always be a Merrill.

It was a Tuesday in late June. It was time. St. Margaret's finally had an opening; Michael took the day off to follow me, chosen to ride in the back of the ambulance with Merrill. We'd then drive home together. Michael had come down to the city from Connecticut the night before; that morning, we parked in the lot where the ambulance was to come. I went into NYU Medical to sign Merry out. We were supposed to meet at the discharge door. There was a delay, so I went downstairs and waited with Michael. Whenever we checked, transport would inform us, "The ambulance is on its way." Neither of us had eaten. We were too bummed out.

Sometime after lunchtime, we were assured the ambulance would arrive momentarily. Michael left to drive up the New York State Thruway since he didn't want to rush. As an ex-EMT, he knew full well that an ambulance emitting the noises it did would drive him mad if he had to follow it. I went inside and waited as told. By the time it did come—it was way too late. Leaving then would mean rush hour traffic, and we wouldn't meet St. Margaret's acceptable window of arrival. I couldn't reach Michael to tell him to turn around or cut the trip short and go home to Connecticut. (There were no cell phones.) He drove the whole way to St. Margaret's, getting lost on the way, only to finally arrive and be told that I'd have to meet him tomorrow in Albany. SNAFU. War term, WWII: Situation Normal All Fucked Up. I felt battle fatigued; Michael took it well.

The next morning, the ambulance ride was grueling. The driver was manic, putting on the siren even if there was the slightest traffic. Hey, we were in NYC, there was traffic. Someplace in the Bronx, I asked them to cut the noise when not necessary. Merrill was filling up with fluids, which needed suctioning with a vacuum tube, and I had to get them to pull over; otherwise, I was jabbing it down into her tracheostomy, and it bothered her. Each time I asked them to stop, it was as if I was causing them to lose some bonus they'd be entitled to if they got us there under time. They must have wanted to make another run in the afternoon; it was that kind of a crew. In motion, we rocked back and forth so hard. It was impossible not to cry the whole ride there.

When we arrived, Michael was waiting, and the woman in charge, whom I told Merrill needed suctioning, said, "We have a policy of not suctioning here at St. Margaret's. However, we will, in this case, given her long rocky ride." And they did.

Michael and I stayed overnight in Albany at some motel, got up, pushed breakfast around on our plates, and went to say good-bye to Merrill. She didn't look good. She sounded very congested, and though I asked, it wasn't their policy to suction. I picked her up, held her wheezing body, kissed her warm little face, and said good-bye, not sure when I'd see her again.

We arrived in Connecticut less than two hours later. It was a beautiful summer day, and as I sat out on the steps leading to the driveway, the phone rang. Michael got up and answered it, then called through the screen door, "Martha, it's St. Margaret's." I looked at him, so sad. "Merrill just died."

CHAPTER 54

Bury Your Baby

This was not the saddest day of my life; Merry's birthday with all my hopes and expectations, kick-in-the-gut realizations, catapulted by the surge of hormones, and a placenta passing, was by far the saddest day and remains so even now, though others come close. I was roiling mad at The Home for Babies for their no suctioning policy. I was mad at the ambulance drivers who raced stupidly over curbs to get around traffic when there was no emergency, dredging up phlegm in Merrill's throat. I was mad for the screwed up scheduling the day before. Michael and I were both exhausted, having endured that life event twice. But I was proud of my Merry, who was a very smart girl and knew how damn hard it was going to be to visit her so far away, in the opposite direction of NYC. She chose to go.

I had chosen to be a vigilant mother in the time given me in NYC, and that time was over. Merrill chose to take matters into her own hands, and in doing so, we separated this turn of the screw from memories of the good times we shared.

St. Margaret's called; I answered. "Mrs. Creamer, do you want an autopsy on Merrill?"

"I suppose we should," I said and asked Michael, who agreed. "But what does that mean?" I asked them. "Will they cut into her...?"

"Yes, they will," came the answer before I finished.

"Cut into her head? Because I want to hold her again. I want to have an open casket." I said this, not asking Mike, but stating what I wanted. I wanted those who had not visited in the hospital to see how sweet she looked, how much she was like my cute baby Michael in his father's uniform jacket, how blonde and seemingly perfect she was with her eyes closed.

"I think it will limit what they can do," the voice said. "But, we'll obey your wishes, Mrs. Creamer."

The autopsy delayed our girl's transport to Marlboro. My high school friend Alan Slattery, now a mortician, took care of the details, even finding Rev. John Chane out at Southborough's St. Mark's Episcopal Church, (Mother's Episcopal rector being out of town) whom Alan knew would be perfect for conducting her service. Many of our friends from Marlboro High attended. It dawned on me as the classes of 1968 and '69 came in that this little death impacted so many. Alene and Debbie, and MVP's staff members made the trip up, some staying with my parents. Michael and I stayed in a hotel. Regina, Alan's wife, remembers that the funeral home was full; the sidewalk, out on West Main Street, and stoop were crowded as well.

Vietnam vets showed up from Massachusetts and Connecticut— Tom Sullivan, Gary, Jim Tackett, local Herd who got the word. After all, Merrill was a casualty of that Conflict, *one of the "afterborns," the collective term used to define the 67,000 disabled children and 40,000 stillborn and miscarried children of Vietnam vets with exposure to Agent Orange.*[1]

When the service was over and the mourners left, Alan let me hold my Merrill's heavy-dead body. I pressed my cheek to her icy temple, and shortly after, I let him take her away. I wouldn't recommend it; it wasn't a Mother's reward. A lesson before cremation.

I had no idea what Michael and I would do next.

---

1 Nicosia, p. 592.

People talk about how hard it is to bury one's child. My sister Dottie and her husband buried theirs. Bernie's brother Tom and his wife Sandy buried a daughter who broke through the ice one winter. My friends Brenda and Linda both buried children very young, both in New Hampshire. My mother, Eleanor Merrill Voutas, buried her first child, then went on to have eight of us. It is an exclusive club that you never choose to belong to, The Bury Your Baby Club. But Beegee was not right from the get-go. Her life, had she lived, would have been miserable, and in leaving us when she did, she made our lives—Mike's and mine—much easier to endure. Though not in the best of shape emotionally, we were gentle with each other and ourselves.

We had to be. We had an odd bunch of close friends, almost none of whom had children, except Abe and Alene, Nancy, who had moved away, Randi Wasserman, and my sister Dottie. Everyone else around us was childless. They hadn't the experience of children to understand. In pain, we're so selective of who can console us: You'll never understand, no matter how often I tell you. As we drove home from the funeral in Massachusetts, a glorious rainbow filled the sky; Michael pulled over, and we huddled and cried.

Then we tried to get on with the tough part—dealing with living. The first couple of weeks after Merrill's passing, Michael and I spent listening to the best of our music at its tweeter-busting best. Henry V, the Kenneth Branaugh version's great soundtrack for one. In between favorite cuts, Michael would quote the Henry verses he'd memorized, "We few, we precious few…" Then Talking Heads, Sting, Night on Bald Mountain, and any jazz from his Michael's Pub days. It was so much easier to share the misery. It brought us closer.

CHAPTER 55

Falling

One night, Mike and I got to talking about another miserable time, about his return from Vietnam, and how his friends treated him afterward.

"Everyone wanted me to feel comfortable, be like the ole Mike," he said, his cigarette balanced in his fingers, "the one who was fun to be with. One night I heard a friend saying, '*Mike's all right. He's okay. He'll be fine; he just had a hard time, he'll get over it.*'"

Mike said, "By their comments, it made me feel that I was somehow—I don't know—acting oddly. I didn't have the distance on the situation to be able to say, Yeah, Mike's all right!"

As Michael drank from his beer; I thought, "Shit, he was only twenty when he came home from the war."

"But I'd never be over it because my experiences made me into a new person," Mike went on, "I was different. They hadn't shared my life in Vietnam. Didn't kill guys. Didn't hear bullets flying past their helmets or pray for support. Hell, I was different from the kid who left in the first place."

I thought about the new war—the Merrill one we'd just survived. How much it changed us.

While Michael had been in the same delivery room on the night our severely disabled daughter was born, he and I had already been torn apart by a difficult pregnancy. All those differences were dropped to deal with Merrill's battle in the NICU. Then, hope of her recovery was deemed futile. I stayed long after. But Michael's training was different as a LRRP medic: he would work on an injured soldier until it became futile. That would free Mike to retrieve his rifle, to fix his mind on the battle at hand, then the-shoot-like-shit alternative action took over, like the one he explained to the vet in DC. That let him survive, at least for the time being. The ten and a half months of Merrill Creamer's life disrupted Mike's combat-honed survival skills, blew off any sense of family, lacerated hopes of bonding, and it undid our sex life. (As I write this, I hear the discordant violin strings of Aaron Copland's *Appalachian Spring*. American and aching but prideful, tethered on the bottom with clarinet runs. I once played the clarinet. Memories from this time come orchestrated.)

Michael made new friends; they largely emanated from Cornwall Package Store, where he'd become a regular. Richard Bramley and his wife Patty, the owners, became good friends, as did Fred Balling, who worked there part-time, and his girlfriend, Verne. Fred and Verne had us over for dinner often. They knew Merrill vicariously. Fred escaped Vietnam via Canada; it still plagued him. Movie houses were few and far between, like news sources: we had no TV in Cornwall, and cable lines were just being run. Michael got his news from NPR mainly; there wasn't great reception in those Litchfield Hills.

He was always great company for his friends; Michael had a library-like mind for the literary and historic. He would have made an unstoppable contestant on *Do You Want to Be a Millionaire?* He might have become rich! His taste in jazz and classical music was inspired. "Listen," he'd say, an audio cassette in hand, waiting for me to arrive from New York on a Friday, "this is Bach played on original instruments." Michael's joy could be enlightening.

Occasionally we'd laugh hysterically at the most banal things like seeing another thru-hiker at the package store and remembering not to ask him home. I longed for nights we sang at the top of our lungs to tapes he played in the living room. We'd drink beer and smoke cigarettes, our salon draped behind gem-green curtains of pine, that blocked the view from down on Rte 4. Other times, the music got us through low times when all that was new was the six-pack from Cornwall Package. We became so enormously bummed out, and all we could do was sleep or recite military code words. (Beethoven's Requiem in the background.)

Surely, I was not the person I was before meeting Michael in DC. Things had happened in the almost six years since then. I became a different person, like Mike, home from War. And for a while, that was binding, in a good sense. Erik Erikson wrote, "Identities tested in fire become a gift to ourselves. People who have created such identities are less vulnerable to future change, better able to handle those matters which extend beyond their immediate existence, and to prepare for the coming turns in the road before they and the rest of humankind actually get there.[1]" I was tested by fire. After Merrill, I brashly thought I could handle anything. In the country, Mike took things as they came. For a while, I believed that would get me through too.

I wrote him a poem— (see page 274)

In late July, we received this note from St. Margaret's House and Hospital for Babies.

> Dear Mr. and Mrs. Creamer:
> Enclosed is what I believe is the final list of those making donations in Merrill's memory. I delayed a bit in writing as letters kept coming in. The total received by St Margaret's was over $1300. These monies will be well used for the special needs of our children.

---

1   Nicosia, p. 594.

You both remain in our thoughts and know that as time passes, you'll continue to cherish your memories of Merrill. She is a well-loved child.

Best regards, Joyce S—, Secretary

A full autopsy might have contributed to Agent Orange findings. At first, I was upset at not permitting it, but Mike explained, "The government would probably refute any finding that admitted they were responsible for Merrill.[2]" He added, "There are too damn many of them."

We held a lunchtime memorial service for Beegee on her birthday, August 2, 1988, which was just enough time for me not to be totally tearful the whole time. It started as a small circle and grew as our working friends entered the church and our circle.

Alene read from her notes—

> In these days of possibility and accomplishment, it is a frustrating experience to want change that cannot be. That with all we can accomplish, and have—the most precious desires are sometimes beyond our reach. As I watched Martha and Merry together, I hoped and prayed for many weeks that Merry would respond more overtly to the gentle and continuous care and love that Martha gave.

---

2   Agent Orange Legislation: After years of advocacy led by VVA, congress enacted the Agent Orange Act of 1991. This legislation empowered the Secretary of Veterans Affairs to declare certain maladies "presumptive" to exposure to Agent Orange/dioxin and enable Vietnam veterans (and some veterans who served along the demilitarized zone in Korea in the late 1960s) to receive treatment and compensation for these health conditions. Service-connected benefits, however, also may be granted for other maladies not recognized as presumptive health conditions. Source: VVA website.

Rock Man

To Michael—alone in the country, with me

Rock man.
Far beyond a rock.
Jazz and guns
And soldiers of fortune.
You have moved my life to this.
Ah, man.
Bastion of morals
Yours alone
And music you share
On this loud night, alone at last.
Do you know
Or is it plain,
That I am caught
Between worlds I thought
Once mine—and now collided
With yours…?
So absolute
And unrelenting
A darker world, you take command
So I
Will stand outside.
(I must),
To know, anew, the choice
I take beside a rock and a hard place.

PHOTO: RON BUCCHINO

As time passed, I dropped judgments and comparisons: this was a child with its own purpose, and Martha, and all of us near her, were part of this transcending experience. Merry's short life on earth instructed me to live my life with more care. That in opposition to efforts to control and expect, her quietness was a lesson in grace, fullness of thought, and the "nowness" of life.

I thank Merry for precious lessons and for making Martha and I sisters.

The service was held at the church where Mike and Me were married, though the Episcopalians of Gramercy Park never came out to console us. While a priest had come to the hospital and baptized Merrill in NICU, there was not a solitary parishioner who recognized me in church throughout our ten-and-a-half-month ordeal, or inquired as to how I was or visited me at home a half-block away. No one said or did anything. Eventually, I extracted myself from a place lacking in love and moved on.

CHAPTER 56

Politics 1988

I'm a politics junky. I like to sit on a comfy couch and watch days of Presidential conventions. I watch Republicans; I watch Democrats. So, it was fine when Michael decided to stay up north during the political season; I had plenty to do at MVP. Business was more challenging; computers changed everyone into a designer. I had to work to win new clients; I was trying to win the 1988 US Tennis Open branding assignment.

The US Open's potential new client asked me to submit sketches for the Dukakis/Bentsen campaign one day. "Dukakis? I'm sorry, my husband is from Massachusetts; he hates Dukakis. My family from Massachusetts doesn't think he's a good governor. I watched the Democratic convention, and I don't know if I even like Dukakis," I said.

"You like George Bush better?"

"No."

"Are you a Democrat?" he asked.

"I don't always vote party lines," I replied.

"You know that George Bush is going to squash the gay movement, don't you?"

"I don't know that."

"Well, he is, and I can't let that happen," he said. "Mr. Dukakis doesn't like his graphics, so we are collecting submissions."

"For his graphics?" That wouldn't matter, I thought; Dukakis' problems were way more extensive than his graphics.

"We're going to have a competition," he said.

"Well, I don't think I can enter, but I know exactly what he would want."

"Huh?" He wanted to know.

"Well, it was the last night of the convention, and Tom Brokaw, commentating on NBC, said something like, 'Mr. Dukakis has influenced the stage design here. He wanted it to be dramatic like a Hollywood set, so it's been built upon a high platform…' on and on…So if I were designing for Dukakis, it would be dramatic: a close-up on an American flag, waving. Then the waving flag is frozen in a freeze-frame. The flag turns into a placard and the type surprints on top." I explained.

"I like it," he said. "You need to enter that, Martha. Please!"

"I have a very conservative husband, and trying to explain to him would be impossible."

"Listen, Martha. You can't let all the progress we gays have made go down the tube. George Bush will decimate us." Again, with this gay bashing. I remained silent because I didn't think it was true, and I wanted the US Open logo. "You know what he needs; it shouldn't be too hard to do some sketches. I need them by Friday; we're meeting over the weekend."

"Okay," I said, trying to be noncommittal.

"Okay? As in okay, okay?" He wanted less non and more committal.

"Okay, I'll see what I can do." He caught me.

"Okay then, and maybe I'll have some news for you about the Open."

Oh, you tease! I didn't get the Open, but I won the damn Dukakis gig, which was the start of *nothing* good. Telling Michael I'd won was like starting WWIII.

"How could you do that?" Mike said. "Now he's gonna win; that asshole is gonna win!"

"He's not gonna win, Michael; that team doesn't even know what they're doing."

"No? They have you. And you're the best there is."

"Well, thank you." He'd never said that. "Michael, I flew up there to present the finished designs this week," I said.

"Did you meet with Dukakis?"

"No, I met with a guy named Snedeker—no relation to Kath—in the mailroom. I walked in, he seemed to be in charge. He took my layouts, came back, said 'Thank you, everybody liked them.' Then a suit came in, said, 'You need to get them printed up now.'"

"Me?" I laughed, "I'm not going to have these printed up; that's for you to do."

"But we're so far behind." (Oh brother, you ain't seen *behind* yet!)

After talking another ten minutes, I could tell they had no idea how to get their graphics printed and out to the states, and I finally said, "' Wait. Listen,' I said, knowing I'd have to solve it, which I preceded to do with states paying individually upfront, Photostats, and FedEx (no Internet). Michael, they didn't have a clue how to make it work. And that's how we left it." I said, "Does that sound like Dukakis is going to win the election?"

"Yeah, cuz, you're helping him, and you're the best," Michael repeated.

"His team can't even figure out how to disseminate his graphics. Can you imagine the shipping cost of printing in one place? That's what they wanted to do. Think about it: how stupid can that be? They could never manage the country! I'm only doing his graphics!"

★ ★ ★

Mike disagreed. He barely spoke to me all weekend, and when I saw him the next weekend, he said: "I made a donation—with my money, mind you—to the Bush campaign."

"Good." I said, "Good for you."

In the end, MVP didn't lose any money and even made a tiny bit. But I too had to vote for Bush in November; Mr. Dukakis would never have worked.

We went from eight Reagan years to another four Republican ones. Thank heavens, or Mike would have had me drawn and quartered.

CHAPTER 57

To Merge or Not to Merge

Michael was still working as a DVOP. He and I talked on and off during the fall about MVP merging with friends Lee and Lyn. They owned a design studio and package design company in Boston, and that way, living midway in Connecticut would make good sense. They might pick up package design work for my clients from NYC whose product lines were extending beyond clothing; I could bring my fashion expertise to Boston, and no longer would I put off vacations or time off. Best yet, Michael genuinely liked Lee and Lyn; beer was plentiful, and we shared intelligent laughter and music.

But looking into companies who want to merge is like researching a pre-nuptial. In the long run, we were very far apart. It tore at our friendship for reasons not worth recounting. While the merger was still a possibility, it consumed much of our emotions. It lasted long enough to drop us far away from Merrill's passing and then back on the game board, into the Reality of Our Situation, which was problematic at best.

Dukakis wasn't our only schism; there was a growing void of things we didn't see in the same light. Some of what had changed in Michael's mind was not even clear to me...

From a letter from Mike to Maryanne: [1]

---

1   Maryanne LeBlanc would share Mike's letters with me after he passed, when I was writing this book.

4 Dec 88

Hello Maryanne…

This won't be a long one. Finally scraped up the guts to sit down and put on paper to you that Merrill died the last week of June…I can't even remember the date anymore. We had just moved her to Albany, which was to be her home.

We had the funeral in Marlboro, where Martha and I have family. I guess we just unconsciously chose that "common ground" rather than Cornwall or NYC, somehow knowing that our paths would part, and we had reached the Junction. The actual decision on it didn't come 'till October. I'll admit that it's mostly me who's the obstacle. Martha wanted me to move down to NYC or thereabouts, settle in and work around her career, and have another baby. Not at all unreasonable when one looks at the situation objectively, I guess. But totally out of the question for this particular individual.

I went back to my job as a Vet's Rep at the Labor Dept. in August. (They called me.) I was hoping that she'd come up here and settle in, leaving the NY scene and finding local clients or a local job. … I won't go into it except to say that Martha is a loving, wonderful person, and I genuinely hope she can find a way of having things she rightfully wants from someone capable of giving.

So, as it stands, I'm going to head out. Hopefully, this time, I realize that I am an incorrigible loner. People must watch carefully and aren't deluded into thinking I can be a part of their lives beyond a good, long-term buddy or a competent and caring co-worker. Many people out there like and respect me, people I've helped as a medic, or counselor, or a soldier. Those who know I put a lot of effort into a job.

I feel good about that. I can handle all the "like" and "respect" that I can earn in this world, and I guess that's the main reason I just keep going for another day. I'm learning, though, that what I can't handle is someone loving me.

I'm trying to get back with (Morrison-Knudsen) in some capacity. ... If that doesn't work out, I'll be looking elsewhere. Keep your eyes open for me, will ya?

This letter has taken me about three hours to write and has left me exhausted, so I'm going to go. I hope everything is going well ... given the "wa-wa," and that you're healthy and happy in body and spirit. I look forward to hooking up again if you're back this way. Maybe I'll even write more often, now that this one particularly difficult letter is history.

Take care, Mike C.

I must confess that I did not read Mike's letter to Maryanne until recently—years into the future—and it makes me realize there is so much I don't remember and can't. There are parts I would swear are lies he made to himself. Living through trauma as Mike and I had, perhaps we got so overwhelmed. Maybe we can't remember, or we remember things differently...but then there's this hard copy, this letter to Maryanne, pointedly showing another truth: The truths of others that are not our own.

This letter was in 1988. It is two years before Mike left. Why did it take Michael more than two years from this letter before he left? Back then, I felt that Michael didn't believe in anything. But his letter portrays him willing to go, and to move on with living, go the way of wanderlust. I don't remember that, or could it be I didn't see? I don't know. It's winter after all, and shortly after this letter, I move out. Maybe Mike hid it from me, encased it in his blustery bravado, saying but failing to act on things Maryanne would not see from so far away.

Not that we didn't both "leave" in those two years, but the memories of what we did and said escape me. It was a time when we didn't write letters, so I have nothing but my memories. I will try to remember:

* * *

The first thing that comes to the surface is I was heartbroken. Without Merry, it was evident that nothing was holding us—Mike and Me—together. We were no longer in the same play. We were bound together in vows, but our emotional arcs were misfiring. While Mike was heading off to Africa again to pick up on his next scene, I was still on stage in the last one: The Mother of Merrill, and then that show was over.

I remember crying in my studio late one evening and Debbie, my old roommate said, "You don't have to be unhappy, you know."

And I listened to her.

"You can change your life," my friend said. "You should think about coming to a Buddhist meeting with me."

I did. Debbie's Buddhism was the Soka Gakkai Buddhism out of Japan. While I didn't know what I was chanting, I sought precisely what Debbie was offering: a community of people wanting the same spiritual reality.[2] *Nam Myoho Renge Kyo*, for the time, sustained me. I had my Debbie, and she was a great comfort—at the office and chanting.

---

2   The Roots of Wisdom; the spirituality of imperfections. Source: online website.

CHAPTER 58

AIDS and Other Losses

Maybe Christmas without the baby Jesus was part of my lack of spirit. Snedeker had finally departed for Dallas to join up with her husband. Dottie was in Annapolis. Michael stayed in Cornwall for his job. MVP was failing; I had to hire a business consultant. The IRS audited me.

But more than anything, AIDS was hitting very close to home: Many men got morbidly sick with AIDS and began leaving us—some fast, some lingering. Clients: Perry Ellis, Laughlin Barker, Bill Robinson, Jim Terrell, Robert Renn, Carmelo Pomodoro, Angelo Donghia, George Stavarinos, Willi Smith, and friends Ray Gill, Thommie Walsh, Arthur Metzgar and Bob Melon. All dead; AIDS hit us deep and hard.

I don't believe anyone can write about NYC in the 80s without explaining the battleground of AIDS. I worked with gay people. I'd danced in discos with my *Vogue* co-worker, Ron and his gay friends. Fashion designers were often gay. More than half of Abe and Alene's wait staff at Texarkana and La Louisiana were gay. These were friends, colleagues, clients, patrons, and lovers of ours. It consumed our hours, wrecked lives, and changed businesses. It certainly changed mine.

Thus, in NYC many people had a situation like mine: We were grieving. People needed to give grieving people some allowance: I called it "The Reality of the Situation." The Reality of the Situation—the life and death of a loved one—made everyone else's Most Important Thing in The World secondary. This reality afforded me—all of us survivors, caregivers—a foot up on prioritizing life. It also gave me a greater understanding of what businesses face trying to carry on when their creative leaders were dropping in the siege of the AIDS epidemic. I am shocked at how little of AIDS is understood thirty years later by a generation that views AIDS as benign.

It was not. It ravaged the design industry. Through my Merrill's tragedy, I knew how long it took when heartbreak strikes, how it consumed hours, and how it triggered other losses—income, energy, customer base. Though Dr. Wasserman and I became close, I missed Kath, and Dottie: I lacked the support of what best friends or the equivalent of a vets' group might provide—that shared sense, unspoken communication of support. Big decisions came down again to me. Business was challenging. It wasn't fun. I was not at the top of my game.

My story, *The Strange Sad Saga of Merrill Donovan Creamer*, maintained half-life, bumping around inside my brain like radon in a house. I guess that's what PTSD is about. When we are hurting, people pass judgment on us. I wish it were easier. I didn't find it to be. Nor did Michael. For him, it must have been unbearable. Like him, I lost years.

A child's passing takes about three years to overcome, that constant impetus to cry when reminded. I learned from Merrill to appreciate what I had, whatever it was worth, *while* it was happening.

I wrote some of what I learned in a letter to my dad:

> 17 Dec 1988
> Merrill taught me many things. She taught me about
> healing and conveyed a powerful message of what it
> means to be well. I wanted so much to find a cure for
> her; I searched with the doctors—and in the process—I
> found *healing*. My baby girl who couldn't talk, taste, or
> swallow taught me about *surviving disappointment*. After
> discovering my hidden patience, (Merrill) spoke to me
> with her inhale, inhale, exhale, how to let go—to relax and

absorb her love…She started me on a long path to find truth and to believe again.

I called her my Buddha Baby—silent and serene. She was powerful; she taught me about motherhood—a full, long life of it in only ten and a half months. She taught me how we can feel that we are totally responsible for a child, yet… life is a private and individual thing. She taught me that *hers* was different from *mine*, and my wishing was just my wishing. I had no power to alter her life.

I learned about love through that little girl. Love I might never have come to know. By her special gift, I felt released of fears that drove me to hate or resent what life had dealt me. And so, she gave me a special peace. We can find tracts of love inside us we already harbor. We can leave behind resentments and pain not worth holding on to. Merrill's with me all the time, even now. She reminds me of a me I liked so much when she was around; the one dealing with life's daily blitz, but touched by this infant, so accomplished at communicating true love. It was an excellent recognition of love for me. Perhaps she is an angel in the truest sense. Maybe because remembering her sheds a loving light on me and brings me to a peaceful state of mind, I have faith that we'll meet again. And we'll be happy.

A Christmas fell in the middle of her life at NYU Medical. Holidays came and went, in NYC everyone doesn't celebrate; decorations could offend. But for parents of sick children, the institutional sameness of the hospital lacked joy and relief. In 1988, I asked if I could decorate the Pediatrics floor. Tina and Cheryl from MVP helped design wreathes constructed of white cotton gloves, stufffed and tied onto forms. A photo of Mickey or Minnie held the center, and a huge red bow tied the botton. We strung them in the halls. As the work wore on, my volunteers were spent of free time; I was back in the hospital, alone again, crying as I finished up.

CHAPTER 59

D Words...

I played doubles tennis weekly out in Queens, hoping it would help me get my body back. (Hopeless.) I have no doubt Depression, and depression-relieving hot wings prepared with smothered butter, caused my weight to soar to delicious heights. Wings and pizza were the only foods I could find to eat near NYU Medical those nights I left Beegee's bedside after 11:00 PM. Two or three nights a week, you'd find me and a few cabbies chawing down wings, each at separate tables, piling on the pounds. I see weight gain in mothers who have experienced similar tragedies—a kidnapping, a child victim of violence—when they share their stories on the news. People live with visible markers of grief; I always give heavy people a nod, a smile.

In the early spring of 1989, Michael came up with the idea to visit our best man, Dave, and his wife Mona, (not their names) who lived in the California Desert. Dave beckoned us with discounted lessons from his hotel's tennis pro. That enticed me. In Mike's mind, Mona and Dave were the epitome of a healthy, modern, childless marriage. This trip was to teach me how sane a childless marriage could be. So, we flew to the desert, for lessons in tennis at sunup. And lessons on love.

Dave and Mona lived just a hop from the hotel Mark managed, in a small oasis of unassuming houses surrounded by unbelievably hot desert. The four of us made with small talk for about a day and a night.

The two of them argued unceasingly. Mona made reservations for us girls to go to the spa at Two Bunch Palms in Desert Hot Springs. I was suspicious of any place that had both Desert and Hot in its name, but I agreed to go once I knew Mona scheduled us for massages and that there were indeed hot springs.

As Mona drove through massive barrel cacti and blue blue skies, she spilled the beans. "I'm filing for divorce." The D-word, I was aghast. "Dave's cheated on me repeatedly," she said.

"Oh, no." I knew it. That smarmy, mustachioed cad.

"I can't tell you how many times he has taken a room at the hotel and pulled double shifts," she said. "Double shifts, my ass. I've had it!"

Back at the ranch, Mike, too, was getting the complete lowdown from Dave, which is why I think Mona planned for us girls to go off and be alone. I was distressed. Mona was supposed to give me advice. I was still trying to figure out what to do with my marital problems.

The hot springs were hot. They whipped those hot-wing toxins out of me to the fainting point. Divorce aside, I chose to count the high points: seeing the desert, feeling the heat, and I came away with a better backhand. On the flight home, Mike and Me grew somewhat closer. Ideal marriages don't really exist; there was no magic peyote for troubles, and we could work on our marriage or not.

We chose to give each other a little space—*If You Love Somebody Set Them Free*—Again, I took Sting's advice to ease up, let go, not hold so tight. It was a countermove I'd learned; it helped whenever Michael pulled away. Both his move and mine served the same purpose, creating space.

CHAPTER 60

Done Deal, 1989

Michael and I were spinning further and further out of orbit from each other, growing further and further apart. Neil Shatan, an early researcher deciphering Vietnam veterans' PTSD, wrote of six characteristics that seemed to be shared by most vets with whom he worked. The first was "persistent guilt that could not be turned off"—guilt at having outlived comrades, maybe those who had been maimed and killed.[1] Michael's survivor's guilt now extended to his daughter.

It had been months since Merrill died, and Michael wouldn't be amorous. He refused to have sex without a condom. "I know you just want to have another baby, and I can't risk that," he said.

"I do not want to have another baby with you. I will go on the pill."

"I know you do, and you'd trick me," he said.

"I would not! How could I? You remember when we visited St. Margaret's, and I asked if a second baby like Merrill was ever born into a family, and that tour woman said, 'Oh yes.' Then she showed us those two brothers. She said, 'That's what their mother wanted to believe!'"

"That a freak kid like that could never come out again?" he said.

"Right, let's call it a freak kid because that's what you thought Merry was, and that's why you stayed away and that freak kid? I love that freak kid, and don't you forget it."

---

1   Nicosia, p. 170

"How could I? I caused it," he cried.

"You caused it? Is that what you still think, even after you saw those babies from the same family?" I was still in disbelief that her condition was due to the War.

"Yeah, Agent Orange." He stood with his arms crossed.

"Agent Orange, well right, it could have been, but those two kids had nothing to do with Agent Orange." I was so in denial.

"You don't know that," Mike said.

"No, I don't. St. Margaret's said, 'babies like Merry come out of two people whose bodies make that combination of...'"

"Abnormalities... Imbalances. Whatever you wanna call 'em," Mike finished.

"I don't want a baby with you, Michael." I walked away.

I kept trying to recover from Beegee, which couldn't be done well around Mike. Having lost one love in Merry, I felt rejected repeatedly by Mike. I was losing my marriage. Mike was adamant, as the following un-dated torn-out journal entry of mine attests, Mike and I were much further away than just talking about another baby. It was a done deal. It confirms I didn't merely imagine Michael's pulling away; it was a tactic he had used since PTSD and Levittown.

> He said so many hurtful things today, but saddest was that
> he felt he always had to withdraw love, affection, the things I
> wanted most (and had just said so) for fear of me becoming
> attached and wanting him to be a father again. He said he
> lived his worst fears being a father. That was stinging, awful,
> and painful.
>
> I should go home now, or to Marlboro. Should, but
> don't know if I can. This is such an awful time for me. I
> do not have an opinion of what I should do and where I
> should be. I feel like Michael now, waiting for decisions
> to be made for him. My face is burning with anger and an

embarrassment of emotions.

I do not want to be a baby, to pout and pull myself away. I am, though, acting hurt and acting out. Just as I did as a kid, this is a setup of sorts, and I have done as much setting up as being set up, so I'm guilty and pained all in the same mouthful ...

[My pen runs out of ink and the rest of the page is blank—how fitting.]

✷   ✷   ✷

I wasn't the only one Mike was pulling away from. Eventually, Mike's job as a DVOP became unbearable. It was logical; it would be hard to work five days a week fixing other veterans' lives. New job postings would come across his desk daily, and when he found one dredging a lake, Mike went for it. He was due to fly to Denver for a national convention of DVOPs and didn't want anything of it.

Mike writes to quit his job:

6/30/89

Dear Mr. Inman:

As I told you this afternoon, I will not be able to attend the July 10-16 session at the NVTI in Denver. I am therefore returning the ticket I received earlier this week.... I'm sorry that I couldn't give more notice; something came up quickly—I got a job offer, and I have to start on 10 Jul or they'll give it to someone else. (That seemed a little juvenile at the end.—MVD)

Thank you for all your support.

Sincerely, Michael E. Creamer

Mike worked alone on a dredge scooping up the vegetation and muck that was suffocating a small lake. He crossed and re-crossed, back and forth, stopping only to tank up or to eat lunch. The dredge emitted so much noise and vibration that it was a surprise Mike's fillings didn't drop out of his teeth. When I visited, I waved frantically from the shore, since the noise alone was enough for the silt to sink, but would not allow my voice to carry. Mike would row a dinghy to shore to pick me up and row back to the dredge and take me onto the deck. He really couldn't stop long; I had to don ear protectors and ride across a few times with him trying to get something said in between sea changes.

I tried again to sell the business, this time to a New York company. It was another disastrous waste of time. We were four months into the talks only to find that the potential new owners thought I would give my business away. "I lost my baby. I didn't lose my mind!" After twelve years of building a business, it didn't make sense to merge. Nothing made sense anymore. Merrill's death anniversary was approaching. I decided to get out of town. I didn't want to be in New York for that. Michael was always morose when an anniversary neared.

CHAPTER 61

Get Me Right Outta Here

10 July 1989: John, my oldest brother, whose suicidal son had been in ICU when Merrill was in NICU, lived in Oregon. Joey had recovered, and it seemed like a good time to go visit. John was a bit of a savant, never graduated from high school, but read a book or two a night. He first married on the rebound in 1964, after the Army of the Vietnam Generation spit him back over a hearing issue.

Every summer, the airlines would offer a "Kids Under 18 Fly Free" promotion. I decided to take Kara, my niece, who had worked for MVP, the summer Beegee came into our lives. Though she finished the very Friday that I went into the hospital, she helped me set up Merrill's bedroom and assemble the crib. She'd been in awfully close proximity to pain. Kara and I deserved that vacation.

We planned to spend a day or two with her cousin in Seattle, then rent a car and drive to John's, camping as we went. Getting off the plane in Houston, the first leg of the trip, I picked up a message in Mike's voice from my home machine: "Don't worry, I'm all right." It was 10 July; in the era before cell phones, we used answering-machines and called them to hear our messages.

I tried to call Michael to no avail and had to re-board a plane for the second leg. I left the phone booth remaining incommunicado. We landed in Seattle to yet another message, "All the phone lines are down; I'm using someone's out on Rte 7. I can't stay on the phone. There's a line of people waiting to use it (shades of Basic Training II). I'm okay though, Mike."

What the heck? I tried to find a TV and asked if anyone knew what happened in northwest Connecticut. Nobody knew; 1989 was a more insular time; things were more regionally separate. Kara's relatives didn't know. Nothing was on TV; channel choices were few, cable was nearly non-existent. Cornwall was another planet.

Days later, Kara and I made it to John's, but still no word on what happened back home. Eventually—*USA Today* showed a small photograph of the destruction in Connecticut of a majestic stand of old-growth "Cathedral Pines." A couple of oddball tornadoes had rolled back and forth in the valley near our house, wiping out the power and telephone lines. I'd heard enough to believe that Mike was fine. But I wasn't sure I was. Sleeping on the ground, I felt a rock, maybe, under my bag. There was no rock. I lay down again. Then felt a lump on my left side under my breast. I would check that out as soon as I got home. News of Cathedral Pines saddened me, and every night the hard rock within me gave me pause.

It was good to see my nephew, Joe, recovered enough from his suicide attempt, driving a car again. Though Kara and I didn't climb right in with him at the wheel, he was healing well. (Since then, we've talked about suicide; it's helped to understand it and his positive attitude after. My brother, John, miraculously decided to take off from work early that afternoon, only to find Joe on the front steps of his house, nearly dead. I know God works in mysterious ways.)

By now, I knew Cornwall was wounded. Arriving back on the east coast, I headed for home. The roads were passable to our house, but everywhere was a piney fragrance, the same that permeated the air in Oregon. Michael drove me around to see the damage. He parked close to the Cathedral Pines; we got out and walked the rest of the way. The fallen trees' diameters were taller by a foot or two than we were. They lay like beached whales, dead on the sawdust shore.

* * *

Before the tornadoes took them out, Michael and I had hiked among them on a century's worth of fragrant needles—the only healing hike that we made together after the death of our daughter. Back then, those Cathedral Pines had filled me with awe. Their fragrance caressed my heart in its most broken state. Now my heart was breaking again.

I wanted to help; I asked Mike, "Are you doing any volunteer work?"

"No," Mike said.

I decided to check in with Richard Bramley down at the package store. Richard sent me up a steep road close to where he and Patty lived; a town crew and volunteers worked there, clearing debris. I parked my Subaru where it would be out of the way of half-fallen "widow makers." I worked for an hour before one of the Cornwall town trucks backed nearly over my car. I drove home, where Mike, surveying the damage to the car, said, "You had to do this so you wouldn't feel left out, huh, Miss Bleeding Heart?"

Mike had forgotten me. *Do you know who you're with?*

The lump in my breast needed addressing, and I didn't want Mike with me at the doctor's appointment. Once scheduled for a lumpectomy, I told Mike over the phone of my doctor's concern for the size and location. "You must be scared to death, not knowing if you're going to die, or if you have terminal cancer," Mike said. He wasn't comforting in the least. My mother came down from Massachusetts, and Dottie came up for the day of surgery. Mom mentioned something she'd heard about breast tumors in women who couldn't have any more children; gee, thanks, Mom. Anyway, it was benign. But the Mike/Martha gap was malignant; we weren't going to get better. By the fall of '89, we started to use the D-word and seriously consider divorce.

Since we're talking D words, let's talk Dredging. That winter, Michael went on leave from his iced-over job. Those months hardened Mike, throwing him back to a housebound version of his former self, smoking cigarettes, and whatever dope he could get his hands on. He drank away his unemployment checks, keeping Cornwall Package Store in the black. With what was left, he sent away for more classical music, tapes by Roger Norrington, Baroque on original instruments. For a conservative guy, Mike listened to a lot of National Public Radio, mostly "Hearts of Space" on Sundays after I'd left for the city.

Maybe the Dave and Mona trip contributed to what happened next. My marriage was over, right? Friends in New York took me out for dinner, where their friend was a waitress. The next time I saw the waitress, she told me the host at her restaurant had asked about me. It had been a severely long dry spell since anyone had asked about me, except in that Sorrowful Mystery way, "Is Martha okay?"

I had just come through the desert with Moses, but it seemed that Michael and I were still stuck in it. And—wait a minute—Moses never made it to Jerusalem. I wanted to make it to The Promised Land! Encouraged by friends, I let my morals down. Or maybe the loose life I'd known in the 70s revisited. I had a fling; I was desperate for love, to be held again and spoken to with kind words. I wasn't proud of myself; things like that can complicate other things. I didn't know, but I opened the door to problems down the road.

The findings of a study completed in 1989 on the VA's Agent Orange program and spearheaded by its new Administrator, Edward J. Derwinski, had yet to be made public. It stated, "'High Combat' vets were four times more likely to be separated from a spouse or divorced than all other Vietnam era vets. It also noted 'serious drinking problems and cigarette habits.' Vets who had seen more combat had more likelihood of developing PTSD, especially those who had come in contact with Agent Orange.[1] I was finding it difficult to share opinions with Michael. Our once very passionate marriage was no longer. Two merger attempts had failed with MVP, and the hopes of us coming together weren't good either.

I telephoned a divorce lawyer. She began by explaining the charges for Divorce I could make: Cruelty, Abandonment, Adultery, Mental Cruelty, Incompatibility. One at a time, she explained the legal meaning. With each, I considered thoughtfully and replied, "No. I couldn't charge Michael in that way, or for that matter, me."

Okay, Abandonment and Mental Cruelty were in the cards, but maybe life had dealt Mike and me the same hand, different suits. In looking at The Reality of the Situation—okay, you tell me, how do you look at someone you love through the eyes of accusation? We had endured awful things, and Divorce seemed unfair to two who had waited as long as we had to find love.

When it came to Irreconcilable Differences, I wondered if it were true about us, when almost immediately I knew that I certainly hadn't put the time and effort into making those differences go away. Either of us could have had our tubes tied, but we didn't. If true love existed— and I believed ours was true love—then Divorce was a cop-out. And realizing the absurdity of Divorce, I began looking for a rental property.

Our house in the country had been essential to my mental health; I could think in the country and revitalize. Because *I* had found our home in Cornwall, I felt a claim to it. Jonas Soltis, the realtor, had told me, "The house is yours." But really, it was because of my Infantryman husband that we won the deal.

I had given Michael space before, and I hoped I was making the right decision now. Then. Whenever. **It took me a long time to get married; it was taking me a long time to get un-married.** I didn't know how,

---

1 Nicosia, p. 592.

and I didn't know what else to do but move out.

I found a quaint, two-story, stone carriage house rental in Somers, NY, a new source of sanity. I gave up the Manhattan apartment. I dealt with my husband: I would pay the Cornwall mortgage, and Mike would pay utilities. We'd both keep the house. We separated our domiciles, planned to do so legally too. In the meantime, I went to Jamaica with my house lawyer, Kathy.

Mike and his infamous Tiger cat, ready for battle in the backyard in Cornwall Bridge.

CHAPTER 62

The Negril Letter

I found a letter to Rev. John Chane from me that I hadn't mailed, only written.

Dear John,

Thank you for your letter. I do know you care, and your caring is what brought me to St. Mark's. Having met with you three times now, I must say each time I have felt a wonderfully genuine love, something not terribly commonplace these days. ...

Michael and I have confronted the vast differences in our lives, and from my point of view, the anger is finally subsiding as to why Michael won't try to get well. My need to get well, join with others, and extend myself is very different from his need to rest and feel secure and sort his options. I realized that divorcing (didn't have to) mean either of us had failed; we could let each other be the separate and different people we are.

It released in Michael a desire to go ahead and get his vocational rehabilitation from the VA. This "voc rehab" has been lingering on the horizon for many years, and he had postponed testing to figure his best future. Releasing

Michael from the vise of marriage has brought him to
a point where he is now eager and going soon to test.
Unfortunately, he could feel free to do that only after we
decided again to split; as he said, "I can choose my career
now without thinking about whether you'd approve or
not." I'm glad he came to that, regardless. He's incredibly
talented and quite able to succeed. I wish him increased
clarity, however long it takes.

I am vacationing in Negril ... and it's a beautiful hot
afternoon in the shade. I've just finished reading Scott
Peck's *The Road Less Traveled*... reading it at this particular
time in my life has been truly gratifying. ... I often felt a
spiritual sense in my daughter's birth and death...I think
having read Peck's work that I instinctively was finding,
evolving if you will, a part of me, a reason for living. One
that encompassed a sizeable spiritual part of me too.

I had been in therapy with a truly gifted and
loving therapist for years. (She) helped me to grow in
many directions. I often brought up a sense of miracle
or Godliness to her, and each time, she dispelled
them.... It's not a big surprise that I landed on your
doorstep that Sunday. Strangely, I blurted out my
biggest upsets in tandem since I'd not exchanged them
with anyone previously. My feeling of not being able to
stay with Michael, and my sense of loss from my NYC
congregation, were both out of my mouth in a moment—
you hardly had time for one of those thoughts! Both seem
connected because I want to grow spiritually and create
around me genuine peace and love.

...I am chanting now with my Buddhist friend,
Debbie, my college roommate, and now my controller.
I feel the experience of focusing on love and happiness

on any given day has been good for me and helped me separate wholly from Michael instead of in parts.

I feel pretty happy right now and ecstatic about Peck's confirming message. I hope to see you soon.

Love, Martha Voutas

CHAPTER 63

Shadowed

It's hard to write of this end-time when I know what happens. I wrote in my journals back then. I wrote poems. I even wrote scenes for a play. Writing now means that I must own up to all that I didn't do. What reconcilable things were overlooked or forgotten? Things that may have contributed to Michael leaving.

Leaving Michael, a part of me felt bruised, darkened. I missed my sweet soldier's letters filled with love. A blackness descended. My friend Alene once said that she felt a blackness in herself at times. I remind her that she was born on the darkest day of the year, the winter solstice, and we laugh it off. But it's a blackness one can't laugh off, probably like the feeling a combat veteran might own, still surviving.

In packing up East 21st Street, I found things to which I no longer related. I didn't fit those Perry Ellis samples, clothes that tall, skinny models wore on the runway. That was a thinner time; I gave them to my thin friends. I found a Tennessee Williams jacket that a friend gave me in trade for money she needed while waiting to be bought out of her apartment. I gave the jacket to someone southern, who'd appreciate it. I also found poems, ones I'd written in sketch pads and tracing paper sheets, when between nursing my business and managing my Beegee, I had no time to write anything longer. The poems reminded me of a love I longed for; I ripped out their yellowed sheets, folded and saved them with journals and notebooks I'd always carried in my handbags.

✳   ✳   ✳

Leaving New York City, I would not miss East 21st Street; Stringfellow's strip club had moved in across the street, and many early mornings, I had to call the police to report some brute beating on some drunken woman or man beneath my French doors. I called so often that after a while, the cops stopped responding.

The details of my Somers habitat remain dim; I was training into the city, parking in the residents' lot. I'd never been a commuter. And it was tough on someone like me, used to rolling out of bed and walking a few blocks to work. Somers itself was as idyllic as Cornwall. There was a loop of about four miles up and down rolling hills that I could speed-walk in an hour. When summer came, and there was still sun enough, I would walk the loop after work. One weekend, determined to find a new route, I walked over eight miles. Having run out of water, I sat on a stone wall, heat-exhausted and alone. I burst into tears and wept openly for what my life had come down to. Living in a dream cottage with green grass surrounding me had long been my image of tranquility. I didn't know the meaning of the word.

CHAPTER 64

Fighting on Too Many Fronts...

On 2 August 1990, President George H. W. Bush ordered the organization of Operation Desert Shield in response to Iraq's invasion of Kuwait. It would have been Merrill Donovan Creamer's third birthday. Like many rumors of war we'd witnessed back in '83, Michael ranted that this new War was not worth losing American servicemen and women over. This was a War about oil, about "bullshit politics and money." Now Mike's Army friends were on alert because of it.

Mike and I had weathered the summer; we were rejoining a little. In September, Ken Burns' *The Civil War* aired on PBS for five consecutive nights. We got together at Fred and Verne's to watch the magic of Burns' showing and telling; how he brilliantly brought the Civil War—do wars really deserve capitalization? —into our living rooms.

I missed a few episodes of *The Civil War*, but Fred had purchased the series on VHS. I borrowed the set, and after late commutes home from NYC to Somers, I would pop in a tape, watch an episode, eat something, drink some wine, maybe talk to Michael on the phone, still in Cornwall, rewind the tape, and then go to sleep.

I wrote Michael a note on the inside of a commercial Hallmark card with a poem entitled:

Our Love was Meant to Be—

11 Oct 90

Dear Michael—

For whatever else happens, I found this card and its sentiment so fitting that I had to drop you a line and say hi, find out how you are.

Recovering from the War gets better and has explained some things about you that I thought of as character flaws. I don't want to sound odd, but some things I thought you should get over, get on with, get away from, get your ass in gear. So much, really. I see now, it is a natural extension of the War. And though I may not be crazy about those behaviors, that's who you are, and I guess I'd better get it.

I do enjoy being with you so much more, so much more of the time lately, and I appreciated changes in you, and the bigger acknowledgments of (from?) you.

Do you want to have a get together for some of your vet friends? If so, let's book it. Do you want to go to Florida? Let's make some plans. Love, Martha

* * *

For Mike and Me, getting along was something I remembered from an earlier time in our lives, after Levittown and after his re-up. We started almost dating and spending some weekend time together. From Somers, it was easy to hop in the car and run up to visit him. It took less than an hour to drive.

Then, in late fall, it happened more than once. In Cornwall, the phone rang, and after I had answered, I heard someone on the other end and a slow hang-up. Another weekend, again, and then a third time, there was a space in which I might have hung up but didn't. On the other end a female voice, asked, "Is Michael home?" I said yes, called him over, and walked into the living room. He hung up quickly. Our phone was in a small mudroom in the entry, the hub of three rooms: kitchen, bathroom, and living room, the busiest rooms in the house. Like Mike's mother's house in Marlboro, a private conversation was hard to pull off there. I let it go.

During the week, when I called from Somers, I remembered several times over the weeks that the phone was busy. Without call waiting, I just had to call back. Sometimes I did, and the line would still be busy long into the night, and I'd give up. Now it was December, I was visiting Cornwall, one more time—the phone rang, and she asked for Michael with minimal hesitation. With that, I asked, "Who is calling?"

"It's Abigail," she said. The name was vaguely familiar. (Not her name.)

"Oh. Sure, I'll get him."

Michael didn't spend much longer on the phone again, but he seemed nervous.

"Who was that, Michael? She's called before, right?" I asked. "Is that why your phone is busy at night when I try to call you?"

He told me the story, including vague parts I'd heard from Mike's clan of Marlboro buddies over our eight years together. It was this: Abigail was Michael's old girlfriend from the west coast. They'd met while he worked a tunnel job in northern California. Mike fell hard. She was the first real love he had, and Michael planned to ask her to marry him.

He was standing as an usher at a wedding and invited her to Massachusetts to be his date. Michael bought a diamond ring and planned to give it to her on the dance floor. After the wedding party's pictures were finished, Michael drank throughout the photo-taking and excitedly went to find Abigail. The story goes that she'd left for a tryst with a male guest. When the trysters returned, Michael stormed off, engagement over. Never begun. Michael had spoken of her briefly, in telling his past to me; I saw the ring once long ago.

We sat down to a disturbing explanation of why she was calling. Top-down with insinuating detail, the way Michael would tell it: She was the mother of two grown kids. She doesn't want more children, (groan—I resented that comment) serves in the National Guard, an OR nurse, waiting to be deployed to Kuwait, scared of chemical warfare. Knowing Mike served in combat, hoping he could take her fears away, maybe give her some advice of what to expect in battle. And she wanted to tell Michael she was sorry (groan) for what she did back then.

"She put ads in a few papers trying to find me," Michael said.

"What?" I asked, amazed at her effort.

"A private investigator called her, said, 'You want me to find him?'" Mike was taken with this Private Eye, *Man from Uncle* stuff. Illya Kuryakin[1] finds Michael Creamer living in Cornwall, Connecticut. Then the calls—many calls, and the romance was rekindling. All the while, it was coming clear—first love, military, going to War, OR nurse, engagement ring. Shit, this was not looking good for me.

"I decided to let it go." Michael avowed. "I told her I was in a committed marriage."

(I wished I felt he was. And it brought up that I hadn't been for that fling of mine.) I was thinking about the odds coming up against me; I was not holding the strong suit.

"She invited me to come down to Florida for Christmas," Mike said, "and I told her I couldn't." I was silent. "She's deploying right afterward."

Deploying. I, former Army Wife, thought to myself. *Wait. What if?* What if she died? Or she was captured? It was untenable to think of what that would become. For Michael? For me?

---

1   The sidekick to "*The Man from Uncle*" TV series, popular in the 70s looked a bit like Michael.

CHAPTER 65

First Love

First love is an important love. My first love, David, was that young man who enlisted in the Navy to avoid Vietnam. Years later, he would find me at Mass Art; he left a note in my mailbox. Afterward, I called and left a message with David's mom. He came back the day I won *Mademoiselle*'s Guest Editorship. As the magazine was informing me that I'd won, David appeared around a corner. It was an amazing moment: *him* showing up again in my life, at the point my life was taking a different turn, around another corner. I romanticized we'd get together after six years apart.

But I didn't return home from NYC. I stayed to make a career. In that first summer in NYC, in my sublet of a photographer's apartment on Lexington Ave, Dottie called me one night to tell me David had died in a fatal car accident out on I-495. I cried and cried at what I might have missed. I still can't throw his letters away. Odd how first loves stay with us to the end.

So, I was stupid. I told Michael to go see her, immediately regretting the words out of my mouth. I said he needed to find out if she was what he wanted. "The question would always be there if something happened to her in Kuwait," I said, "I don't want to stand in the way of you finding yourself." It might seem altruistic, maybe. During my own fling, I had found everything I needed to come back to our marriage and move to Somers to give Michael some space. Now, he needed to find that for himself.

I didn't stop to think that he had just said, "I told her I was in a committed marriage." I didn't listen to his words; I didn't feel in a committed marriage. I was basing what I was saying now on my previous actions, the apple of which I had partaken, and the confusion and fear of losing him. Now, I offered him a bite and his Eve to go with it.

Michael made plane reservations and flew to her.

He came back confused. He loved Abigail. He loved me. Now I loved him more than ever; I pleaded for Michael's commitment. Silly, silly girl.

Ron kept sending me photographs he'd taken of Mike over the years; by his hair, this is a Mike I didn't know, but I had seen the depression and sadness often. Seems right about here.

"You mentioned something about you having your chance to find out," he said to me. "What did you mean?"

I couldn't answer him honestly; I wanted him back too badly. Maybe my truth would weigh in her favor, and he would leave me for her. I just wasn't sure in what way.

CHAPTER 66

Gone

In which words come, but no sentences, nor paragraphs. Just anguish and words.

He said, "You'll never be happy because you want another child.

I told him, "Not so."

He insisted on wearing a condom with me.

The Persian Gulf was flooding in. "We shouldn't go."

He went back to the group at the VA.

He went to protests and stood in the light of Litchfield bonfires and called talk radio to be heard!

Don't go.

She wrote to him. The nurse about to deploy.

He went to her at Christmas. It might be the last he'd ever see of her.

Chemical warfare.

He came back confused.

He asked me, "Why didn't you serve? *Why don't you enlist?*"

I still had Fred's *Civil War* tapes in Somers. After watching one, I would rewind it to be ready for viewing when Fred got the videos back. I was sad, alone again, and I made it worse, watching Episode 7, or "Most Hallowed Ground." It was a dreadful, awful, sorrowful chapter, one Michael and I had viewed together, about the prisoner of war camps in both the south and the north, where men had barely a chance of surviving as whole men. That night, I stopped the VHS player and swore I would never watch that again, and rewound to the beginning.

Michael didn't answer phone calls for days, so I drove up. Radio talk of the War-about-to-happen filled the car, nearly suffocating me.

Michael fumed and smoked and drank beers. What can I do?

"Come to New York with me," I said.

Pushing me against the fridge, "I'll come down after you stop working with all the Jews."

The Jews?

"It's a War for oil and the Jews, and when you have nothing to do with them, I'll come down."

He stared at me with raging eyes.

I was afraid of him at that moment. Never before. I got away and drove to Richard and Patty's house.

I called the Vet Center in the morning.

His counselor told me, "Stay away; give him some space."

I had been.

I went to work for a long day. Then another; no word. Next day, my friend Lee was in town on business, and we had dinner together. He came up to spend the night in Somers. I called Michael to join us, but he didn't answer. I went to the VHS player to put in a new tape, but Episode 7 was not rewound. I stopped, sure I'd done it already.

Richard went a few days later to check on Mike. Once, he'd driven by, and Mike's car was up in the tree line; there's no road there.

("I can look out for invading troops from here…he once told me." Yes, I remember that.)

A day later, Richard pulled up the driveway; that's where he found Michael, dead on the ground.

Monday, 4 Feb. 1991. I'd gone to work on Metro-North. That night I had an exercise class in NYC. It was a small class; we would work out with a few people. Then I caught the subway up to Grand Central. I ran, I remember; I didn't want to be late getting home; staying late meant fewer trains. I caught my train, rode up, walked to the Somers lot in Katonah, found my car, and drove home.

Key in the lock; the phone was ringing. It was the Connecticut State Police, they told me, "Mrs. Creamer? This is the State Police. Stay there, please; we have someone on the way to talk to you."

"Can you tell me, is it about my husband?"

"Yes. But we'll be right over. Is there someone you can stay with till we get there?"

(It has to be bad.)

I crossed the path to my landlord's house.

My landlady mentioned that a few days back, "Michael was in your house during the day. (He often visited, so it hadn't mattered.) He stayed for some time while you were at work."

$$* \; * \; *$$

I remembered that *Civil War* tape, the one about POW camps in the player, but it wasn't where I'd left it; I always rewind.

He'd watched Episode 7. *Not that episode.*

Now it made horrible sense.

I waited until the Trooper came, and we walked back to my living room.

He told me, "Your husband Michael shot himself; he is dead."

(When you hear about unexpected death, you're outside yourself. Just like Michael had told me years ago, "Merrill is dead." Or Dottie calling to say, "Patrick drowned.")

"I'm sorry to have been the one to tell you. Call your Cornwall friends." The Trooper said, "They want to come down to get you."

While I waited, I called Michael's brother, Steven; I told him I was going to call his mom, and that she might need some help. I waited a bit, then called Michael's mom. I apologized for all I contributed. Suicide makes one feel guilty.

"You kept him alive for nearly ten years." Dot Creamer added, "Michael wouldn't have survived."

I didn't.

I called Peter, who said, "I'm so grateful he went alone and didn't do damage to anyone else."

"Me too," I said, "it was just what I was thinking."

Mike told me the AR-15 and Uzi had been sold off, not the weapons one should have around a house with children. Without children.

I called Debbie, "I won't be coming to work."

My sweet Debbie, my college bud, my bookkeeper, *Myoho Renge Kyo* Jewish Debbie, I could never stop seeing my Jewish Debbie.

Fred and Verne and Patty and Richard came for me.

I packed a bag, for what it was worth, I wouldn't change clothes.

We rode north; they told sweet stories of Michael and we cried.

We went to Fred and Verne's to talk, then Richard and Patty took me home to sleep.

I lay on my back on their living room sofa, crying, and I saw Michael come through the glass of the window that looks out over the mountain side of their house.

I felt his presence and thought in that moment that God knows everything.

When you come into His presence, He tells you what it is you need to know.

Michael was there learning everything he needed to know.

My eyes were open wide.

* * *

I see it like this—those nightmares of war never fully subsided in Michael. The books on the shelves lining the back wall of our living room in Cornwall were filled with war stories, war glories, strategies, and tragedies. Eternities of conflict. Even I contributed a picture book, *What Did You Do in the War, Daddy?* and last Christmas' companion book to Burns' *The Civil War*. Mike's massive *Vietnam: Order of Battle*, recounting every American and ally unit's actions. And before it was business-chic, *The Art of War* by Sun Tzu. There was a drawing of Michael in uniform I had drawn in Conte crayon, and his framed photo with VP George Bush face down on the mantel. War surrounded us; it finally overtook Michael Creamer.

It was too late for us to hear the new findings, that "PTSD and other neuropsychiatric wounds of war, change your electrical/chemical reactions in the body and have psychological manifestations, which are only starting to be understood.[1]"

Our friends placed this notice in the local paper:

> CORNWALL—Our good friend, Michael Creamer, took his own life a few days ago. Michael was a veteran of the Vietnam War, 173rd Airborne Brigade. He was one who saw the most dreadful casualties of that War while treating our torn and broken soldiers. Michael could not endure the pain and casualties of another ground war. He tried in desperation to serve in the Persian Gulf as a medic, knowing the horror of the wounded. He felt he could deal with the situation by being there; he could not deal with it while being here. Michael hopes that the troops coming back this time will receive the respect and admiration that

---

1   Nicosia, p. 621. That, according to Rick Weidman, one of the VVA's co-founders.

the Vietnam veterans did not receive until it was too late. He earned two Purple Hearts, a Bronze Star, and numerous other decorations.

We salute Michael—a complex, compassionate, and beautiful soul…A casualty of two wars.

Michael will be buried in Arlington National Cemetery. He will be remembered by his friends, Fred Balling, Richard Bramley, Verne Henshall, Pat Bramley, Dusty Sandmeyer, George Charleton, and Martha Creamer.

On February 6th, I read Michael's suicide notes. The state troopers watched over my shoulder as I read. It reminded me of having my drug habits examined through Merrill's baby blood in NICU. Looking for collusion. Mike had a way of getting his "word" out; he documented his life in everything he did. His suicide note was a protest of the Persian Gulf War; it was clear.

> *I'm sorry… I know many people will be hurt by this. But this new War has brought up too many nightmares of the last War for me, and it has become unbearable. I don't think I could again endure the pain of mass casualties produced by a ground war, and this is the only way out.*
>
> *When the survivors of this War come home, please treat them with the admiration and respect we Vietnam vets never received until it was too late.*
> Michael E. Creamer
> Combat Medic, N/75th Rangers + Co. B (Medical)
> 5 May '70 – 23 Jan '71

CHAPTER 67

Witness

Michael left three contact names at the end: Mine, Dot Creamer's, and Abigail's. Three to bear final witness. But no one was there to witness the killing. He did that alone. He left another kind little note that he tacked on the door to the house, "Please don't let the cat out, he'll be spooked," which of course didn't save the cat from being spooked and getting out. Gentleness doesn't factor into police investigations. Troopers explained, "We were told he might have booby-trapped the door. He's a Vietnam Vet." Right, I said, same old, same old. I wonder how long that tiger cat watched over Mike from the kitchen window before anyone came. The police swung the door open. I would search forever for the cat.[1]

I read the three "please contact" names. Dot Creamer, his mother, I had called last night; it was up to me to call Abigail. Someone loaned me a mobile phone. I did it.

"Oh, Martha," Abigail said, as if she knew me. "Why did he have to do that?"

Days later, when I could be brave enough to go into our house, I found letters on the coffee table that Abigail sent Michael; he had left them out, besides his suicide note, where the police returned it. That's when I formed the theory of the colliding dreams.

---

1   Years later, Tiger's ID collar was turned in to Richard at the package store. A jogger found it. Richard gave it to me.

His dreams had crossed.
With her dreams of War.
His dreams of War and his dreams of her.
Colliding at night.
Becoming a dream of her
and him at war.
From which they'd not escape.

Abigail called me a day later to ask about funeral arrangements, to send flowers. I told her I had read in her letters her innermost fears of War, fears of being without him in a warzone. She knew there was no way Michael could protect her. He tried to re-enlist and couldn't. Abigail froze as she had before, during the clandestine calls to Cornwall, before I knew it was her on the line. Struggling to find her voice, Abigail demanded I send her letters back immediately, not to make copies of them. I sent them the next day. I didn't want copies. I wanted Michael. Off the phone.

There were flowers from her days later at the funeral home.

"Hello, Martha, this is Tom Brokaw.[2] "

"Hello," I said, "Richard Bramley said you might call."

"I hope you're okay with me calling directly. I own a house in Cornwall, and I saw the notice that Richard and your friends put in the paper regarding Michael. He gave me your number, and I was hoping that I could write a short piece about Michael's suicide."

"Why?" I silently inferred.

---

2   For younger generations, Tom Brokaw was the senior-most newcaster for NBC NEWS. He explains the rest.

"My brother served in Vietnam, so I know a little about what you might have been dealing with, especially with Desert Shield…"

"Yes. We can talk." He was coming from a good place.

"I want to get this into *The New York Times*. Many veterans across America are having trouble with the prospect of going to War again, and I think we could reach a lot of people that way."

"Sure. Let's." I paused, "Mr. Brokaw, I just want… Well, I've been interviewed before and… I just want to make sure you get all the details right. I need to know that you'll run it by me, not to edit you, but to make sure the facts are correct. Can we do that?"

"Absolutely. I'll hand off to my secretary when we finish. She'll get you a fax before it runs," he stated, "—can you talk now?"

"Sure," I said.

We did.

CHAPTER 68

Arlington Monologue

I knew he wanted Arlington. Mike left his DD-214 (two-fourteen) out with the suicide notes, so it was pretty straightforward. The 214 is the US military service discharge, listing his time in and his medals. I put it all together, and that's what I thought he chose. *"I can be buried in Arlington,"* he'd told me repeatedly. When I told his mother, she was dismayed about the distance from Massachusetts to Arlington. It would be hard to get there regularly. I explained my reasoning; she left it up to me.

It's a cold February day; the sun this day keeps coming out from behind big white clouds to reveal true-blue beneath. I didn't want to be late today, so I asked my brother-in-law, Bernie, to drive me to the cemetery early, as the others were just getting it together back in Annapolis. Bernie reminds me in the car ride that part of his job in the Army was to accompany caskets of Vietnam KIA from where they landed in California to their hometowns. His role was like official Pall Bearer. Numbing, I'd imagine, dealing with death, though he says to me, "It wasn't every day." I worry this might bring it all back for him.

For all the crap Mike suffered, for the current conflict he died protesting, they've picked a shitty plot for him to fall into. Over there, low on the horizon there's the Pentagon, a stone's throw away. You can almost sense its war machinery ticking away. It makes me smirk, but what I wanted to do when I saw it so nearby was to scream, "Stop This Stupid War," which wasn't a very Jackie Kennedy, grieving-widow kind of thing to do.

When it's over, after the three-volley gun salute and the echoing duet of "Taps," they fold this up into a triangle (Holding up a flag.), and they hand it to the widow. *Me.* That's when you realize you are a Widow. And honestly, it's humbling. Jackie Kennedy humbling.

Back in Massachusetts, at the funeral home, I had asked to touch him once more, like I held my Beegee. I reached under this flag they had just handed to me and into the coffin. Michael's thigh was rigid as a statue beneath his dress uniform. I couldn't touch his face. I knew enough not to ask if there was one.

CHAPTER 69

In God's Hands

It is the most sorrowful thing I know to take a phone call and hear that your child is dead. I knew that. Michael's mother said the night I called to tell her Michael had shot himself, that I saved him back in DC, in 1982. I told her I didn't save Mike. Every failure I had with Mike came racing to the fore. Years before, on a different call, she told me I was the answer to *her* prayers. Back then, I knew that God put us together, timed that parking space to open up, and the pee or not to pee at the Lincoln Memorial, which Michael and I both wrote about in separate pieces—observing life, taking notes, both wanna-be writers. "God put us together," I told her. First, Mike was lifted up by Frank Baker and the rest of The Herd, the night before. They got him to "STAND IN THE DOOR;" I was the parachute.

Standing before The Wall, and the Lincoln Memorial or the concession stand, and watching gathering Vietnam vets, their families and their supporters, was the first time in my life, as a thinking, fully-aware adult, that I was in that "zone," which is not really the right word for it. It is not sports-like, nor entirely ethereal. I believe it comes from finally knowing oneself well enough to go for things. Then you feel it when it happens. I hope everyone gets to feel that.

Unless we're health professionals, or medics, or first responders—they call them that today—we do not have the power to save someone else's life. Only God does. The burden of thinking we can is unrealistic;

it doesn't make for a great marriage. If we believe it for a single moment, it creates a lopsidedness that will throw love's intricate workings out of kilter. What we can do is pick up a ball and run with it. Each of us picks both the ball and the direction.

Like I told my friend Bruce Plotkin, the day Michael left to go to Penn Station, and I went to find him there, I had to try to help. Vinnie and Peter did their parts in saving Michael; they had to move their friend Michael along and onto the bus where he might find his own, and he did. Michael found the men with whom he shared that awful, powerful experience of War, the one Ken Burns quotes by Oliver Wendell Holmes: "They ...shared the incommunicable experience of war..." Their "...hearts were touched with fire." And those people primed Michael to find me.

Ron Bucchino saved Mike's life, found the ad for a medic's job in Africa. Wrote letters back, when Mike was far away; applauded his manhood, and spurred on his sense of humor. And with that, more letters. Ron and many of his friends shared Mike's letters with me after he died, so I could get to know him beyond the person I married. Afterward, Mom C. sent Mike's letters from Vietnam.[1] It worked towards closure for me when he was gone. None of us individually saved Mike; just helped shape his choices. Threw him balls, life-lines.

Dot Creamer, Michael's mom, was also a victim of a cruel abandonment by the combat veteran she married. She learned to drive, made a living, and taught herself how to cope, facing the unforeseen. She survived the combat of abandonment twice. After Dot lost her husband, she taught her family what she could; then prayed novenas for Mike when she didn't know how else to help. The VVA rep, Jim Tackett, who helped him file for disability, saved Michael. And Sully too—one broken man to another. They saved each other, back and forth. And don't forget Maryanne.

---

1   Mike wrote to the family, especially his dad, from Vietnam.

Men and now, more women who serve in combat are the only ones who know and can understand. Ann Jones tells us, "So much we need to know about the cost of war lies right there in the things that parents and their soldier kids, or wives and their soldier husbands, or men and their soldier wives don't speak about.[2] "

It is their truth: drawn, carved, sketched, acted and written from another perspective, different from ours. Mike wrote to me from Fort Campbell, "I don't know if you will ever truly understand, no matter how many times I tell you." Everything about Mike's Vietnam experience was Mike's and the men he served with. And no, I couldn't ever understand. Just dealt with the aftermath, the emotional numbing, his and what had spread to me. I stood with him while I could.

MARTHA: Hello, is this Tom Brokaw?

BROKAW: Yes, it is.

MARTHA: Hi, Tom, this is Martha Creamer; I've been trying to reach you.

BROKAW: I'm just finishing it up. *The New York Times* has agreed to run it on the Op-Ed page on President's Day.

MARTHA: Great. Say, I haven't seen a copy yet.

BROKAW: Yes, well, they decided to move fast, and we haven't had a chance to get it to you. I'm sorry.

MARTHA: Can you read it to me now?

BROKAW: I can, (pause) sure.

MICHAEL CREAMER,
A CASUALTY OF 2 WARS
By Tom Brokaw

---

2   Jones, p. 96.

All of us, in one way or another, have been living, first with the prospect of War, and then with the reality of it since the Iraqi invasion of Kuwait. For many veterans of Vietnam, this has been an especially anxious time. Many of their worst memories have been reawakened. The Persian Gulf has become their second War as it plays out graphically and continuously on television, radio, and in the press.

Michael Creamer was one of those veterans. He grew up in a South Boston working-class family and served as a medic with the Rangers in Vietnam, winning two Purple Hearts and a Bronze Star for his valor during long, dangerous patrols.

When he returned, he had trouble leaving his terrible experiences behind. He dropped out of nursing school when an assignment to emergency-room surgeons provoked a nightmare of broken bodies and horrible wounds from his combat days. He returned to his mother's home and the life of despair common to post-traumatic stress disorder victims –depression, bouts of violence, and thoughts of suicide.

Friends, other veterans suggested that he confront his past by attending the dedication of the Vietnam War Memorial in Washington. That trip was the beginning of a halting recovery. He met his future wife at the ceremony. She persuaded him to join a veteran's outreach program.

As his confidence returned, he decided to re-enlist in the Army. An injury during ... training short-circuited his career plans, so he returned to New England and began to work with other troubled veterans, counseling them on their problems, helping them find work.

By all accounts, he was extremely effective. One veteran, Tom Sullivan, was deeply distressed and out of work until Mr. Creamer eased him back onto a path of hope and confidence.

Now working in public transportation in Connecticut, Mr. Sullivan says simply, "The man saved my life."

Yet the day-by-day counseling took its toll. Dealing constantly with the flashbacks of other veterans, Mr. Creamer could not escape his past. So, he quit and took a job on a dredge, restoring a lake in northwestern Connecticut where he had settled on a wooded hillside. He and Martha went to see "Dances with Wolves" last fall, and he told her he related to the Kevin Costner character who leaves the War to go out west to kill himself.

MARTHA: Wait. That's not right.
BROKAW: You said he related to "Dances with Wolves," didn't you? I have it in my notes.
MARTHA;   I did, but what he was reacting to wasn't suicidal. What he couldn't cope with was that people outside of War didn't understand what he'd been through. He pulled away from the world like Kevin Costner's character did because the world couldn't comprehend him not participating in it.
BROKAW: I see. Okay, I can fix that, I understand. Let me go on…

Life wasn't perfect. He and his wife, Martha, were often separated. They lost their only child to birth defects. He occasionally sought help in group therapy at a Hartford veteran's center. Still, to his friends and neighbors, he seemed on the mend.

Richard Bramley, a soft-spoken country wine merchant, remembers going to the film "Henry V" with Mr. Creamer and coming away deeply impressed with his friend's knowledge of contemporary and ancient military history.

"Here was a guy," Mr. Bramley said, "whose life was so altered by the military and yet he was fascinated by it."

Then Iraq invaded Kuwait. Desert Shield turned to Desert Storm. Mr. Creamer and an untold number of other troubled Vietnam veterans again began to suffer flashbacks of the horror of their War. Counseling centers reported a sharp increase in veterans seeking help.

Television coverage of this War is much more vivid than it was during Vietnam, the first so-called living-room war. This time, in their living rooms, Vietnam veterans were seeing bombs, missiles, and antiaircraft fire as if they were back on the field of battle. One man at a Texas counseling center, said, weeping, "It brought back memories – and it kept sticking in my mind – of the people I buried in B-52 bomb holes."

In Connecticut, Mr. Creamer, extremely conservative in his politics, was obsessed by the War. On the Friday night before the Congressional vote authorizing force, he stayed up until 3 A.M. dialing members of the Connecticut delegation.

He removed from his fireplace mantel a picture of himself in uniform with George Bush. He attended a prayer vigil with his friend Tom Sullivan on the common in Litchfield.

Mr. Creamer talked to anyone who would listen about his fears of a ground war, yet he tried to join the Army a third time, thinking his experience as a medic would be needed.

Counselors around the country have encountered similar reactions from other veterans: fear, anxiety, and a compulsion to re-enlist.

Martha Creamer, who had been living apart from her husband, decided to visit a week after the bombing of Baghdad began. She recalled that before dinner Mr. Creamer was listening to the radio and then...

"He just blew…kicking furniture, throwing a beer can. He had me up against the refrigerator in the kitchen. For the first time, I was frightened of Michael. Always before, I had been frightened for him."

She urged him to return to the therapy group and called his counselor before she left on a business trip. He saw the counselor the next day; although he seemed confused, he promised to return soon. Instead, he drove back to his home in the woods just east of the Housatonic River. He wrote letters to friends …pinned on his Ranger black beret and arranged his driver's license and Ranger identification card at his side. When this was all in order, he picked up his shotgun and killed himself.

MARTHA: Thank you, Mr. Brokaw. It's very touching. The rest is fine. Michael would have liked it.

On Feb. 7, 1991, three days after Michael took his life protesting America's entry into another ground war, government Publication 102-4, referencing the linkage of PTSD and Agent Orange exposure, stated: "High Combat" vets suffered 72 percent higher suicide rates than other Vietnam era vets.[3] 72%?! It's like a swear word.

In rebuttal to Mr. Brokaw's opinion piece on Michael Creamer, which appeared in *The New York Times* (and syndicated by UPI), *The Times* would publish an almost immediate letter-to-the-editor, denying that any higher suicide rate existed for Vietnam veterans. There were those—then and still—who lobby against Vietnam veterans' lives, holding onto the separate mindsets that ripped our generation down the middle.

---

3   Nicosia, p. 593.

CHAPTER 70

Aftermath of Wars

Maybe it was a play; all the lines were written already. We met in a theater group originally—Mike on one side of the pushcart, Me on the other. Ballast. Perhaps the prequel to the epic Michael envisioned of our lives coming together is this. He and I cast to tell the story of what it means to fight in combat and what it means to come home from War, and how to deal with the unimaginable birth and death of a child poisoned by chemicals of War. Maybe I needed to bear Beegee so she'd offset Baby Michael, standing on that ottoman, in his father's uniform, somewhere in South Boston where young men courageously race off to fight Wars and come home lacking explanations, losing themselves for War's sake.

There are many wars that Michael Creamer fought.

The War of expectations that young men inherit from their fathers, (mothers)...

The War of heroics witnessed on the intimate screens in our living rooms—"Combat" and news footage from a war zone, or NCIS...

The War Mike physically fought, in Vietnam...

The punishing return from War, his homecoming at San Francisco airport...

The War from which his father could not escape;

The War that caused John to leave his family ...

The War of abandonment that trespassed on and snapped Mike's own recovery...

The savage civil War "Doc" Creamer narrowly escaped in Zaire...

The mindless Baby Killer War that forced his retreat from nursing school ...

The chemical residue of War that wrought havoc inside Merrill Creamer's infant brain as well as Mike C.'s body...

The torture of War a veteran experiences, seeing another sorrowful episode...

The War against veterans' need for services and readjustment, that labeled Vietnam vets crybabies from the highest office in the land. That declared their physical ailments meaningless—one that continues to deny the echoing existence of the horrors of War—back then, now and whenever we'll fight again.

Collectively, War has not changed.

War strips us of our patriots, of those who seek a moral ground and fight for it. Born leaders lost. For as long as we continue to fight wars, it will take coming home from one before we can understand what Michael wrote from Fort Campbell while seeking closure: "War is an abomination. To think that man aligns himself into separate blocs and leaves no real avenue for the settlement of differences other than squandering his resources and butchering his youths is terrifying."

Yes, Michael...butchering our youths, is terrifying. At whatever age. It hurts.

Postlude

I's been a long time since Michael took his life protesting Desert Storm. I'm not as vehement, not as enmeshed in his death as I once was. Frequently, I have wondered if there were anything I could have done besides the unloving things I *did* do that would have left Mike alive. I remembered that last fall when we were starting—maybe—to get back together, that Mike read to me, or quoted, or gave me something to read. It was an article, a discussion, something about the brains of wo/men who go to a brutal war, and their brains reconfigure themselves. Something about the pressure, or the Agent Orange, the medication, or maybe all the weed vets smoked, that shifted one's neural pathways so that one doesn't think the same way anymore. (I should look it up, but I want to get this thought together.) That made me love Mike again, but there were times in those 3003 days that I was less than loving.

I was sad and angry after his death. My sister Dottie came up from Maryland after the burial in Arlington and stayed an entire month with me. We borrowed a laptop from Natalie, a Cornwall Bridge friend, and I read Mike's letters aloud, we laughed, drank wine, and Dottie and I entered them into the computer. Many of his friends supplied letters he'd written to them; it was helpful to know who Mike was beside the person I believed him to be. I didn't go into our house for about three and a half weeks. I would hunt for the cat outside in the low slope above where the old red barn used to be. I saw him once, his tiger body perfectly camouflaged by the spots of snow on leaves. Dottie and I finally braved the Cornwall house; I hadn't been in since the police brought me in, showed me the suicide notes Mike left us.

When Dottie went home, I worked with the governor of Connecticut on an *ad hoc* committee creating a safety net for our Vietnam vets troubled by Desert Storm. Suicides prevailed nationwide. (Still Prevail.) We were doing our best to catch them, save them. I'd leave my studio in Manhattan and drive up three hours to the meetings on Wednesday nights, all fired up from the white-knuckle-rush out of NYC to Hartford. I worked on a personal grassroots campaign to make Veterans Day a time to celebrate our living vets; built my list, and sent the flyer out to people whom it seemed I'd just written thank-you notes from Mike's funeral…And all of that was too much.

I couldn't help thinking about Mike's words though, every time I found a letter of his. I was caught in the imagery he wrote with such embodiment. And that's how this book finally came into being: The story of our time together, Mike and Me, and the world and wars that shaped around us. Shaping us too.

Afterword

A Remembrance
The Right Reverend John Bryson Chane DD
8th Episcopal Bishop of Washington DC

The memory of Mike's death and subsequent funeral has never left me. Since his funeral on a cold gray New England day in February,1991, my journey has taken me from Southborough, Massachusetts to San Diego, California, to Washington DC, then following my retirement, back to San Diego.

(Rev. Chane continues to serve the Episcopal Church as an Assisting Bishop in the Diocese of San Diego and as Senior Advisor at Washington National Cathedral's Center for Global Justice and Reconciliation for Interreligious Dialogue. The Center's work involves the Middle East.)

Following Mike's suicide, while serving as Rector of Saint Mark's Episcopal Church in Southborough, I spoke with Martha Creamer and the Slattery Funeral Home in Marlborough to immediately travel to western Connecticut to identify her estranged husband Mike's body at a morgue. Traveling back to Marlborough in Martha's car, with her and her friend Debbie Schuman MacRae, we followed the hearse bearing Mike's body. We drove slowly through a snowstorm; there was plenty of time to get to know Martha better and learn more about Mike's decorated military service as a medic and Army Ranger.

Mike's story was overwhelming and gut-wrenching: two tours of duty in Vietnam, serving part with a MASH unit, then as a Ranger. He was wounded, received the Purple Heart and other medals for bravery. I kept thinking of the horror he must have experienced every day with the broken, mangled bodies of the wounded, the dying, and the dead. My memory would not release me from having to identify Mike. His head had been blown half away by a self-inflicted blast from a rifle. And there his body lay unceremoniously on a cold slab in the morgue. He was wearing his Ranger dress uniform, his jacket covered with medals.

Mike had been following Operation Desert Shield's opening on national media with several other combat veterans in early 1991. Each of the men in his vets' group battled the demons reawakened by Desert Shield. Living through the horrors of serving their country with distinction during the Vietnam War put them on common ground. Each had been traumatized by deep depression and Post Traumatic Stress Disorder (PTSD) caused by exposure to war's haunting violence. He and Martha owned a house on the rural western border of Connecticut and New York. Mike had become estranged from his wife and grew more deeply depressed after their only child was born with abnormalities probably caused by Mike's exposure to Agent Orange in Vietnam. *(Rev. Chane officiated at the funeral of Merrill Creamer in June, 1988.)* Mike blamed himself and took that guilt with him to his grave. As Desert Shield kicked over to the ground war of Desert Storm, Mike and his brother veterans had been monitoring the radio coverage of the opening air war against Iraq.

It began on January 16, 1991. With the night sky illuminated by SAM missiles fired by Iraqi forces and the massive explosion of bombs dropped on Iraqi soil by American warplanes seen live on television, it looked like a Fourth of July fireworks show gone horribly wrong. I could not imagine what it must be like for others who had personally experienced such horror during Vietnam.

That night, I gathered in the dark with a small group of clergy from Southborough, in front of the Community House on Main Street and with others from the town, we prayed while holding lighted candles high in the sky. The clergy who had gathered left to return to their churches and rang their church bells as a collective witness calling for life over death, peace, and an end to the carnage of Desert Storm. I had little thought of Mike and Martha, but events would sadly bring them both back into my life, never forgotten.

Two weeks after the opening airstrikes, Mike determinedly put on his Army dress uniform, his jacket with medals proudly pinned to it, his Ranger beret, and went out to the backyard of his house. Mike, clutching a rifle, pulled the trigger and took his own life.

During the mid-1960s, I became actively opposed to the war in Vietnam. I became an SDS member (Students for a Democratic Society) at Boston University and worked in Boston's South End and Roxbury doing community organizing. I left the Episcopal Church as a congregant because it was not speaking out actively and collectively against the war. I had lost my faith in organized religion.

As preparations for the 1968 Democratic National Convention in Chicago took place, the SDS was fracturing into the Weathermen. Violence was proposed instead of peaceful, non-violent student activism. I left the SDS, and I began to feel that lasting change, and the ending of the Vietnam War would never come through acts of violence but must come through engaging in the War on Poverty, changing hearts of those elected to lead the United States. It was then that I began to read the teachings of Jesus, Muhammad, the Prophets, Gandhi, and the Buddha. I entered a seminary of the Episcopal Church. I was ordained a deacon in 1972, a priest in 1973, and then consecrated bishop in

2002. God is always full of surprises!

War changes us. For me, as a young priest, it brought back memories of classmates from Winchester High School in Massachusetts and college in Ohio, who, between 1962-1963, lost their lives in Vietnam. To this day the memory of them still haunts me. Being Christian, my response to Mike's suicide was that his life was changed forever by seeing so much death while caring for the wounded in his MASH unit. In Mike's case, it was not about who he was, so much as what he had to do as an Army medic who served his country with honor, but who experienced the unimaginable horror of War beyond even a good definition of what Biblical Hell looks like. The only way he could express his anger at his life that had been torn apart by war and his child born and physically impaired by his exposure to Agent Orange was to take his own life. I believe suicide is an action taken more out of anger, not aimed so much at loved ones or friends. Done so because the person who takes their own life bears such anger-producing guilt, intolerable pain, isolation, and depression. Mike's suicide note attests to such. It shares those horrors with other veterans suffering the debilitating effects of PTSD. It is the voice of those who feel isolated, alone, and deeply depressed; those not receiving the support nor treatment upon returning to the United States, the country that sent him to War.

Martha was worried as we drove towards Michael's mother, a devoted Roman Catholic, how Mike's suicide would factor into the Church's take on sin. How could anyone judge Mike's death as a sin from a Christian perspective? The real sin was Mike not getting the appropriate care after he returned from Vietnam. There is only compassion in the broadest Christian tradition for a lost body and soul. Those who die in the name of a loving God are considered saints. There is no judgment, nor is there any prolonged sorrow or pain, but only the gift of life everlasting.

During our long car ride to Marlborough, Debbie, born Jewish but practicing Buddhism, asked, "Where does the soul go when a person dies?"

Jewish interpretation of the Law and subsequent teaching and writing views life as of great value, that in the strictest (Orthodox) understanding, suicide and euthanasia are forbidden. There is a heaven, so to speak; Jewish theologies tend to view the afterlife and heaven as a place where one goes with the Messiah's return. Many Jews believe in heaven and view death by suicide as a tragedy on life's journey and not a sin. Again, there is no judgment.

Buddha taught that through reincarnation, one is reborn after death. Again, there is the understanding of re-birth in that the soul of the person or the self can ultimately be free, liberated, no longer suffering, and in a state of Nirvana. Also, no judgment, but compassion, forgiveness, and embracing a love lost are the core of the Buddha's teachings.

For Mike's funeral that gray day in February of 1991, *The Boston Globe* columnist Mike Barnicle was in Marlboro to cover it. I remember Army Rangers in uniform, several of them in tears, and the haunting words and music of "From a Distance[1]" made famous at that time by Bette Midler, Martha asked if Alan Slattery had a tape player and Martha played it through the funeral home speaker system. It was moving; there was barely a dry eye.

---

1   (Martha was given a cassette tape that Jim Tackett, Mike's VVA Counsellor played for her when he came to explain the benefits she was due after Mike's death. Martha loved it; Tackett gave it to her. It was the original version, sung by its creator, Nanci Griffith.)

In the many years that followed Mike's death, I was elected to serve the Washington DC Diocese as their bishop, yet I could not bring myself to visit the Vietnam Wall. If I did, I knew that I would not be able to hold it together emotionally. Eventually, I did go, and when I found the names of my high school and college friends who had lost their lives in that war, I teared up. A kind park ranger came over and asked if he could help make rubbings of my classmates' names. I gave him their names, and he returned a few minutes later with their names debossed on papers that I could take home.

During the years 2002-2011, I served as the Bishop in Washington. I had a colleague who was a reservist in the Army National Guard. When the unit was called up for active duty, he spent about a year in Afghanistan. As a clergyperson, he was Chaplain to his unit. It was hard. Stationed at a MASH facility, he witnessed the daily horrors of War: the wounded, maimed, and others in the throes of death. One night he called me from basecamp, expressing the stress he was experiencing and the need to share that experience. He eventually would connect with the Chaplain for the Armed Forces; he was able to speak with him about the challenges he and others were facing in caring for those severely injured or killed. Upon returning from his tour of duty, he sequestered himself in a quiet space for three months, not returning to his Church but to reflect and write about the experience until he had time to process it all. On occasion, we would connect, sharing a few of his experiences from Afghanistan. I never pressed him but wondered if he had the opportunity to share the trauma of his experience with a professional counselor. His experience, and the always-present memory of Michael and his suicide, was, for me, a painful reminder of the horrors of war and war's crippling effect.

By coincidence, one Sunday, while on a Bishop's visit to a parish in the Diocese, I met a young active-duty naval officer and psychologist. We began talking about returning veterans from Iraq and Afghanistan who suffered from debilitating PTSD. Eventually, I had the chaance to meet with her and several other active-duty military personnel to discuss their hope to establish a program for returning veterans who had acute PTSD. Some soldiers, wishing to remain in the service were afraid to share their acute symptoms within the VA system (fearful that doing such could impede their promotion, or even worse, label them as having a "weakness," questioning their mental fitness, or their ability to serve the country with a "black mark" on their service records).

Much of this work started as I began the process of retiring as Bishop of Washington. I heard that an alternative program for support and care beyond the VA's embrace has since evolved.

During my time in Washington, to escape the Diocese's busyness and the culture of Washington, my wife Karen and I would go to a (hide-a-way) restaurant located in the basement of the Capital Hilton. Franny O'Brien's Stadium Lounge was a special place; started in the 1960s by Fran O'Brien, a professional football player for the Washington Redskins (now the Commanders). His nephew and a close family friend managed the restaurant; it had a large, private back room. I learned that it was a gathering place for returning service personnel who had been wounded in Iraq and Afghanistan and were undergoing treatment at Walter Reed National Military Medical Center (also called Bethesda Naval Hospital). The restaurant would charter a bus every Friday evening and bring in wounded veterans, including their families visiting Walter Reed. The owners asked me if Karen and I would meet with the veterans and their families and spend some time with them on Fridays. We did so gladly!

One evening, we stood outside the Capital Hilton and waited to receive veterans to O'Brien's when a marine was gently lifted down from the bus onto a wheelchair. His young wife joined him. Talking with them, we learned they had been married a few short months before he shipped out to Iraq; he was twenty-years old, and his wife was nineteen. Stepping on a land mine, he had lost both limbs above the knee and part of his right arm. In God's name, I kept thinking about how this young family would survive their challenges in the years to come after leaving Walter Reed. The young marine, when I asked him how things were going at the hospital, said, "Don't worry, I'll be alright. I'm alive, ain't I? And I am married to the most beautiful gal in Texas."

The restaurant manager had served as a chopper pilot in Vietnam and evacuated countless severely wounded and dead soldiers from the battlefield back then. On one mission, his chopper was shot down, and he, too, joined the severely wounded. After his discharge from the service, he continued to suffer from PTSD and was still battling those demons as he ran the restaurant. He never forgot what it was like to return to the United States, feeling helpless and untreated for his PTSD symptoms. His self-prescribed therapy was to open his restaurant doors to veterans returning home, wounded from combat. It was his way to help speed their recovery, letting them know they were respected, understood, and honored for their service. Not only did the restaurant pay for everything and anything on the menu that they and their families wanted, but they could spend the entire evening in the backroom just relaxing together and being away from the hospital.

Mysteriously, the restaurant lost its lease from Capital Hilton just before I retired, and closed its doors. Some say the restaurant was too close to the White House and connected to the Capital Hilton. It was too close for the public and politicians to witness the scene of maimed and wounded veterans getting off a bus and entering the restaurant every Friday. In closing Franny O'Brien's Stadium Lounge, the owners began again, caring for the uncared for, starting a nonprofit housing corporation to build homes for returned, wounded veterans and families.

* * *

I left the Church long ago during the days of rage against the Vietnam War. But in the end, I came to understand that God never leaves His people alone. My friend Graham Nash of Crosby, Stills, and Nash often says, "No one has the right to take another's life in the name of God." Graham's words reflect a way of thinking that must—sooner rather than later—be at the very heart of every nation's existence on this fragile earth, our island home. It must form the way governments and states engage with one another beyond the violence of War, which destroys human life. If we do not act, who will be the next Michael in a contemporary story of anger, depression, grief, and loss?

Martha's journey and mine, connected by Mike's death, divergent and separated by time and distance, continue to follow similar paths of reflection and pain. Mike's tragic death will never be a dated story. It lives in the conscience and hearts of many in this country. Aging as we are, thousands have lost a child due to war. Today, many continue to lose sons, daughters, husbands, wives, and lovers to the ravages of war, or like Michael, they return forever changed. Life for all of them will never be the same. Long ago, Mike's death gave me the energy to raise up the needs of those who sacrificed much and received little in return from the country they courageously served. War is Hell! But sometimes, by experiencing Hell, if one looks long and hard enough, one can begin to see that we can overcome with care, compassion, understanding, and thankfulness to those who gave their lives for the cause of freedom.

Live on, Michael!
In Christ's peace, power and love,

The Right Reverend John Bryson Chane DD
Eighth Bishop, Episcopal Diocese of Washington, DC

August 27, 2018

Appendix

Appendix I

The Mademoiselle *Entry that won Martha Voutas her Guest Editorship*

WATER, FIRE, EARTH AND AIR
The Passage of Time and Other Things

Three days after the Kent State killings, a baffled and sensitive art student wandered out to seek solace in an older, married friend. She found confrontation, spite, and a National Guard husband. That student was me. That friend is gone. And four years later, that confrontation lingers.

Four years ago, I marched a straight path through the soot-covered doors of Massachusetts College of Art. Following me were my freshman peers and earthly crew holding in their sweaty palms orientation literature and the future of the Art World. That talent that bound us together on the eve of our college careers, today still flows in our veins. What flows in our memories has bound us together for life.

Our similarities were inherent. We had been nurtured through high school on policy—not protest. Our high school yearbook was covered in standard Naugahyde (padded blue) with a panther embellished in gold. Inside was never a mention of clenched fists. No air of dissent. Every girl wore a bra for senior pictures, and every boy was clean-shaven with close-cropped hair.

My guidance counselors discouraged me in my venture into the Arts, as my records and tests indicated I was "perfect teacher material." The art field was crowded and filled with fags and freaks. It was best to avoid the whole scene. So, I decided to go to art school. For spite—I swore I'd show them all—as well for the realization of my talent and the need to express it.

What I expected were fags and freaks; what I found was something else: Massachusetts College of Art, being a State School, had for too long been traditioned by staunch scholastic politicians and tenured pedagogues from the "Old School." By September '69, a liberal coup was in effect, and we all fell victim. The great god, IBM, was moving in and bringing with him a new (young) President and a new (young) Dean of Students. The irony of these two major moves canceled each other out of relevancy. In the halls, they passed us by with smiles, and in the classrooms, they passed us on with punches in our cards.

The wind of change that whistled through the dimly lit halls of Mass Art brought cumulus clouds of seemingly airy spirits. From above, what appeared fluffy and round from below was flat and shallow. (With a 73% chance of rain.)

Our new hierarch-administrators deemed from their vantage point that we were traveling with the times. We were floating downstream with little fear of rapids. The marking system was washed out. Enrollment quotas were flooded. And the once familiar faculty faces were swamped with new ones. The fresh wetness was exhilarating while, at the same time, totally confusing.

The irrational storm of the war was burrowing a raging river that fed from the mountains of Vietnam into our placid stream of unconsciousness. At the tributary marked "Cambodia Crossing," the tides were changing. Perhaps our liberal attitudes were surfacing, but in the Spring of '70, questions needed answering.

Before the answers came, the waterfall did. Kent State plunged Mass Art into chilly waters. Exhilaration flashed to revolt: Our liberal leaders who were so quick to jump with the times now pleaded for time. Organizers crammed us into overcrowded auditoriums calling for action. We were all too willing, as independent thinkers of the new generation echoed in unison, "Cambodia No!"

As canvasses gathered dust in the studios, a fiery student populace gathered black arm-banded in the streets. Had it not been for some quick-thinking faculty and our neglected talent, we might still be there. Many did stay, but many more sought more creative means to bring about change.

Within 24 hours, Massachusetts College of Art's striking students had phoenixed from the fire and set up a Graphic Communications Center serving the Strike. We vented our anxieties not by throwing stones at the "pigs" on Hemenway Street but by shooting staples into silk-screen frames and pulling ink-loaded squeegees across paper donated by the Student Mobilization Committee.

Our system, our liberal system, was smashed! For sanity's sake, we had created a system of our own. Collegiate cohorts across the nation were splashing in the muck of a muddy revolt while Mass Art's airborn (sic) physical launch spanned the mud to wharf upon an evasive but grounding soil. Mentally, we were less successful.

I can't help but think that one Massive cop-out on the parts of administration, faculty, and students resulted in the academic policies of the Strike. Administrators, red-faced and cool-footed, left all classroom decisions to faculty and students. Since marks were already obsolete (Pass/No Credit had joined us in January), this move was only a secondary buck-passing appeasingly timed. Faculty left the decision to the student while half-heartedly encouraging the Strike and more heartedly encouraging an early vacation.

Students were left with the following options:

1. If two-thirds of all work was completed, a student could select to receive a "P" (pass), and that left two sub-options:
   a. Work for peace.
   b. Go home and hibernate for the summer.
2. Students who were not in favor of the Strike could continue studies provided:
   a. Faculty members decided their classes would be in session, and
   b. Said students weren't roughed up by those in favor of the Strike
3. Students who were interested in completing work and felt compelled to participate in the Strike could opt for "I" (incomplete), which would be made up during the first six weeks of the resuming semester. (Whenever that was to be, "…this Strike could go on for years.")

Need it be said that whatever one chose, the Strike had been chosen. I, of course, drifted with the current. Four p's and one i. My last hold-out was Painting Techniques 1. My conscientious frustration drove me to the haunted Annex studio, an abandoned warehouse for used canvas, where I sat down and cried with one of the few totally concerned faculty. That teacher and that lost friend had more to do with my state of mind than I did. I decided occupational therapy was a need, indeed.

I spent hours covered to my elbows in red ink that sunk into my skin and numbed my senses. Day after striking day, my senses, companions, and enthusiasm dwindled. Finally, in late May, when a 4-member work team had reduced itself to one, I, too, went home.

I had hoped that as a sophomore, I would graduate from the confusion to conviction. Instead, my mind had remained suspended in an endless freshman year. I wasn't alone. The rebuilding process was as strange as the transitional one.

In September of '69, only tradition had to be cut away, and most of us were ready to be updated. Our hunger for Student Rights had been thus assuaged long before the "Berkley Syndrome" stalked the other campus communities. Now, in September '70, we had to back up, cool the pace, and regain some semblance of order.

Puzzlement: If Mass Art almost lost me, the most conscientious of students, how many more felt the ordeal of returning? As a returning sophomore, I had lost much less than the graduating seniors. My fears were unlike theirs, who were stepping into a world that they did not want nor they them. "Should line 'em up and shoot the whole bunch." (This, my mentor's National Guard husband had yelled as I left.)

When studies resumed, all seemed quiet on the Mass Art front. It was as if we had been reincarnated. My forehead felt like a clean-wiped slate. But why didn't anyone want to talk about it? Talk to me about it? Or just talk to me! I had no intent for conspiracy, just some rational conversation. Those refugees from the rationale who couldn't cope, or wouldn't cope, just stopped coming to classes. If they had come back at all. Promising painters were now pushing brooms, picking up the debris of a drop-dead senior year.

My "I" lost its appeal and became an "NC" (no credit). I would not venture back into the wilds without escort. Besides, I thought that if someone noticed that dried red ink under my fingernails, they might turn me in as a traitor. I projected my concern on the future. Selecting a major field of study and passing in the correct IBM cards allayed my tensions and lifted us to a cloud of noncommittal.

Here I surmise that our institutional embarrassment at having been so easily swayed now gave cause to the survival tactic of apathy. My own personal feelings were handled quite differently. As I lost sight of a sense of self-determination, I gained an unsightly 25 pounds. As the war swelled to unreasonable proportions, the body of this writer grew to wholesome extremes. Bouncing from class to class, I changed my major twice in two years. I realize now I was asserting my decisive powers in the only capacity this deaf-eared world would allow.

I have survived. Through thick and thin, I have survived. Though I doubt these past four will go down in my diary as the best years of my life. With the Vietnamese ceasefire, most American minds will be purged of the guilt of the war. With our senior cease-studies in June, the halls of Massachusetts College of Art will be completely purged of the guilt of the Strike.

We are the Children of the Strike
And we were struck to the core
Winds of change…
…waters of havoc…
Fire of revolt.
What earthly timbre rings in our minds.

Appendix II

Two of Mike's letters from Zaire

12 May 75—#3
Mike Creamer 1-01
Constructeurs Inga-Shaba
B.P. 15698 Kinshasa
Rep. Du Zaire

Hello Ron,

Received your letters the other day, one marked #1 and a handwritten one predating that. Thanx for the paper and envelopes, but don't try to send a pen. The Bastards will open the letter and I'll never get it, okay? Glad you enjoy the pump.

The big problem about me being over here will come after I return—I already have too much swagger for a guy my size. People will get aggravated at me walking around all of the time in bush jeans, boonie boots, and a safari hat, and carrying an ivory cane or something. I suppose it is valid, though. It's not like I'm a tourist here or something. Do you know that I'm an actual resident of Zaire now, with papers and a driver's license and the whole bit? Another first: The only one of us to actually ever reside in a foreign country—in Fucking Africa, no less. Oh, well.

Sometime soon I'll be sending you a paper about getting me some music. Sure is quiet over here without McCoy Tyner's magic fingers pounding away. Zairois music is a big bust. African bubble-gum. No feverish, throbbing drum music, boiling your blood, no primeval voices screaming up images from the past. Just La-La-La Mobutu La-La, and shit like that.

Ah well, think I'll crap out. I've had Malaria for 3 days now, you know. Leaves one a bit piqued, to say the least.

Take care
Servus Diabolicus Dei,
Mike C.

23, 27 May 75—#4
Mike Creamer 1-01
Constructeurs Inga-Shaba
B.P. 15698 Kinshasa
Rep. Du Zaire

Hello once again,

Still not a whole hell of a lot going on here. Those two broads (*note: Mike could be very disrespectful—he is in this letter. MVD*) arrived, and it's having a detrimental effect on the camp already. What a Fucking stupid maneuver that was.

Had a few beers tonight at Dr. DeCooman's home in Matadi. He's the young Belgian doctor at Amiza Clinic. His house could be described as a modest mansion I suppose. On a hill overlooking the city, pool in back, the whole bit. I want to invite him out to Tombangadio for supper sometime this week, let him see how the other half lives.

The situation is getting rough for medical supplies here—most of them come from Belgium, and they're not getting along too well with Mumbles right now. Every order gets returned, with a little note saying, in effect, "Fuck you." The Zaire is only a little bit more solvent than Monopoly money on the world exchange right now, and frankly, I don't think this project is going to finish. The whispered word here is that we'll be home by June 30th, but that sounds a bit extreme. By October 30th sounds highly likely. I don't really care one way or the other, to tell you the truth. Mumbles came out with a statement this past week that "the only religion in Zaire will be my government," and promptly ordered all the missionaries out of the country. Seems a bit rash, since they operate about 70% of the medical facilities here.

Okay, have something to write about, finally. A bunch of us went on a little expedition Sunday. Drove down to near Matadi, and then took a path about 15 clicks into the hills, to find what was rumored to be an old Portuguese grave. What a day! One of the guys who works for us in Matadi Port, "Jesse" James, had looked for this thing before, a few months ago. He apparently told some of the people in the back villages that "Jesse" was English for "hello," and driving through the villages all the kids were going nuts, waving and yelling, "Jesse! Jesse!" … Anyhow, we finally hit the furthest point accessible to the 4WD pickup, and started hiking down this 45-degree slope. Jesse had said that the thing was supposedly 300 meters down, but we went well over a click and saw nothing. Then Jesse and I left the main party and hiked on down another 200 m or so, and found it. There was a group of fishermen living in caves on a rocky cliff above the Congo River and we had to climb, hand-over-hand, down vines the natives had set for about 20 feet.

There it was—the Portuguese emblem and some undecipherable writing carved into a rock 10 feet above these wicked rapids, by the first European to find this river, Cao, in Fucking <u>1406</u>! (Or maybe it was 1604.) Anyway, the rest of the group, Bill W., Mark M., Chuck A., Bill S., the Two Broads, and their Mother came down to the top of the cliff, and we all smoked what would have been about a hundred bucks worth of Hash in Boston. Now comes the Bitch. (Incidentally, on the way down, I slipped and fell, breaking my beer bottle, and Tom later put 16 stitches in my hand.) The climb up wuz practically vertical for a click and a half. Halfway up, the B. Woman crapped out, and I had to charge back to the top, get water and salt, stumble back down, and then practically <u>carry</u> her up the hill. I was <u>Dead</u>. The climb back up took 3 hours all told. Jesse, Mark, Chuck and I were doing alright, but the others had no business being on that hill (or probably even in Africa). It was pitch black on the trail back to the road, and we saw an owl with a 7-foot wingspread. HUGE!! Anyway, kids, that's the exciting story of the rediscovery of the Cao marker by two stoned Vietnam Vets on the Congo River.

Let me tell you 'bout Elvis Presley. The first day that Jesse got to Matadi Port (Jesse incidentally, would immediately remind you of my friend Don K.). These two Zairois dressed like Zoot-suiters walked up to him and the tall one said, "Hello, my name is Elvis Presley and this is Mick Jagger, and we work for you. Can you help us to be American pop-men?" ... What a trip—I see him occasionally at the dispensary. Last week he came up to me and said, in good English, yet, "Doctor, I must ask you a question. I want to grow a beard. Mr. Larry F. at Matadi Port," (biggest beard I've ever fucking <u>seen</u>!) "says that all American pop-men must have beards. Does Mr. Larry F. tell the truth? My beard does not grow."

Christ, I about <u>DIED</u> laughing. Elvis Presley saw one of the new broads to-day, and went nuts. "Mr. Mike Creamer! Mister Mike Creamer! Make it so that I may meet this woman! I want to make her crazy for me, and we will live like Euell Gibbons in Arizona." What an absolute <u>trip</u> this guy is! God!!

Hopefully, I might be going to a new camp called Sona Pangu soon. Way out in the boonies. By the end of the month it'll be at full strength with 12 Americans, 12 Italians, and hopefully me. Tombangadio is hard to tolerate anyway, but recently it's been unbearable. No f'ing family status at Sona Pangu.

So far, nobody's written except for you and one from Hoyt. Didn't realize that paper shortage was <u>that</u> bad.

I'm about ready to write off any hope of hearing from Karen. Almost two months now and <u>nothing</u>. I really should know better by now, shouldn't I? Imagine that. I'll have been here 2 months this Sunday. Time sure is moving. (But not fast enough.)

If I don't get out of Tombangadio soon it'll be all over for me here. The damned families are flooding into this place, and there are too many fucking rug rats for my taste—always teasing and being bitten by the dog, or sticking a finger into the fan, or some shit like that. I had to suture one up the other day, and I damn near started with a good lock-stitch mattress suture on his mouth. If I had wanted <u>that</u> shit, I would have stayed in Boston and become a fucking social worker.

Oh, well, Buddy, you're the bright light in the gloom to the west. Keep them cards and letters comin' in. Mail call's pretty grim otherwise. I'm not at all homesick, just Tombangadio sick.

Take care, Mike

Appendix III

The Fight for Dak To

By Mike Creamer
(Printed by permission, Turner Publications)

In late October of 1967, captured documents and information given by enemy defectors revealed that the North Vietnamese Army was building up for a major offensive in the Central Highlands. Furthermore, the NVA division, composed of some five seasoned regiments, moved into Vietnam for its sanctuary. Its target was the Special Forces camp at Dak To, a troublesome obstacle in the NVA infiltration route to the densely populated, rich-rich Coastal plains. A key element of their plan, intended to give them a propaganda victory, was to draw an American reinforcing unit away from the open lowlands to the eerie, remote mountains and "annihilate" it. The first part of the North Vietnamese plan went like clockwork: They did draw away a unit. The second part blew up in their faces: That unit was the 173rd Airborne Brigade.

The Herd, minus the 3/503rd Infantry and D/16th Armor, which stayed to continue operations on the coast, was put under the operational control of the U.S. 4th Infantry Division and began Operation "MacArthur" in early November. Constant, massive sweeps were made through the steep mountains to "Find, Fix, Fight, and Finish" the teeming North Vietnamese. There was heavy contact nearly every day, and fire support ranging from mortars up to B-52 bombers was used with good effect to shatter the concentrated enemy forces. The fighting swirled and eddied throughout the thickly jungled hills for almost three weeks until the North Vietnamese decided that they had had enough and began slipping back across the Cambodian border to lick their wounds. The American units kept up the pressure, searching for and trying to block the enemy escape routes. One NVA regiment held in reserve, the 174th, was ordered to dig in on a remote hill and make a last-ditch stand so that two other regiments could make good their escape. The chosen hill covered bamboo and tangled triple-canopy jungle that concealed precipitous "lung-buster" slopes. The hill had no name and was known only by the map marking its height in meters: 875.

The 2/503rd found itself on Hill 875 on Sunday, November 19th. Throughout the weekend, they found some enemy basecamps in the area, and the men had a feeling that something big was about to break loose. They were right. Delta company reached the crest of the hill around midday. As the company began to push off across a ridgeline that was the hill's dominating feature, it became embroiled in a fight against a large, strong, and cleverly concealed system of trenches and bunkers. Several men were lost.

Alpha Company began to move back down the hill to clear a landing zone to evacuate the wounded and get supplies and ammo. A large NVA unit caught them with a swift and vicious flanking attack as they negotiated the steep slopes. Realizing that the company could not hold off this onslaught, Alpha's commander ordered his stunned unit back up the hill to rejoin the Battalion.

One paratrooper, PFC Carlos Lozada, knew that the withdrawing troops would be cut to pieces unless someone remained behind to cover them. He ignored the pleas of his comrades to pull back and instead held his ground, a grim, solitary figure lashing machine-gun fire into the NVA who were by now, closing in on three sides from only yards away. Before he fell mortally wounded, his blazing M-60 killed at least twenty of the enemy and disrupted their attack, allowing his buddies to escape the trap without being slaughtered. This heroic and selfless act won PFC Lozada the Medal of Honor.

The Sky Soldiers called for an airstrike to soften up the NVA positions and began regrouping for another assault. The three companies of the Second Battalion linked up and, assuming a regiment surrounded them, established a fifty-yard perimeter on the crest of the hill. "Jesus, they were all over the place," one trooper later told *Newsweek* correspondent Edward Behr, "in bunkers and tied to trees and everything."

Luck, however, had abandoned the paratroopers. One supporting F-100 Supersabre fighter-bomber swooped in low and released a 500-lb. bomb too soon. It crashed into the small perimeter and exploded, killing more than twenty unprotected paratroopers and wounding dozens more. The North Vietnamese, however, were relatively untouched by the airstrike. Their bunkers were, in some cases, thirty feet deep and protected by yards of earth and logs. Gloating, they took full advantage of the tragic mishap.

Rippling sheets of automatic weapons fire tore into the American position, punctuated by the crash of mortar rounds. Wave after wave of NVA troops attacked furiously. The desperate troopers hung on tenaciously, fighting for their very lives. Eleven of the Battalion's thirteen medics were dead, and only one was about to work on the mounting number of wounded. Father Charles J. Watters, the Battalion's dedicated chaplain, did what he could to fill the gap, exposing himself time and again to drag wounded paratroopers back from the perimeter to hurriedly scraped holes in the ground. Finally, he, too, was struck down by the murderous hail of fire and spent his final breaths giving the last rites to his dying boys. Father Watters became the second paratrooper of the 173rd to win his country's highest award for valor that day.

Meanwhile, the Brigade Commander, Brigadier General Leo Schweiter, directed the effort to aid his besieged troops. Airstrikes pounded the swarming enemy on an average of once every fifteen minutes. The gunners of the 3/319th Artillery filled in the gaps, slinging rounds into the smoking breeches of the 105mm Howitzers until their arms ached and went numb. The artillerymen had their hands full as well: North Vietnamese regulars attacked the firebase and were driven off only when the gunners cranked their pieces down and let go at point-blank range. Helicopters braved curtains of fire in successive attempts to resupply the paratroopers and rescue the wounded, but the cunning NVA gunners drove them off every time, crippling ten choppers. A relief force, the 4th Battalion of the 503rd, set out from a firebase a mile and a half away, stripped off all but their essentials to give them as much speed as possible.

On the crest of 875, the cauldron boiled on throughout the night and into Monday. The men were out of food and water now, and the wounded moaned hopelessly through parched lips. Men burrowed in between the bodies of dead buddies to gain some meager protection from the constant rain of hot steel and the bitter chill of the Highland night. "They were hitting us with mortars and recoilless-rifle fire all night," said one survivor. "Everybody was trying to get underground. Every time you tried to dig, you put your shovel into somebody. The dead were everywhere." Still, the troopers held. It was hold or die.

The 4/503rd relief column fought doggedly against backbreaking terrain, a feverishly determined enemy, and an ever-diminishing element of time to reach their brother troopers before they were overrun. The first rescuers reached the perimeter at dusk on Monday, but the enemy fire was so intense that it took until ten o'clock that night for the entire force to get into the tiny position. The scene, ghastly beyond all belief, shocked the relieving paratroopers. More than seventy dead lay in the confined area, sprawled face-down in the torn earth or staring sightlessly up into the moonlit sky. The wounded begged for water, but the men of the 4th Batt had none to give. They had drained their canteens during the torturous climb up the hill. Torn fragments of flesh and strips of blood-sodden clothing, both American and North Vietnamese, lay on the ground and hung from the splintered trees. Eight of the 2nd Battalion's officers were dead, the other eight wounded. The enemy fire now died down a bit. Perhaps they were demoralized by the reinforcements or were waiting for an ammo resupply, but the rest of the night passed in relative quiet. It was to last very long.

At dawn on Tuesday, the mortars began slamming in again. Flat-trajectory fire from recoilless rifles whip-cracked in as well, churning the already blasted earth. The NVA would put in five or six rounds at a time from positions as close as a hundred meters away and then moved before their positions registered for the U.S. fire support. The troopers worked frantically to deepen their holes.

Wounded men were hit over and over again. A scout dog handler and his beloved German shepherd perished together in the same hole. One platoon that had started up 875 on Sunday with twenty-seven men was down to nine by noon on Tuesday. Jet aircraft streamed in at treetop level to lay huge, whooshing fireballs of napalm as close to the paratroopers as thirty meters. Peter Arnett, a veteran AP correspondent, was with the troopers now, and his dramatic on-the-scene dispatches electrified Americans at home, riveting them to the front pages.

Late on Tuesday afternoon, a landing zone was finally cut near the base of the hill, and the wounded started out for evacuation. Men who were peppered with shell fragments carried the legless in litters rigged from their ponchos. Blinded troopers stumbled down the hill, their hands on the shoulders of men in front of them. The helicopters began to land, and it took two hours for the 140 injured paratroopers to be lifted out. All the while, enemy mortar men pumped rounds into the jungle, searching for the landing zone. More choppers came in, carrying food, water, and desperately needed ammunition. The Brigade's Combat Engineers came in too, carrying demolition charges and flamethrowers. There was still a ridgeline to be taken. The massive fire support hadonly begun to crack the enemy's diabolical fortress. Everyone knew that the stubborn bunkers would have to be taken out one by one, man to man. Technology had exended itself. This was an infantry fight.

The survivors of the two decimated battalions refilled their ammo pouches, greedily wolfed down their first food in days, and began to look with new resolve at the enemy positions. They might be exhausted and bloody, but they were far from finished. They were still paratroopers, and now it was the enemy's turn to suffer! As the food filled their growling stomachs, the flickering fires of a reborn Airborne spirit began to fill their hearts.

As the last light of the day faded away, a new light blazed on the hillcrest; it was that of the flamethrowers. Under cover of darkness, with the heavy torches, grenades, and courage bordering on the supernatural, the troopers advanced over the terrain that now resembled a haunted moonscape. One obstinate bunker fell, and then another. The fighting was brutal and bitter, with no quarter asked nor given. An American grenade thrown into a bunker would be answered by the Vietnamese. Enemy soldiers howled desperate counterattacks from zig-zagging trenched to be cut down by popping M-16's. Foes died within feet of each other.

The carnage continued through Wednesday. Slowly the NVA realized that they could not win against the hollow-eyed, clench-jawed demons that they faced. They could kill them, but they could not stop them. The remnants of the NVA regiment began pulling out, carrying their wounded and their hundreds of dead with them. Resistance began to light. When the 173rd made its final assault just before noon on Thursday, only a last die-hard squad remained to oppose them. It was over.

The weary paratroopers sat and contemplated the blood-soaked hill. Each man looked to whatever greater force he thought had enabled him to survive while so many had died and offered numbed gratitude.

It was a fitting time to do so.
It was Thanksgiving Day.

Later, outside the medical tent at the Dak To camp, which he had just left after talking with the wounded, one of the Herd's Sergeant Majors told a magazine reporter about the battle. His voice kept catching with emotion. "Those kids in there," he blurted out, "they kept holding up their thumbs and saying 'Airborne.' They're good kids." Then he turned away and wept.

Written in 1983 by Michael Creamer for the 173rd's yearbook

Acknowledgments

This book required a lot of help, first, let me thank Mike's friends who sent their collections of letters from Zaire to me after his death. They were: Mike Yuoska, Ron Bucchino, Debbie Valiante, and Richard Hoyt. Mike's mom, Dot Creamer, sent me his Vietnam letters.

To Peter Connors and Vinnie Fricault, for getting Mike on that bus to DC, a big thanks. To Nancy Secrist, my friend with a car, and to Heavenly Father who opened the parking space that November day in DC, thanks. To The Soldier on the Hill, *Do you know who you're with?* You set the tone for me to love and revere Mike in a way I perhaps wouldn't have without meeting you. To Frank Baker and the rest of the 173rd Airborne Brigade (Sep) for helping Mike, off the bus in DC, and afterwards at your reunions, giving him the spit and vinegar to write his essays. To Turner Publishing for rights to reprint those essays.

To Maryanne, whose love for Mike and letters from him filled the gaps I needed to know. Ron for his stories and photographs, and for answering my questions, and to Randi Wasserman who shared her loss at a time when doctors didn't do that stuff.

To early readers, my husband Dennis who heard my stories, *ad nauseum*, thanks for bearing with me. Lily too. Some of you read my book multiple times, thanks: especially Dottie Glynn who ID'ed missing stuff, Linda Bacon, Patsy Grace, Ron Bucchino, Alene and Abe delaHoussaye, Bruce Plotkin, Debbie Schuman MacRae, Richard and Patty Bramley, John Voutas, Jim Tackett, The Right Reverend John Bryson Chane, Judy Beck Roy, our theatre director, Bernie Glynn, Linda and Steven Creamer, Nan Barrett, Katherine Snedeker, Bob Barsamian, Tone Lowe, Dan Crowley, Steve Brignoli, Joanne

Wojtusiak, and Lee Vaughan early reader and final proofreader. Thanks too, Butch Kamataris who read my words and dedicated a park bench in Mike's name in Marlboro, given by the class of 1969. Alan and Regina from Slattery Funeral, thanks for moving our story forward.

To friends since departed: The vets on The Wall and those who passed later. Tom Sullivan, Frank Baker, Gary Millard, Dusty Sandmeyer, Nancy Secrist, Brenda Heath, Donna McIntosh, Dot Creamer. It would have been so great to talk to you all again. I miss you. Collectively. Respectfully.

Patsy Grace held a very early reading in New Orleans which gave me strength and comments, greatly altering my way of writing; I knew I just had to speak from the heart after your friend called me a wordsmith. Jerry Sullivan, my lawyer, who read the book and gave me loving encouragement towards the end, thanks. Thanks, Jan Scruggs for "The Wall," *et al.*

Editors Kurt Opprecht, who read more than once, once for free, (I owe you) and N. West Moss, who won the Faulkner competition (Nonfiction) the year *Mike & Me* was shortlisted, you were terrific and patient. With you, I made big cuts, and I really needed to do that! A special thanks to Rosemary James from the Faulkner Wisdom Competition, and to her late husband, Joe. I hadn't entered a competition since *Mademoiselle Guest Editorship* (1973), and believe me, it was the way to go.

Thank you John Chane for bringing us into the future. Your Afterword brings relevancy to *Mike & Me*. War never stops echoing. Pray for Ukraine.

To my agent, Langtons International. I appreciate the effort, Linda and Lyndsey. Thanks to Pat Addis for sending me to Linda. Thanks to Darlene Swanson, the book fixer, who did exactly that!

I thank especially my book editor, Marcia Rockwood, with whom I worked through all those feelings/corrections. Marcia was one of the people asking for more of Me. It was, after all, *Mike & Me*, and I was missing Me. She believed in the arc of a love story and worked to refocus me. Marcia is more than an editor; she was my guide through this process. I love her for all she contributed.

Lastly, my daughters Merrill, always with me, and Lily who was/is my muse. And most of all, my husband Dennis Donegan, who came out of retirement to support me—financially, spiritually and lovingly. Thank you with all my heart, Dennis. The witch was right.

Importantly, I must acknowledge the thousands of men and women lost in the war between Vietnam and America. On both sides. The ones lost in battle, in action and afterwards, as prisoners, by suicide, as afterbirths (hopeless babies). Those suffering from the effects of PTSD, which is very real, from self-medicating, from the many diseases the War let loose on those courageous people and their children.

I wish y'all ended war.

You didn't. And it's not your fault.

Finally, for those left feeling alone by suicide, *it's not your fault.*

Pray for Peace. Amen.

CPSIA information can be obtained
at www.ICGtesting.com
Printed in the USA
BVHW041421090523
663838BV00008B/444